The Taiwan Economy in Transition

The Taiwan Economy
in Transition

Shirley W. Y. Kuo
Professor of Economics
National Taiwan University

Westview Press / Boulder, Colorado

Copyright © 1983 by Shirley W. Y. Kuo

Published in 1983 in the United States of America by
  Westview Press, Inc.
  5500 Central Avenue
  Boulder, Colorado 80301
  Frederick A. Praeger, President and Publisher

Library of Congress Catalog Card Number 82-63192
ISBN 0-86531-611-2

Composition for this book was provided by the author
Printed and bound in the United States of America

Preface

The Taiwan economy has undergone a successful transition in the postwar period—transition from agricultural to industrial, from traditional to modern, and from backward to advanced economy. This book explores and illuminates broad dimensions of the transition growth of the Taiwan economy for the period 1951—81. It deals in depth with all major aspects: key issues of the early period; labor absorption and income distribution; trade, prices and external shocks; technical change; and economic policies. The coverage of these topics is extensive, so as to give readers a comprehensive outlook of the development of Taiwan after the Second World War.

Facts and causes of Taiwan's successful transition growth are intensively analyzed on a basis of both micro- and macro-economic theories. Particular attention is paid to the analysis of the quantitative aspect of each topic. The quantitative analyses are made by various types of methods: input-output analysis, regression analysis, differentiation, simple comparison among time series data, etc., depending on the need.

This book contains fifteen chapters. The earlier versions of some of the chapters were presented at international conferences. Some of the chapters are the result of writings done under the auspices of the World Bank, the Council for Asian Manpower Studies, or the Japan Economic Research Center.

My general approach in economic analysis, I believe, reaps

the benefit that I derived from my former days at M.I.T. under Professors Robert L. Bishop, Paul A. Samuelson and Robert M. Solow. In the long-term preparation of this book, I have profited greatly from the comments, advice and support of Professors Bela Balassa, Hollis B. Chenery, John C.H. Fei, Walter Galenson, Shinichi Ichimura, Gale Johnson, Hisao Kanamori, Simon Kuznets, Kazushi Ohkawa, Harry T. Oshima, Gustav Ranis, Miyohei Shinohara, S.C. Tsiang, Larry E. Westphal, and my colleagues at National Taiwan University, among whom I wish to mention especially Professors Yen Hwa, Chen Sun and Tzong-shian Yu. Most recently I have received penetrating comments, based on careful readings of the manuscript, from Professors Mitsuo Saito and Winston W. Chang. These comments have been particularly helpful in improving the final draft of the manuscript. I assume sole responsibility, however, for the analyses and conclusions of the study.

Shirley W.Y. Kuo
October 1982

Contents

PART V. ECONOMIC POLICIES

1

Introduction

The Taiwan economy has undergone a successful transition in the postwar period — transition from agricultural to industrial, from traditional to modern, and from backward to advanced economy. The rapid industrialization and export expansion have brought, in their wake, higher per capita income, stable prices, full employment, improved income distribution, and better quality of life. This book explores and illuminates broad dimensions of the transition growth of the Taiwan economy for the period 1951–81.

Transition into modern growth is usually accompanied by both profound structural change and growth acceleration[1]. In the case of Taiwan, the share of primary industry in the GNP dropped from 32% to 7% over the last three decades, while the share of secondary industry increased from 22% to 51%. The rapid growth increased the net domestic saving ratio from 5% of the NNP in the 1950s to more than 10% by 1963, which made it possible for the economy to reach "the take-off" stage and to continue sustained growth after the termination of U.S. aid in 1965. Land reform and agricultural pricing policies implemented in the 1950s greatly contributed to agricultural diversification, which paved the way for rapid export expansion of the food processing industry.

1

The Taiwan economy experienced hyperinflation from 1946 to 1949. Prices rose at an annual five-fold rate in 1946–48 and then accelerated to about a 30-fold increase in the first half of 1949. Successful stabilization policies brought this rapid inflation rate down to an average annual rate of 1.9% in the 1960s. Although the inflation rate fluctuated significantly in the 1970s in the wake of the oil crises, it was once again curbed by early 1982.

At the beginning of the 1950s, the government was faced with a difficult choice between inward-looking and outward-looking policies. Both policies were problematic. For the former, the size of the domestic market itself was apparently too small to support a sustained growth. For the latter, there were not enough surpluses of rice and other agricultural products for export, and the quality and cost of simple manufactured products were not competitive in the international market. Import controls were implemented in the early 1950s, prompted by a trade deficit and the desire to protect infant industries. However, easy import-substitution development came to an end around 1958 due to the limited size of the domestic market and other reasons. The development strategy was then turned toward export promotion, which has since greatly contributed to the successful development of the Taiwan economy.

Foreign trade has been the decisive factor in the island's very fruitful development process. Particularly, it has greatly contributed to rapid economic growth and the achievement of full employment. By 1981, the shares of exports and imports in the GNP had increased to 49% and 46%, respectively. The pattern of foreign trade has revealed the natural evolution of the transition growth of the economy in terms of the commodity content of exports and imports, and has also revealed the natural selection of trading partners as governed by the law of comparative advantage. In the early period, food processing was the most important industry in leading exports. By the 1960s, however, its place in exports had been taken over by textiles. The electrical machinery industry emerged and grew rapidly in the 1960s, although it was not able to continue such a rapid expansion in the 1970s. Due to historical and geographical reasons, Japan was formerly the major market for exports. Sales to the U.S. increased much more rapidly, however, and that market replaced Japan after 1967. Rapidly growing exports to the U.S. encouraged a government policy to diversify overseas markets. As a result, the growth rate of exports to the U.S. decreased in the 1970s, while that to Japan and Europe increased.

The rapid industrialization of the 1960s successfully absorbed labor, both newcomers and the originally unemployed. Full employment was achieved by 1971. The existence of gaps between the modern and traditional sectors appears to be a necessary adjunct to the course of development. Nevertheless, the Taiwan economy had a more equitable income distribution than other developing countries, and the distribution continued improving over time. This was chiefly attributable to the rapid labor absorption and industrial decentralization.

Technical progress accounted for about half of the nonagricultural growth in Taiwan in the 1950s. This contribution declined, however, to about 30% in the 1960s and to 10-15% in the 1970s. This change deserves serious attention. The service sector comprised about a half of the annual GNP during those years. The service sector is characterized by a dual character in that it exists not only for itself, but also for other industries; its positive external contributions to other sectors in terms of structure and linkages, therefore, were important to Taiwan's successful development.

This book attempts to make an intensive study of the facts and causes of successful transition growth of the Taiwan economy. Its five parts focus on five important aspects of the island's economic development: key issues of the early period; labor absorption and income distribution; trade, prices and external shocks; technical change; and economic policies. In Part one, those issues that were critical to overcoming the problems of the early development period are examined. They include such macro financing aspects as savings, investment, and U.S. aid, as well as micro sectoral analyses of land reform, agricultural pricing policies, multiple cropping and agricultural diversification. Part two addresses the issues of labor absorption and full employment, female participation in development, and urbanization and income distribution. In Part three, the discussion focuses on how trade affected economic growth and employment, on a comparison between the export performances of the ROC, Japan, Korea and Hong Kong, on cost-price changes occasioned by external shocks, and on growth and stability in the wake of the oil crises. Part four examines technical progress in the nonagricultural sectors, and particularly technological and structural change in the service sector. Finally, Part five discusses the changing overall policy setting, i.e. from the stabilization policies of the early 1950s to import substitution, then to export promotion in the 1960s, and finally to the problems and policies of the 1980s.

NOTE

1.   Douglas S. Paauw and John C.H. Fei, *The Transition in Open Dualistic Economies: Theory and Southeast Asian Experience* (Yale University Press, 1973).

PART I

2

Savings, Investment and U. S. Aid

Savings and investment are the core of development. The savings ratio in Taiwan was under 5% of NNP during the 1950s, but it increased to exceed 10% of NNP by 1963. Because of this, the Taiwan economy was able to reach "the take-off" stage and to maintain a sustained growth after the termination of U.S. aid in 1965.

But why did the savings ratio increase? What were the decisive factors contributing to the increase in savings in this early period? What role did U.S. aid play? And how was the investment spent? These are the questions that will be studied in this chapter. The period of observation is 1951–65. 1951 is chosen as the starting year because this is the year when the economy recovered to the pre-war level and, at the same time, most of the statistics begin only in 1951. 1965 is chosen as the ending year because this is the year when U.S. aid was terminated.

I.   Review of Savings and Investment, 1951–1965

Savings are the main source of investment. In a closed economy, investment is completely determined by the ability to save. However, in an open economy, domestic investment can exceed domestic savings by foreign aid and net capital inflow in the form of foreign investment and foreign loans etc.

Foreign aid is different from foreign investment and loans in that it is an inflow of transfers that the economy does not have to pay back. Therefore, in the national accounts of the Republic of China, foreign transfer payments (mostly U.S. aid) are treated as a part of domestic savings. However, the economy's ability to save can only be identified after these foreign transfers are subtracted. In this chapter, savings net of foreign transfers will be referred to as "domestic savings," and the savings inclusive of transfers will be referred to as "disposable domestic savings."

1. Changes in the Domestic Savings Ratio

According to Professor W.W. Rostow, if a country's net investment comprises more than 10% of the national income, then the country is regarded as having satisfied one of three conditions for "the take-off."[1]   For a country which receives no foreign capital, the 10% share of net investment to national income is equivalent to the 10% share of net domestic savings to national income.   However, for a country which receives foreign aid and loans, domestic investment is often greater than domestic savings.   The Taiwan's case showed that in the early stage of development, when the saving radio in NNP was still very low, the investment ratio was already higher than 10%. Considering the importance of a structure which subsequently permits a high rate of savings, the condition for "the take-off" is bound to be the domestic savings ability.   In this respect, Taiwan did not satisfy the condition for the take-off before 1962, because the average ratio of net domestic savings to the national income from 1951 through 1959 was only 5%, and from 1960 to 1962 it was 8% on the average. The ratio jumped to 13.4% after 1963.   Thus, one can say that the economy began to meet this necessary condition in 1963. In the analysis of Taiwan economy, 1961—63 is often used as the demarkation period for Taiwan's economic take-off.[2]

Table 2.1   Ratios of Domestic Savings and Investment

(%)

Year	Ratio of Net Domestic Savings to NNP	Ratio of Net Domestic Investment to NNP
1951	5.3	10.9
1952	5.2	12.5
1953	5.0	11.1
1954	3.3	13.5
1955	4.9	10.2
1956	4.8	13.3
1957	5.9	12.5
1958	5.0	13.6
1959	5.0	15.7
1960	7.6	17.0
1961	8.0	16.9
1962	7.6	14.5
1963	13.4	15.0
1964	16.3	15.3
1965	16.5	20.4

Source: Directorate-General of Budget, Accounting and Statistics, Executive Yuan, *National Income of the Republic of China, 1981.*

2. Sources of Disposable Domestic Savings

Dividing disposable domestic savings into three categories — private savings, corporate savings and government savings — we find that all of these three were in positive figures. However, government savings were positive all throughout the period simply because it received a considerable amount of transfer payments from abroad in the form of U.S. aid. When these transfers are subtracted, government savings before 1964 become negative, showing that the government was in deficit prior to 1964.

Private foreign investment was almost nonexistent before 1960. U.S. aid started in 1951 and ended in 1965. The annual

Table 2.2   Sources of Disposable Domestic Savings
(U.S. Aid and Domestic Savings)

(NT$ million)

Year	Disposable Domestic Savings	Private Disposable Savings		
		Private Disposable = Savings	Domestic Private + Savings	U.S. Aid to Private Sector
1951	1,290	519	483	36
1952	1,812	330	303	27
1953	2,253	520	484	36
1954	2,112	523	524	−1
1955	2,860	802	778	24
1956	2,748	986	994	−8
1957	3,178	1,173	1,170	3
1958	4,208	1,655	1,299	356
1959	4,830	1,712	1,355	357
1960	7,063	2,871	2,670	201
1961	8,492	4,010	3,422	588
1962	6,854	4,534	3,949	585
1963	11,205	7,230	6,667	563
1964	14,266	10,151	9,668	483
1965	16,243	9,400	8,792	608

Source: Same as Table 2.1.

Government Disposable Savings			Corporate Savings	Year
Government Disposable = Savings	Domestic Government + Savings	U.S. Aid to Government Sector		
458	−244	702	313	1951
939	−87	1,026	543	1952
1,134	−112	1,246	599	1953
1,185	−257	1,442	404	1954
1,515	−125	1,640	543	1955
1,076	−357	1,433	686	1956
1,059	−218	1,277	946	1957
1,781	−282	2,063	772	1958
1,932	−485	2,417	1,186	1959
2,492	−518	3,010	1,700	1960
2,392	−957	3,349	2,090	1961
1,177	−432	1,609	1,143	1962
1,202	−24	1,226	2,773	1963
1,475	1,153	322	2,640	1964
2,690	1,983	707	4,153	1965

amount received during this period was US$1,372 million on the average. It was an important source of disposable domestic savings, as it comprised 40% to 68% of the disposable domestic savings realized before 1961.

3. Allocation of Investment

During these fifteen years, gross investment comprised 15% to 20% of the GNP, with an increasing tendency. Fixed capital formation increased from 11% to 16% of the GNP. Percentage distributions of gross investment between the private and public sectors and the growth rates of investment are shown in Table 2.3. The growth rate of private investment far exceeded that of public investment all throughout the period 1951–65. Due to its accelerating growth, private investment increased its share rapidly from 45% in 1951 to reach 68.7% in 1965.

Table 2.3   Gross Investment in Private and Public Sectors

(%)

Period	Percentage Distribution				Growth Rate	
	Private Sector	Public Sector	Public Enterprises	Govern- ment	Private Sector	Public Sector
1951-56	53.4	46.6	34.7	11.9	12.0	7.8
1956-61	50.6	49.4	37.0	12.4	16.7	10.8
1961-65	63.1	36.9	25.9	11.0	19.7	6.4

Source: Same as Table 2.1.

Fixed investment by industrial origin shows considerable change, with its weight shifting from agriculture to industry. The secondary industries enjoyed a larger share of investment after 1955. U.S. aid was distributed in the following order: electricity, mining and manufacturing, transportation and communications, and agriculture. The percentages shared by each industry were: electricity 31%, mining and manufacturing 26%, transportation and communications 15%, and agriculture 10%. It is also noted that capital goods in the form of machinery and equipment comprised about 40% of total investment almost every year (the highest proportion); construction was next, followed by non-residential buildings, dwellings, and transport equipment.

Table 2.4   Fixed Investment

(%)

Period	Percentage Distribution		
	Primary Industry	Secondary Industry	Tertiary Industry
1951-56	24.0	35.6	40.4
1956-61	19.5	39.4	41.1
1961-65	17.9	38.9	43.2

Source: Same as Table 2.1.

Table 2.5   Types of Capital Goods

(%)

Period	Dwellings	Non-residential Buildings	Construction	Transport Equipment	Machinery and Other Equipment
1951-56	11.1	21.9	20.1	7.1	39.8
1956-61	11.7	20.0	18.8	9.6	39.9
1961-65	10.9	20.5	19.5	10.7	38.4

Source: Same as Table 2.1.

4. Capital Stock

To provide a credible time series for capital stock is not an easy task.   At the present time (1982), the only available "officially published" capital stock data in Taiwan is a CEPD publication[3] that gives the capital stock of 1975. Since net investment for every year and deflators are available from the DGBAS national accounts,[4] we can calculate a time series for capital stock data by subtracting the net investment for every year prior to 1975, and then adding the net investment of every year later than 1975, all in constant prices. The capital stock series thus obtained, however, provides peculiar information such as that the manufacturing capital/output ratio decreased gradually from 2.87 to 0.39, and the manufacturing capital/value added ratio dropped from 7.69 to 1.46, over the thirty-year period of 1951–79. Therefore, we would prefer to refrain from using these capital stock data, although they can be considered official data.

Since our analysis deals with the economic situation of the early period prior to 1965, the capital stock data compiled by the present author in 1967, based on the adjusted 1961 census and the adjusted CIECD industrial survey,[5] may better serve the purpose. By regressing output on this adjusted data, the net marginal fixed capital coefficients for the whole economy, the nonagricultural sector and the secondary industry are estimated as shown in Table 2.6. The marginal fixed capital coefficients for the whole economy and the nonagricultural sector were both 1.2 over the 1951–65 period, and that of secondary industry was 1.48.

5. U.S. Aid

Scholars who have studied U.S. aid consider the assistance extended to the Republic of China as a successful example of aid utilization.[6] U.S. aid started in 1951 and ended in 1965. Aid was used mainly to expand the infrastructure, including electricity, transportation, and communications, because high levels of education and sanitation already existed in Taiwan.

Table 2.6   Net Marginal Fixed Capital Coefficient

(at 1964 prices)

Period	Industry	Regression	Standard Error of Capital Coefficient	R^2
1951-65	Whole economy	K = 1.2038Y + 81,615	0.0348	0.9893
1951-65	Nonagriculture	K = 1.2100Y + 73,892	0.0363	0.9884
1951-65	Secondary industry (CIECD adjusted data)	K = 1.4818Y − 62	0.0437	0.9888
1951-65	Secondary industry (Census data)	K = 1.4807Y + 3,835	0.0435	0.9889

Source: Shirley W. Y. Kuo, "Economic Development of Taiwan — An Overall Analysis," in Kowie Chang ed., *Economic Development in Taiwan*, (Taipei: Cheng Chung Book Company, 1968).

Foreign investment other than U.S. aid was very rare before 1960. U.S. aid comprised more than 30% of domestic investment each year, sometimes reaching more than 50%, and was the main financial source of domestic investment before 1961 (See column (2)/(3) of Table 2.7).

From the standpoint of the overall economy, we see from Table 2.8 that the distribution of U.S. aid investment from 1951 to 1965 was: public enterprises, 67%, private enterprises, 6%, and mixed enterprises, 27%. The public enterprises which used larger shares of U.S. aid were: electricity, transportation, and communications. As to the investment provided by local currency project aid to the manufacturing industry, we find that the distribution was: public enterprises, 22%; private enterprises, 32%; and mixed enterprises, 46%. Regarding the distribution of U.S. dollar project aid in manufacturing investment, the figures show a higher percentage for public enterprises and a lower percentage for private ones: 49% and 32%,

Table 2.7   U.S. Aid and Foreign Capital Inflow as a Percentage
of Domestic Savings and Domestic Investment

Year	Domestic Savings	U.S. Aid and Foreign Capital Inflow	Domestic Investment	Ratio of Domestic Savings to Domestic Investment	Ratio of Foreign Capital Inflow to Domestic Investment
	(NT$ million)	(NT$ million)	(NT$ million)	(%)	(%)
	(1)	(2)	(3)	(1)/(3)	(2)/(3)
1951	1,193	586	1,779	67.1	32.9
1952	1,586	1,057	2,643	60.0	40.0
1953	2,034	1,190	3,224	63.1	36.9
1954	1,930	2,111	4,041	47.8	52.2
1955	2,700	1,298	3,998	67.5	32.5
1956	3,158	2,366	5,524	57.2	42.8
1957	4,244	2,111	6,355	66.8	33.2
1958	4,411	3,047	7,458	59.1	40.9
1959	5,295	4,437	9,732	54.4	45.6
1960	7,889	4,729	12,618	62.5	37.5
1961	8,935	5,048	13,983	63.9	36.1
1962	9,506	7,227	13,733	69.2	30.8
1963	14,838	1,112	15,950	93.0	7.0
1964	19,880	−791	19,089	104.1	−4.1
1965	21,979	3,567	25,546	86.0	14.0

Source: Same as Table 2.1.
Notes:
  1. Domestic savings refer to the savings generated domestically, exclusive of foreign transfer receipts.
  2. As U.S. aid was terminated in 1965, column (2) only includes foreign capital inflows after 1961; before that year, it refers mostly to U.S. aid.
  3. An extended series after 1966 is shown at the end of this chapter as note 7.

respectively. Thus, the contribution of U.S. aid to the private sector was through both infrastructural construction and direct aid to the manufacturing industry.

Table 2.8   Distribution of Project Aid (1951–1965)

		Percentage of Distribution		
Item		Public Sector	Private Sector	Mixed
Whole economy	U.S. dollar project aid	79.5	6.9	13.6
	Local currency project aid	59.3	5.6	35.0
	Total	66.7	6.1	27.2
Manufacturing industry	U.S. dollar aid	48.9	32.4	18.7
	Local currency project aid	22.1	32.2	45.7
	Total	41.0	33.0	26.0

Source: Calculated from CIECD data.

II. Factors Contributing to High Savings

The achievement of a high savings rate in this early period was a decisive factor for the successful development in Taiwan. In this chapter, we try to examine causes of the rapid increase in the saving ratio based on a typical economic theory. That is, saving is a function of income and interest rate. It is a fundamental natural phenomenon that the propensity to save increases as income increases. We also note that at lower income levels, saving will possibly increase as interest rates rise. Reflecting this theory, Taiwan's postwar experience showed that factors contributing to the higher savings rate were a speedy growth of the economy and high real interest rates. In addition, sound government fiscal policies also provided a considerable portion of domestic savings. These points will be successively elaborated below.

1. Speedy GNP Growth

The Taiwan economy was restored to its prewar level by 1951, and after that the economy grew at a high speed. The average annual growth rate of the GNP between 1951 and 1955 was 9.7%, between 1956 and 1960, 7.0%, and between 1961 and 1965, 10.1%. Such a high GNP growth rate generated higher incomes, which naturally reduced the propensity to consume and increased the propensity to save.

2. High Real Interest Rates

One of the characteristics of the 1950s was a high interest rate policy that was adopted as an anti-inflation measure. The inflation in Taiwan immediately after World War II was serious. Prices rose at an annual five-fold rate during 1946—48 and then accelerated to about 30-fold in the first half of 1949. "Preferential interest savings deposits" were introduced in March 1950 as an important stabilization measure. The preferential deposits offered a monthly interest rate of 7% for one-month time deposits which, compounded, amounted to 125% per year. Compared with the then prevailing one-year time deposit rate, which was only 20%, the preferential interest savings deposits offered a very high rate for a one-month duration. It is obvious that the high interest rate attracted a large amount of deposits. The ratio of the amount of the preferential deposits to the money supply was 34.3% in 1952—55, and 24.6% in 1956—58.

Although the interest rate was brought down gradually, the interest rate in real terms was generally high during the 1952-65 period. The high real interest rate was realized because of two factors: a high nominal interest rate and a lower inflation rate. Actually, the hyper-inflation was overcome by 1952. The inflation rate was brought down to 8.8% in 1953 and 2.4% in 1954, although it took several more years to really overcome high price increases. Thus, the success in price stabilization contributed greatly to the increase in savings.

Table 2.9 Real Interest Rate (1951—1965)

(percent per annum)

Year and Month		Nominal* Interest Rate	— Inflation Rate (by WPI)	= Real Interest Rate
1951	Mar.	69.6	66.0	3.6
1952	Apr.	63.8	23.1	40.7
1953	Apr.	42.6	8.8	33.8
	Jul.	34.5	''	25.7
	Oct.	26.8	''	18.0
1954	Jul.	21.0	2.4	18.6
1955		''	14.1	6.9
1956		''	12.7	8.3
1957		''	7.2	13.8
1958		''	1.4	19.6
1959	Jan.	20.7	10.3	10.4
1961	Mar.	19.0	3.2	15.8
	Jun.	15.8	''	12.6
1962	Aug.	14.4	3.0	11.4
1963	Jul.	12.7	6.5	6.2
1964	Mar.	11.4	2.5	8.9
1965		''	−4.6	16.0

Source: Economic Research Department, The Central Bank of China, *Taiwan Financial Statistics Monthly* (Dec. 1956, 1961 and 1966); Directorate-General of Budget, Accounting and Statistics, Executive Yuan, *Commodity-Price Statistics Monthly, Taiwan Area, the Republic of China* (June 1982).

Notes:
* 1951 Mar.: Three month rate of preferential deposits.
1952 Apr.: Six month rate of preferential deposits.
1953 Apr.–1958: One year rate of preferential deposits.
After 1959 Jan.: Two year rate of fixed savings deposits.

3. High Government Savings

The sources of disposable domestic savings have been shown in Table 2.2 above. It is very impressive that government savings registered a large amount, and that government savings even exceeded private savings for the period 1952—56. The high rate of government savings was not likely a result of heavy taxation, but was possibly the result of very restrictive government consumption. For, tax revenues were a very low percentage of GNP:10.0% in 1951–55, 11.7% in 1956–60, and 10.1% in 1961–65.[8] The income tax was particularly low; the business income tax and individual income tax combined comprised only 1.53%, 1.56% and 1.17% of the GNP, respectively, in those periods.   A large part of agricultural surplus was collected to the government in the form of a "hidden rice tax" through government's rice collection paid at the government's purchasing price, which was far lower than the market price.   The hidden rice tax exceeded the total income tax of the whole economy almost every year before 1963 (see Chapter 3 for the details).   Thus light taxation enabled the industrial sector to retain a large part of its profit for further investment. However, restrictive government consumption basically made it possible to have light taxation.

The high rate of government savings was possible because of sound fiscal policies which were implemented with a firm determination.[9] The determination to cure inflation and to maintain balanced budget can be seen, for example, in the statements of Mr. Chen Chen, the then Governor of Taiwan Province and the later Prime Minister.[10]

As the bitter lesson of inflation was well taken by the government, the issuance of paper currency was strictly controlled.   The annual budget was carefully prepared and executed.   In addition to the reform of the monetary system, several important measures were taken by the government to counter the problems of increasing public expenditures. These measures were to: launch a tax reform program, increase monopoly profits, speed up the disposal of properties received from the Japanese, gradually increase the spendings for positive purposes and reduce the items for passive purposes in the budget, try hard to maintain a balanced budget, and establish a sound budgeting system.[11]

From the above observations, we know the following: The Taiwan economy started to grow at a high rate right after World War II with its investment comprising more than 10%

of its NNP every year.   During the 1950s, however, the savings rate was low, only being around 5% of the NNP.   U.S. aid was the main financial source that made up the gap.

A high percentage of investment made the economy grow fast which in turn brought the savings rate to a high level. The economy reached "the take-off" stage in 1961—63 as the savings rate started to exceed 10% of the NNP then.

The growth rate of private investment was much higher than that of public investment although a greater portion of U.S. aid was spent on the public sector.   The contribution of U.S. aid to the private sector was through both infrastructural construction and direct local currency project aid to the manufacturing industry.

Factors contributing to the generation of a higher savings rate were essentially a speedy growth of the economy, a high real interest rate, and a firm determination and implementation of sound government fiscal policies.

U.S. aid was really an indispensable key factor in the economic development of Taiwan.   However, such financial injection was only to be a "necessary but not sufficient" factor. That U.S. aid could have helped bring such tremendous achievements in Taiwan was greatly due to the diligent and economical character of the Chinese, political stability, and the efficient policies implemented by the government.

NOTES

1. According to Professor Rostow, "the take-off" is defined as:
    "for the present purposes the take-off is defined as requiring all three of the following related conditions: (1) a rise in the rate of productive investment from say 5% or less to over 10% of national income (or net national product (NNP)); (2) the development of one or more substantial manufacturing sectors, with a high rate of growth; (3) the existence or quick emergence of a political, social and institutional framework which exploits the impulses to expansion in the modern sector and the potential external economy effects of the take-off and gives to growth an on-going character. . . . In short, whatever the role of capital imports, the preconditions for take-off include an initial ability to mobilize domestic savings productively, as well as a structure which subsequently

permits a high marginal rate of savings."
in W.W. Rostow, *The Stages of Economic Growth* (London: Cambridge University Press, 1960), p. 39.

2. In addition to the condition of savings rate, the following points are also taken into consideration:

1) The monetary reform was successfully achieved by 1961, as the average annual rate of price inflation came down from 10.5% in 1952−60 to 2.0% in 1961−65 and 2.9% in 1966−70.

2) In 1961 the multiple exchange rate was abandoned, and the simple exchange rate became effective.

3) The real wage rate, having remained nearly fixed, began to rise rapidly after 1961.

4) The rate of labor absorption into the nonagricultural sector, having kept pace with the increase in total population, started to exceed population growth rapidly after 1962.

5) The rate of investment in the manufacturing sector accelerated after 1961.

3. Council for Economic Planning and Development, Executive Yuan, *Survey on Capital Stock, 1975* (September 1980).

4. Directorate-General of Budget, Accounting and Statistics, Executive Yuan, *National Income of the Republic of China,* various years.

5. The author's estimations of capital stock are based on the Census held by the Department of Reconstruction at the end of 1961 and the unpublished industrial and service survey held by Council for International Economic Cooperation and Development at the end of 1964. Capital stock of tertiary industries estimated by the Census is only one-fifth of that estimated by CIECD because its coverage was not complete. The drawback of the Census data of secondary industries was said to be mainly in the ambiguity in definition; for example, the failure to distinguish net and gross figures. Data are adjusted in the author's estimation. Shirley W. Y. Kuo, "Economic Development of Taiwan − An Overall Analysis," in *Economic Development in Taiwan,* Kowie Chang ed., (Taipei: Cheng Chung Book Company, 1968).

6. Neil H. Jacoby, *U.S. Aid to Taiwan: A Study of Foreign Aid, Self-Help, and Development* (New York: Frederick A. Praeger Publishers, 1966).

7. Extention Table 2.7 U.S. Aid and Foreign Capital Inflow in Percent of Domestic Savings and Domestic Investment (1966–1981)

Year	Domestic Savings (NT$ million) (1)	U.S. Aid and Foreign Capital Inflow (NT$ million) (2)	Domestic Investment (NT$ million) (3)	Ratio of Domestic Savings to Domestic Investment (%) (1)/(3)	Ratio of Foreign Capital Inflow to Domestic Investment (%) (2)/(3)
1966	26,988	−252	26,736	100.9	−0.9
1971	95,545	−6,366	69,179	109.2	−9.2
1972	100,893	−19,811	81,082	124.4	−24.4
1973	141,021	−21,648	119,373	118.1	−18.1
1974	172,565	42,760	215,325	80.1	19.9
1975	156,397	22,650	179,047	87.3	12.7
1976	226,477	−10,246	216,231	104.7	−4.7
1977	267,867	−35,672	232,195	115.4	−15.4
1978	340,349	−62,757	277,592	122.6	−22.6
1979	403,019	−10,877	392,142	102.8	−2.8
1980	479,534	21,735	501,269	95.7	4.3
1981	526,730	−18,836	507,894	103.7	−3.7

Source and Notes: Same as Table 2.7.

8. Exclusive of government monopoly revenues.

9. Virtually observers of this early period seem to be in agreement in this case.   See, for example, Erik Lundberg, "Fiscal and Monetary Policies," in Walter Galenson ed., *Economic Growth and Structural Change in Taiwan, The Postwar Experience of the Republic of China* (Cornell University Press, 1979).

10. T.F. Ho, *A Biography of Mr. Chen Chen,* Anti-Communist Publisher, pp. 172-175, 1965.

11. Kowie Chang, Ming-jen Lu, Teh-an Hsu, "Fiscal Operations," in Kowie Chang ed., *Economic Development in Taiwan* (Taipei: Cheng Chung Book Company, 1968).

3

Effects of Land Reform, Agricultural Pricing Policy and Economic Growth on Multiple Cropping and Agricultural Diversification

The multiple cropping system, which is a special feature of agricultural development in Taiwan, enables farmers to grow two or more crops a year on the same piece of land. Usually, multiple cropping includes two rice crops with one, two, or three other dry land crops. This intensive use of land not only increased land productivity and crop production, but also provided employment opportunities for the farmers, thereby absorbing surplus labor that existed before 1971.

Agricultural diversification was manifested in the decreasing share of rice and the increasing share of other higher value products in total agricultural production. The fast agricultural diversification was essential for the rapid growth of the food processing industry which behaved as the leading manufacturing industry during the 1950s and the early 1960s.

Thus, multiple cropping and agricultural diversification were important features of the agricultural development in Taiwan before the 1970s, which was the period of labor surplus and food processing development. Land reform, agricultural pricing policies, and rapid growth of the economy made significant impacts on these two important features. The present chapter is aimed at studying the effects of land reform, agricultural pricing policies, and economic growth on the intensity of multiple cropping and agricultural diversification. Since they were especially important features for the period before the

1970s, our observations will be confined to the period 1952–1971.

I. Definitions of Multiple Cropping and Diversity Indices

1. Multiple Cropping Index

The multiple cropping index measures the intensity of land utilization. It is defined as:

$$\text{Multiple cropping index} = \frac{\text{Cropping area}}{\text{Cultivated area}} \times 100$$

When the multiple cropping index is more than 100, it means that a piece of land is cropped more than once in a year. The multiple cropping index increased from 171.9 in 1952 to reach a peak of 190.0 in 1966, and decreased to 179.3 in 1971 as the economy moved closer to the stage of full employment.

The intensification of multiple cropping was also manifested in a rapid increase in the number of working days per hectare of land. The number of working days per hectare of land increased from approximately 170 in 1948–50 to about 260 in 1963–65.[1] Larger labor inputs to the cultivation of the new crops resulted in more intensive cultivation of land. The shift toward such labor-intensive and higher value crops as vegetables and fruits, and away from complete dominance by the traditional crops of rice and sugarcane, paved the way for the rapid expansion of the food processing industry in the 1950s.

2. Diversity Index

The agricultural diversity index measures the degree of diversification of agricultural products. It is defined as:

$$\text{Diversity index} = \frac{1}{\sum \left(\dfrac{\text{Value of each product}}{\text{Value of total product}} \right)^2}$$

Thus, the greater the diversity index, the greater the degree of diversification.   The diversity index of agricultural products, based on 118 products, increased significantly between 1952 and 1971, from 3.54 to 7.03.   Over the period 1952–71, the share of rice in total agricultural production decreased from 50% to 29%, while the share of higher value products, such as vegetables and fruits, increased from 50% to 71%.

Fig. 3.1   Multiple Cropping Index and
Agricultural Diversity Index

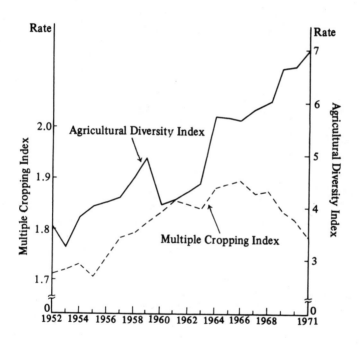

Table 3.1   Multiple Cropping Index and Diversity Index

Year	Multiple Cropping Index	Diversity Index A (based on 118 products)	Diversity Index B (based on 7 products)
1952	171.9	3.54	3.55
1953	172.5	3.18	3.18
1954	173.8	3.81	3.82
1955	171.2	3.99	4.02
1956	175.5	4.07	4.09
1957	179.0	4.21	4.23
1958	179.9	4.61	4.64
1959	181.5	4.95	4.98
1960	183.5	4.01	4.01
1961	185.8	4.13	4.15
1962	185.3	4.31	4.34
1963	184.7	4.43	4.46
1964	188.0	5.75	5.80
1965	189.3	5.67	5.72
1966	190.0	5.67	5.72
1967	187.4	5.85	5.91
1968	188.2	6.04	6.11
1969	184.3	6.69	6.79
1970	182.7	6.67	6.80
1971	179.3	7.03	7.16

Source: Department of Agriculture and Forestry, Taiwan Provincial Government, *Taiwan Agricultural Year Book,* various years.

Note: Also see Note 2 at the end of this chapter.

$$\text{Diversity index} = \frac{1}{\Sigma \left(\dfrac{\text{Value of each product}}{\text{Value of total product}} \right)^2} = \frac{1}{\sum_i \left(\dfrac{y_i}{Y} \right)^2}$$

$$\text{Multiple cropping index} = \frac{\text{Cropping area}}{\text{Cultivated area}} \times 100$$

II. Effects of Land Reform

Land reform in Taiwan has produced significant effects on the economy. Among the many effects, those on multiple cropping will be examined in this study.   Land reform in Taiwan was carried out in three phases: rent reduction, sale of public land, and the "Land-to-the-Tiller" program.

The rent reduction program was implemented in 1949.   It legally limited the amount of farm rent on private tenanted land to 37.5% of the harvest.   Before the implementation of this program, tenant farmers in Taiwan had to pay a land rent amounting to more than 50% of the total harvest.   Therefore, the new rental rate reduced the land rent paid by tenants by more than 15%.   The program also provided farmers with more security on lease contracts.

The sale of public land to tenant farmers was successfully implemented in 1953, followed by the redistribution of excess private tenanted land to the tenant-cultivators.[3]   The area transferred from landlords to tenants through the public land sale program, and the area bought by the tenants through the "Land-to-the-Tiller" program, amounted to 71% of the total area of public and private tenanted land.[4]

The most significant factors which contributed to multiple cropping as a result of land reform are as follows: (1) change in tenancy conditions, (2) change in the size of landholdings, and (3) change in production patterns.   These will be analyzed one by one.

1. Changes in Tenancy Conditions

After land reform, tenancy conditions were altered significantly.   The ratio of owner-farmers to total farm families increased from 36% in 1949 to 60% in 1957.   Owner-farmers and part owner-farmers owned more than 83% of the total farm land in 1957.

The incentive to make extra efforts in cultivation was strong after the land reform.   First, after rent reduction, the tenant not only benefited from lower rents but also from increased production beyond standard levels.   This tended to encourage multiple cropping.   Second, the superiority of an owner-farmer system over a tenancy system was obvious as seen from a basis of per family, per person and even per hectare income.   The farm income of the tenant was only three-fourths that of the other two categories. Therefore, significant changes in tenancy conditions provided a strong incentive for production increases, and facilitated the more efficient utilization of the agricultural labor force.

Table 3.2   Farm Yields by Category of Farmers in 1963

(NT$)

Category	Per Family	Per Person	Per Hectare
Owner-farmer	34,853	4,019	26,998
Part-owner	39,095	4,274	25,252
Tenant	29,877	3,038	17,754

Source: Chi-lien Hwang, *Wages and Incomes of Agriculture Workers in Taiwan* (Taipei: National Taiwan University, The Research Institute of Rural Socio-Economics, 1968).

2.   Changes in the Size of Landholdings

Land reform led to an equalization of property and a smaller-scale farming system. Before the implementation of land reform, landholdings of more than 3 hectares comprised 42% of the total area; after the implementation, they dropped to only 23% of the total area. Conversely, landholdings of 1 hectare or less, which originally comprised 25% of the total, increased to 35% (Table 3.3). This indicates that land reform resulted in a reorganization of the economic structure of the farm in the direction of smaller-scale farming. The smaller size of farm units naturally brought about more intensive use of labor, and, consequently, more labor-intensive production of vegetables and fruits.

3.   Changes in Production Patterns

After land reform, the farmers had greater choice regarding the cultivation of crops because, as owner-cultivators, they were under no obligation to produce rice for rental payments.

Table 3.3   Changes in the Size of Landholdings Before and After Land Reform

(ha; %)

Farm Size	Pre-reform (1952)		Post-reform (1955)	
	Area	%	Area	%
Below 0.5 ha.	67,511	10	92,146	14
0.5 – 1.0	102,577	15	146,042	21
1.0 – 3.0	227,890	33	285,627	42
3.0 – 10.0	175,064	26	124,113	18
Over 10.0	108,108	16	31,642	5
Total	681,150	100	679,570	100

Source: T.H. Lee, "Government Interference in the Rice Market," *Economic Essays,* Vol. 2 (Taipei: National Taiwan University, Graduate Institute of Economics, 1971).

Thus, the land reform tended to reduce the relative share of rice production and to increase the share of other crops, including vegetables, fruits, livestock and poultry. Moreover, technological changes in agriculture after land reform were largely centered on the intensive use of land with more labor input.

Table 3.4   Indices of Land and Labor Productivities in Agricultural Production

(%)

Year	Land Area	Land Productivity	Labor Input	Labor Productivity
1950	100.0	100.0	100.0	100.0
1955	100.7	121.5	107.6	113.2

Source: Same as Table 3.3.

In short, after land reform, changes in tenancy conditions, in the size of landholdings, and in production patterns all greatly contributed to the development of multiple cropping farming and agricultural diversification.

III. Effects of Agricultural Pricing Policy

Agricultural pricing policy was a very important factor contributing to Taiwan's past agricultural diversification, which was mainly characterized by the decreasing share of rice and the increasing share of other higher value products in total agricultural production. The share of rice declined from 50.2% in 1952 to 29.1% in 1971, while that of other products increased from 49.8% to 70.9%. More broadly, the share of common and special crops dropped from 78.5% to 48.1% during the same period, while the share of fruits, vegetables, and livestock products increased from 21.5% to 51.9%.

Table 3.5   Share of Rice in Agricultural Production

(%)

Year	Rice	Agricultural Products Other Than Rice
1952	50.2	49.8
1955	45.9	54.1
1960	45.5	54.5
1965	36.8	63.2
1970	31.7	68.3
1971	29.1	70.9

Source: Department of Agriculture and Forestry, Taiwan Provincial Government, *Taiwan Agricultural Year Book,* various years.

Agricultural pricing policies were mainly implemented through governmental action in the markets for rice, sugarcane, and other agricultural products. The effects of such actions were manifold. First, by various methods of compulsory rice collection, the government controlled the supply of rice and kept a large part of rice consumption from going through the market mechanism. Thus, it contributed to the stabilization of the price of rice. Second, by purchasing and collecting rice at a price relatively lower than the market price, the government

Table 3.6   Change in Agricultural Structure

(%)

Year	Common Crops	Special Crops	Fruits	Vege-tables	Live-stock	Common Crops and Special Crops	High Value Agricultural Products
1952	61.6	16.9	3.0	4.1	14.4	78.5	21.5
1955	57.5	17.1	2.6	4.1	18.7	74.6	25.4
1960	58.1	13.9	3.3	4.5	20.2	72.0	28.0
1965	47.0	13.8	8.5	6.1	24.6	60.8	39.2
1970	40.7	10.1	8.3	11.3	29.6	50.8	49.2
1971	37.9	10.2	8.7	11.1	32.1	48.1	51.9

Source: Same as Table 3.5.

made huge profits. These profits in fact had the nature of a "hidden rice tax." Third, by offering guaranteed prices for the production of sugarcane, corn, mushrooms, asparagus, etc., the government encouraged the production of agricultural products other than rice. Thus, as the result of agricultural pricing policies, rice production relatively declined and other production increased instead.

The effects of agricultural pricing policies on agricultural diversification will be examined from the following points of view: (1) governmental action in the rice market and the "hidden rice tax", (2) impact of the "hidden rice tax" on agricultural diversification, and (3) the government's guaranteed price policies for other agricultural products.

1. Governmental Actions in the Rice Market and the "Hidden Rice Tax"

In Taiwan, the production, distribution, and marketing of rice were under the special direction, supervision and strict control of the government. The Taiwan Provincial Food Bureau (PFB) was the agency in charge of the implementation of policies related to food crops, mainly paddy rice. The annual rice production in Taiwan was disposed of in three different ways: first, part of it was retained by the farmers to be used as seed and for their own consumption either as food or as feed; second, a large share was collected and purchased by the government for rationing, export, and other uses; and third, the remaining part was sold in the domestic free market through ordinary commercial channels for the consumption of the general public.

During 1950–59, the share of rice under government control amounted to 62% of the total, while in the later period of 1960–70 the share dropped to 53%.[5]   For marketing control, all business activities of farmers' associations and private rice dealers were under government supervision. All rice dealers had to be licensed and follow regulations set by the PFB.

Huge incomes for the government in the form of a "hidden rice tax" was generated through land taxes, compulsory purchases, the rice-fertilizer barter system, and land prices paid in kind.   It will be proved later that the "hidden rice tax" was the main cause of the faster agricultural diversification in the 1950s, thus contributing indirectly to the development of the food processing industry.   The mechanism and collection of the "hidden rice tax" will be described below.

(1) Land Tax Payment in Kind

The government stipulated that taxes on paddy fields, and surtaxes, must be paid in rice. The rates of land tax were different according to the grade of land. In addition, compulsory rice purchasing, in a certain proportion with land taxes, was made by the government at an official price which was only two-thirds of the wholesale market price of rice.

(2) Rice-Fertilizer Barter

Rice-fertilizer barter was implemented through the period 1948–71, and was the most important program as it contributed more than a half of the "hidden rice tax" every year before it was abolished in 1972. The program was undertaken on an area basis by the district offices of the PFB; however, the actual distribution of fertilizer and collection of rice were entrusted to the township farmers' associations. The barter ratios between rice and different chemical fertilizers were adjusted by the government from time to time, but the ratios were high in terms of the amount of rice exchanged for one kilogram of chemical fertilizer.[6]

The fertilizer barter program was successful mainly owing to the government's monopoly on chemical fertilizer distribution and also to the farmers' strong demand for these materials, as the farmers were technically well trained in the application of chemical fertilizers. Other commodity barter programs were for cotton cloth, bicycles, soybean cakes, etc. But they failed because the barter ratios were unrealistic and the commodities involved were not government monopolies. Therefore, they have long been suspended.

(3) Other Rice Collections

In addition to the rice-fertilizer barter program, the government extended short-term production loans to the farmers in exchange for rice. The loan repayments, including interest, were made in rice at the average farm price of rice after harvest.

The rental rate on public farm land was 37.5% of the annual yield of the main crop raised on the land. The payment of rent was made in rice if that was the main crop.

The payment of the land price to the landlords under the "Land-to-the-Tiller" program consisted 70% of land bonds in kind.

All these collections were paid at the government's purchasing price, which was far lower than the market price. Thus, the government's gain through the difference in its purchasing price and the market price, multiplied by the total amount of rice obtained through this kind of rice collection, is here referred to as a "hidden rice tax."

Actually, the government collection of rice played two important roles. First, it stabilized the price of rice throughout the two periods, and consequently that of other commodities. Second, the government collected a substantial amount of tax through this operation. The share of rice collection by each kind of operation and the total amount of the "hidden rice tax" are listed in Tables 3.7 and 3.8.

Table 3.7   The Amount and Shares of Rice Collection

Year	Total Rice Collection	Land Tax Payment in Kind and Compulsory Rice Purchasing	Rice-fertilizer Barter	Collection Through Repayment of Loans	Land Price Repayment
	(1,000 m.t.)	(%)	(%)	(%)	(%)
1952	429	33.6	60.6	5.8	–
1955	519	21.0	60.0	6.6	12.4
1960	466	28.7	62.9	4.9	3.5
1965	653	30.1	60.8	7.6	1.5
1970	499	39.5	56.2	3.9	0.4
1971	450	44.6	50.7	4.6	0.1

Source: Compiled by JCRR, based on data from PFB's Financial Operating Statements.

The government's extra gains through rice collection totalled a large amount. As can be seen from Table 3.9, the hidden rice tax exceeded the total income tax of the whole economy many years before 1963. It reached more than twice the agricultural land tax every year before 1961, with only 1954 as an exception. However, the relative burden of the hidden rice tax decreased gradually after 1964. After 1969 even the absolute amount of the hidden rice tax decreased rapidly, and the ratio of the hidden rice tax to the total income tax was only 8.5% in 1971 because the government purchased rice at a relatively reasonable price and at the same time, income tax collections increased.

Table 3.8   The Extra Gains in Value Through
Rice Collection (Hidden Rice Tax)

Year	Farm Price	Government Purchasing Price	Difference Between Farm Price and Gov't Purchasing Price	Total Extra Gains Through Rice Collection (hidden rice tax)	Hidden Rice Tax as a Percentage of the Total Income Tax of the Economy
	(p) (NT$/m.t.)	(p₀) (NT$/m.t.)	(p−p₀) (NT$/m.t.)	(p−p₀) x q (NT$ million)	(%)
1952	1,868	1,071	797	342	107.2
1955	2,698	1,663	1,035	537	106.1
1960	4,913	2,788	2,125	991	104.6
1965	5,045	3,375	1,670	1,091	82.5
1970	5,555	4,418	1,137	568	14.3
1971	5,574	4,658	916	413	8.5

Source: Farm price: based on *Taiwan Agricultural Year Book*; Gov't purchasing price: based on *Taiwan Food Statistical Abstract*; but the gov't purchasing price was multiplied by 0.92.

2.   Impact of the "Hidden Rice Tax" on Agricultural Diversification

Let us now examine the impact of the "hidden rice tax" on agricultural diversification.

The change in the share of rice production relative to other agricultural products will be observed.   The share of rice production Q, will be first explained by (1) the relative price of rice in terms of the ratio of the price of rice to the price of other agricultural products P; (2) relative rice consumption in terms of the ratio of rice consumption to other agricultural consumption C; and (3) relative exports in terms of the ratio of the export of rice to the export of other agricultural products X.

The counterparts of the regression, Equation (1), are listed in Table 3.10.

Table 3.9   Hidden Rice Tax

Year	Hidden Rice Tax (1)	Total Income Tax for the Whole Economy (2)	Agricultural Land Tax (3)	Ratio of Hidden Rice Tax to the Total Income Tax (4)=(1)/(2)	Radio of Hidden Rice Tax to the Agricultural Land Tax (5)=(1)/(3)
1952	342	319	118	107.2	289.8
1953	598	293	210	204.1	284.8
1954	275	332	147	82.8	187.1
1955	537	506	225	106.1	238.7
1956	489	576	230	84.9	212.6
1957	604	573	251	105.4	240.6
1958	568	683	270	83.2	210.4
1959	594	831	276	71.5	215.2
1960	991	947	318	104.6	311.6
1961	1,158	897	400	129.1	289.5
1962	935	790	507	118.4	184.4
1963	956	949	569	100.7	168.0
1964	1,042	1,248	590	83.5	176.6
1965	1,091	1,323	640	82.5	170.5
1966	1,107	1,328	653	83.4	169.5
1967	1,191	1,599	808	74.5	147.4
1968	1,136	2,184	1,064	52.0	106.8
1969	645	2,992	1,082	21.6	59.6
1970	568	3,977	1,088	14.3	52.2
1971	413	4,868	1,178	8.5	35.1

Source: Income Tax and Agricultural Land Tax: based on Department of Statistics, Ministry of Finance, *Yearbook of Financial Statistics of the Republic of China, 1972*; Total Hidden Tax: based on the calculation as shown in Table 3.8.

$$(1)   Q = a + bP + cC + dX$$

The results in Table 3.10 show that the coefficient of determinant R^2 was rather high for the 1961–71 period, while it was very low for the 1952–60 period. This indicates that the explanatory factors of the relative decline in the rice

Table 3.10 Statistics of Equation (1): Share of Rice Production as a Function of Relative Price of Rice, Relative Consumption of Rice, and Relative Export of Rice

Period	a Constant Term	b Coefficient of Relative Price of Rice	c Coefficient of Relative Consump- tion of Rice	d Coefficient of Relative Export of Rice	
1952-60 t value	0.2018	0.0225 (0.1963)	0.0306 (0.4873)	0.0245 (0.8845)	R^2: 0.279 D.W.: 2.019
1961-71 t value	0.2825	−0.0913 (1.1826)	0.0800 (0.9852)	0.0580 (1.1219)	R^2: 0.783 D.W.: 1.270

Sources: Q and C are calculated from JCRR, *The Food Balance Sheet*; P is from DGBAS, *Commodity-Price Statistics Monthly, Taiwan District, The Republic of China*; X is from Department of Statistics, Ministry of Finance, *Monthly Statistics of Exports and Imports, The Republic of China*; T is from Table 3.8.

share of the two periods are different, and that there must be some other factor or factors involved in the relative decline of rice production in the 1952–60 period. After the "hidden rice tax" T is added to the equation as one of the explanatory factors, as seen in Equation (2), we find that the coefficient of determination of the 1952–60 period increased tremendously from 0.279 to 0.743, and that of the 1961–71 period increased from 0.783 to 0.838.

$$(2) \qquad Q = a' + b'P + c'C + d'X + e'T$$

With the t value of 2.6944, the "hidden rice tax" was the most significant factor explaining the decline in the share of rice production in the 1952–60 period. In the later period, the most important factor which contributed to the decline in the share of rice production was the decline in relative rice consumption. The hidden rice tax still had its effect on the decline

Table 3.11   Statistics of Equation (2): Share of Rice Production
as a Function of Relative Price of Rice, Relative
Consumption of Rice, Relative Export of Rice,
and Hidden Rice Tax

Period	a' Constant Term	b' Coefficient of Relative Price of Rice	c' Coefficient of Relative Consump- tion of Rice	d' Coefficient of Relative Export of Rice	e' Coefficient of Hidden Rice Tax
1952-60	0.1952	0.1020	0.0018	−0.0107	−0.0194
t value		(1.2439)	(0.0416)	(0.4714)	(2.6944)
		R^2: 0.743		D.W.: 1.708	
1961-71	0.2609	−0.0732	0.1388	0.0570	−0.0093
t value		(1.0000)	(1.6065)	(1.1801)	(1.4308)
		R^2: 0.838		D.W.: 1.356	

Source: Same as Table 3.10.

in the rice share, though its importance decreased.

In short, the government's "hidden rice tax" collection was the most powerful factor contributing to the decline in rice production in the 1952−60 period. In the 1961−71 period, it continued to be influential, although its importance declined. On the whole, the relative price of rice and the share of rice export were not crucial to the decline of the rice share throughout the two periods, although the decline of the relative price of rice had some influence on the share of rice production in the 1952−60 period.

3. Pricing Policies for Other Agricultural Products

(1) Pricing Policy for Sugarcane

The sugarcane required for supporting the sugar industry was drawn from two sources: the government-owned Taiwan Sugar Corporation's own plantations, and private cane growers.

During the period 1953—69, private cane growers accounted for 69% of the total planted area. For better utilization of land each farmer had to estimate the relative advantage of raising different competing crops. If he wanted to plant cane in the following crop year, then he had to sign a contract with the Taiwan Sugar Corporation and become one of its "contract cane growers." The contract specified a certain percentage of the grower's sugar that could be retained by him for sale on the domestic market. Farmers generally sold a regulated part of their sugar on the domestic market at a monopoly price which was higher than their cost of production. When the international free market price of sugar was lower than their production cost, the loss was made up by a high price in the domestic market generated by the Corporation's limited supply. In most of the years between 1951 and 1965, the farmers' retained percentage was about 40%. But when production was expanded to levels exceeding 900,000 m.t., due to high prices in the international sugar market, as in the years 1957 and 1963—64, the percentage of farmers' sugar for home consumption was successively lowered to 35%, 30% and 26%. Since 1968, however, cane growers have been allowed to retain 50% or more of their sugar for sale on the domestic market.

(2) Hog Production

Hog production accounted for the second highest value of production of all of Taiwan's farm products, second only to paddy rice. In addition to money income directly generated from the sale of hogs, there were some supplementary earnings from the utilization of surplus or residual resources of production, and from the yield of by-products. By 1971 over 90% of the hogs in Taiwan were raised by individual farmers as a subsidiary farm business. Their primary purposes were (1) to get additional cash income directly from selling hogs, (2) to get hog manure for enriching the soil and thus increasing crop yields, (3) to utilize surplus farm family labor for livestock production, and (4) to use residual food materials together with some non-saleable farm products for feeding hogs.[7]

The hog-raising business in farm households opened a

sideline field for utilizing such surplus labor as females and elderly persons to do productive work. The residual foods in all rural households and some non-saleable by-products on most of the farms, such as potato vines and leaves, were used as supplementary feed for hogs.

Hogs from all rural areas passed through the hands of local hog dealers to reach urban slaughterhouses. The Taiwan Sugar Corporation sold its hogs directly to domestic slaughterhouses and export markets. All the slaughterhouses were public organizations managed by municipal offices, township agencies or Farmers' Associations, which regulated the supply and demand of hogs so as to stabilize hog and pork prices. Thus, the control of hog prices was accomplished indirectly through control of the hog supply.

(3) Major Vegetables

There were more than 40 varieties of vegetables produced in Taiwan during this period, and the great majority of them were sold on the domestic market because of their perishable nature. However, mushrooms and asparagus comprised a great portion of vegetable production, and were mostly produced for export. In 1971 mushrooms comprised 27.4% of the total vegetable production, and asparagus made up 25.6%. Most of these were exported in canned form. Because their production does not require a large area of farm land, especially in the case of mushrooms, the production of these products relies heavily on the demand rather than supply. Approximately 87% of the annual production was processed into canned mushrooms, of which about 93% was exported to foreign markets during 1961–69. Asparagus was first brought into production in 1963 and expanded rapidly after 1965, owing to a drastic increase in export demand. Land is not a limiting factor in asparagus production. This suggests that whenever export demand rises and prices are favorable, the industry may expand appropriately. On the average, approximately 88% of the total canned asparagus was sold to foreign countries during the period 1963–69.[8]

In order to insure a stable price and to encourage farmers to produce   mushrooms, asparagus, and other crops, the government purchased these products at certain guaranteed prices and distributed them to processing factories.   The purchasing and distribution were mostly handled by Farmers' Associations. The guaranteed price mechanism covered sorghum, citrus, corn, pineapples, onions, etc.

In short, past agricultural pricing policy greatly contributed to the reduction in the share of rice production and the increase in the share of other products.   It contributed greatly, therefore, to agricultural diversification.

IV. Effects of General Economic Growth on Agricultural Diversification

In addition to land reform and agricultural pricing policies, general economic growth also had a significant impact on agricultural diversification.   Effects of general economic growth on agricultural diversification will be discussed in this section from the following aspects: (1) changes in agricultural demand as a consequence of overall economic development, (2) relative change of nonfarm income vs. farm income, and   (3) labor migration from the agricultural sector to the nonagricultural sector caused by industrial growth.

1.   Changes in Agricultural Demand

The past experience in Taiwan was characterized by a percentage decrease in rice consumption and, conversely, a relative increase in other agricultural consumption.   Showing the same tendency, the percentage of consumption of common crops and special crops decreased and that of fruits, vegetables and livestock products increased rapidly. Thus, as a consequence of economic development, agricultural consumption diversified greatly.

The diversity index of the domestic consumption of food is shown in Table 3.13.   Domestic consumption is defined as domestic production plus import minus export minus change in

Table 3.12   Domestic Consumption of Major Agricultural
Products in Percentage of Total Consumption

	1952	1960	1971
Common crops	59.8	59.7	46.5
Rice	39.9	39.1	24.0
Sweet potatoes	8.3	7.8	5.1
Wheat	3.5	4.6	3.4
Special crops	1.8	1.4	2.1
Fruits	2.2	2.4	4.5
Vegetables	3.8	4.0	5.8
Livestock	32.4	32.5	41.1
Pork	16.8	16.1	16.9
Beef	0.3	0.3	0.9
Poultry	1.8	1.7	6.6
Eggs	2.5	2.6	2.3
Fish	10.0	10.5	12.5
Milk (fresh)	1.0	1.3	1.9

Source: JCRR, *The Food Balance Sheet.*

inventory.   The index of domestic consumption shows that there was a great diversification in the period 1961–71.

Another factor that contributed to agricultural diversification was the diversification of exports. The diversity index of agricultural exports can also be found in Table 3.13. It shows that export diversification occurred only in the second period, 1961–71,   though it then proceeded at a rapid pace. The growth rates of three diversity indices are shown in Table 3.14. All the three diversity indices show a higher growth rate in the second period, 1961–71, than in the first period, 1952–60.

A regression analysis shows that production diversification was highly correlated with consumption diversification throughout the two periods. When the export diversification is also taken into account in the regression as a factor to explain diversification of production, the coefficient of determination is increased.   However, in the first period, the sign of the statistic is negative and the t value is rather small. This means

Table 3.13   Comparison of the Diversity Indices of Agricultural
Production, Domestic Consumption and Exports

Year	Diversity Index of Production	Diversity Index of Domestic Consumption	Diversity Index of Exports
1952	3.54	4.74	2.02
1953	3.18	3.73	1.44
1954	3.81	5.32	2.00
1955	3.99	4.96	2.15
1956	4.07	5.39	1.81
1957	4.21	5.56	2.12
1958	4.61	6.02	2.08
1959	4.95	6.12	1.83
1960	4.01	4.90	1.88
1961	4.13	5.32	2.87
1962	4.31	5.67	2.39
1963	4.43	5.46	3.27
1964	5.75	6.08	2.58
1965	5.67	6.04	5.26
1966	5.67	5.95	5.49
1967	5.85	6.34	6.59
1968	6.04	7.00	6.51
1969	6.69	7.52	6.58
1970	6.67	8.25	7.14
1971	7.03	8.37	7.23

Source: Based on Department of Agriculture and Forestry, Taiwan Provincial
Government, *Taiwan Agricultural Year Book*; JCRR, *The Food Balance Sheet.*

Notes:

1. Diversity index of production = Agricultural diversity index
2. Diversity index of domestic consumption

$$= \frac{1}{\Sigma \left(\dfrac{\text{Value of each agricultural consumption}}{\text{Value of total agricultural consumption}} \right)^2}$$

3. Diversity index of exports

$$= \frac{1}{\Sigma \left(\dfrac{\text{Value of each agricultural export}}{\text{Value of total agricultural export}} \right)^2}$$

that export diversification contributed to agricultural diversification only in the second period.

Table 3.14   The Growth Rates of Three Diversity Indices

		(%)
	1952–60	1961–71
Diversity index of production	3.84	5.39
Diversity index of domestic consumption	3.35	4.71
Diversity index of exports	0.83	12.72

Source: Same as Table 3.13.

(3) $Y = k + fF$
(4) $Y = k' + f'F + gG$
(where Y: diversity index of production
        F: diversity index of domestic consumption
        G: diveristy index of exports)

2.   *Relative Change of Nonfarm Income vs. Farm Income*

The per worker earnings in both the agricultural and non-agricultural sectors are listed in Table 3.16: (1) The per worker earnings in the nonagricultural sector were always higher than those in the agricultural sector owing to the higher productivity in the nonagricultural sector. (2) In the first period, the increase in farm income was 1.06 times that in nonfarm income, while in the second period, it turned around to become 89%. (3) The average growth rates of agricultural income and non-agricultural income during the first period were 16.7% and 14.1% respectively, while those in the second period reversed to 7.0% and 8.4%. (4) The yield per hectare of land showed a lower growth rate in the second period than in the first: 6.6% and 16.7%, respectively.

All these factors were detrimental to agricultural production. The relative deterioration of farm earnings was one of the major causes in accelerating the emigration of farm labor, and thus it decreased the degree of multiple cropping in the later stage of the second period.

Table 3.15 Counterparts of Equations (3) and (4)

Period	k Constant Term	f Coefficient of Diversity Index of Domestic Consumption		R^2	D.W.
1952-60	0.5213	0.6778			
t value		(6.8258)		0.869	2.150
1961-71	0.2357	0.8284			
t value		(6.3576)		0.818	0.788

Period	k' Constant Term	f' Coefficient of Diversity Index of Domestic Consumption	g Coefficient of Diversity Index of Exports	R^2	D.W.
1952-60	0.9858	0.7552	−0.4501		
t value		(6.4109)	(1.1571)	0.893	2.509
1961-71	1.0564	0.5606	0.1834		
t value		(2.6607)	(1.5542)	0.860	1.517

Source: Same as Table 3.13.

3. Labor Migration

Labor migration out of the agricultural sector into the industrial sector has been a continuing phenomenon as a result of industrialization in Taiwan. The rate of emigration was particularly fast during the period 1966—70. Table 3.17 shows the net immigration or emigration by type of area. The net immigration rates to metropolitan and industrial areas were 12.1% and 17.4%, respectively, during the period 1966—70. The rates were much greater than in the period

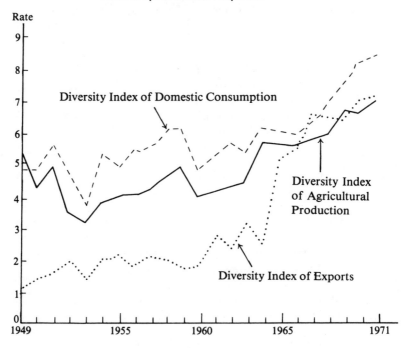

Fig. 3.2   Diversity Indices of Agricultural Production, Consumption and Exports

1951–55 (7.0% and 7.5%, respectively), and also in the period 1961–65 (9.8% and 13.4%, respectively).

These three areas, i.e. rural mixed, agricultural, and predominantly agricultural, had a net emigration of labor. The migration rates were extremely high during the period 1966–70. The migration rate from the predominantly agricultural area was as high as 24.7% a year.

Thus the rapid emigration of agricultural labor, together with the decline in the relative income of the agricultural sector, finally caused a decline in the degree of multiple cropping.

V. Conclusions

(1) Land reform has produced significant effects on multiple cropping in the following ways: changes in tenancy con-

Table 3.16   Agricultural vs. Nonagricultural Incomes

Year	Ya/A ($/ha.)	Ya/La ($/pers.)	Yn/Ln ($/pers.)	Yn/Ln − Ya/La ($/pers.)
1952	5,973	3,316	7,706	4,390
1955	9,196	5,097	12,659	7,562
1960	19,016	10,029	21,976	11,947
1965	27,874	14,849	34,178	19,329
1970	36,168	19,583	48,233	28,650
1971	37,308	20,200	53,029	32,829

Source: Directorate-General of Budget, Accounting and Statistics, Executive Yuan, *National Income of the Republic of China* (1972); Council for International Economic Cooperation and Development, Executive Yuan, *Taiwan Statistical Data Book* (1972).

Notes:
1. Y: income; L: labor; A: agricultural land; *a*: the agricultural sector; *n*: the nonagricultural sector.
2. The definition of farm income by the *National Income of the Republic of China,* DGBAS, is different from that by the JCRR.

Table 3.17   Percentage of Migration by Type of Area

(%)

Area	1951-55	1956-60	1961-65	1966-70
Metropolitan	7.0	8.1	9.8	12.1
Industrial	7.5	12.0	13.4	17.4
Rural mixed	− 9.3	− 7.4	− 9.0	− 9.8
Agricultural	−12.1	−10.6	−12.2	−13.6
Predominantly agricultural	−14.9	−17.6	−19.4	−24.7
East coast	11.3	3.7	7.6	−12.8

Source: Paul K. C. Liu, "The Population of Taiwan: 1945-1990," Sino-American Conference on Manpower in Taiwan (Taipei: Academia Sinica, China Council on Sino-American Cooperation in the Humanities and Social Sciences, 1972).

ditions, changes in the size of landholdings, and changes in production patterns. After land reform, the ratio of owner-farmers and part owner-farmers to the total family increased tremendously. The change in tenancy conditions provided a great incentive to produce more, and made possible the more efficient utilization of agricultural labor. Land reform caused an equalization of property and a smaller-scale farming. The smaller size of the farming unit naturally brought about a more intensive use of labor and, consequently, more intensive multiple cropping farming. After land reform, there was a freer choice of crops for the farmers because owner-farmers no longer had any obligation to produce rice for rental payments. Thus land reform led to a reduction in the relative share of rice production and an increase in the share of vegetables, fruits and livestock. Further, the technological changes in agriculture after land reform were largely centered on the intensive use of land with more labor input, thus accelerating multiple cropping.

(2) Past agricultural diversification was mainly characterized by the decreasing share of rice and the increasing share of other crops. Governmental action in the rice market mainly took the form of land tax payment in kind, rice-fertilizer barter, and other rice collections. All of these collections were made at the government's purchasing prices, which were far lower than the market prices. Thus the government collected a "hidden rice tax." For many years before 1962, the "hidden rice tax" exceeded the amount of the total income tax paid by the whole economy. However, the ratio of the "hidden rice tax" to the total income tax decreased gradually after 1963 and particularly after 1969. It comprised only 8.5% in 1971 due to the decrease in the "hidden rice tax" and the relative increase in the income tax.

The government's "hidden rice tax" collection was the most powerful factor contributing to the decline in the share of rice production in the period of 1952–60. In the second period, 1961–71, it continued to be influential, but its importance declined. The relative price of rice played a comparatively significant role in the 1952–60 period. On the whole, the relative price of rice and the share of rice export were not crucial to the relative decline of rice production share throughout the two periods, although the decline of the relative price of rice did have some influence on the share of rice production in the 1952–60 period.

(3) The government controlled the production of sugarcane by offering a certain percentage of sugar to the cane growers to dispose of as they wished. Farmers generally sell a regulated part of their sugar on the domestic market at a price higher than their cost of production. The government offered a guaranteed price for major vegetables and fruits in order to encourage their production. The encouragement of hog production was accomplished mainly through control of the hog market by provision of an appropriate supply of hogs to the market.

(4) Effects of general economic growth on agricultural diversification are discussed mainly from three points of view: (a) changes in agricultural demand as a consequence of overall economic development, (b) relative change of nonagricultural income vs. agricultural income, and (c) labor migration from the agricultural sector to the nonagricultural sector caused by industrial growth. The diversity indices of domestic consumption and of agricultural export were calculated along with the index of agricultural production. The index of domestic consumption shows that there was a great diversification in the period 1961–71. Export diversification occurred only in the second period, 1961–71, and at a rapid rate. All the three diversity indices showed a higher growth rate in the second period of 1961–71 than in the first period of 1952–1960. A regression analysis shows that production diversification was highly correlated with consumption diversification throughout the two periods. Export diversification contributed to agricultural diversification only in the second period.

(5) The per worker earnings in the nonagricultural sector were always higher than those in the agricultural sector. The increase in agricultural income was faster in the first period than in the second period. And the yield per hectare of land showed a lower growth rate in the second period than in the first. All these factors tended to discourage agricultural production. The relative deterioration of agricultural earnings was one of the major factors leading to accelerated emigration of farm labor, and it thus reduced the degree of multiple

cropping in the later stage of the second period. Labor migration out of the agricultural sector to the industrial sector has been continuing as a result of industrialization in Taiwan. The rate of emigration was particularly fast during the period 1966–70.   The emigration rate from predominantly agricultural areas reached 24.7% a year during the period 1966–70. Thus the rapid emigration of agricultural labor, together with the decline in the relative earnings of the agricultural sector, finally caused a decline in the degree of multiple cropping after 1967.

NOTES

1. You-tsao Wang, "Agricultural Development," in *Economic Development in Taiwan,* Kowie Chang ed., (Taipei: Cheng Chung Book Company, 1968), p. 176 ; Wen-hui Lai, "Trend of Agricultural Employment in Postwar Taiwan" (paper read at Conference on Manpower in Taiwan, 1972, Taipei).

2.   The diversity index A in this table includes 118 varieties of agricultural products, while the diversity index B includes only 7 leading agricultural products. The difference between the two calculations is very negligible, indicating that the diversification in these 7 products is representative. The 118 products and the 7 major ones are as follows:
   Total agricultural products (118 items): Rice, Sweet Potatoes, Barley, Wheat, Millet, Barn-yard Millet, Sorghum, Indian Corn, Soybeans, Other Beans, Fresh Edible Sugar Cane, Sugar Cane, Tea, Tobacco, Coffee, Peanuts, Sesame, Rapeseed, Arrow Root, Cassava, Ramie, Jute, Cotton, Tachia Rush, Triangle Rush, Pineapple fiber, Perfume Plant, Cymbopogon, Sisal, Derris, Bananas, Pineapples, Ponkan, Tonkan, Citrus Sinensis, Wentan Pomelos, Tou Pomelos, White Pomelos, Ambari Hemp, Peppermint Flax, Flowerseed, Wenchow Oranges, Valencia Oranges, Lemons, Grapefruit, Other Citrus Fruits, Longans, Mangos, Areca Catechu, Pomegranates, Prunes, Peaches, Persimmons, Papaya, Water Apples, Grapes, Loquats, Radishes, Other Root Vegetables, Ginger Taro, Potatoes, Onions, Scallions, Garlic, Other Stem Vegetables, Cabbage, Leaf-mustard, Mustard, Water Convolvulus, Parsley, Other Leaf and Flower Vegetables, Oriental Pickling Melons, Cucumbers, Watermelons, Guardmelons, Squash, Egg-appies, Asparagus Beans, Water Chestnuts, Lichees, Bamboo Shoots, Plums, Asparagus, Cauliflower, Garlic Bulbs, Pears, Carrots, Other Fruits, Liu-cheng, Peas, Tomatoes,

Other Fruit Vegetables, Mushrooms, Mushmelons, Buffalo, Yellow Cattle, Indian Cattle, Western Cattle, Hybrid Cattle, Hogs, Goats, Sheep, Horses, Deer, Chickens, Ducks, Geese, Turkeys, Milk, Skins, Honey, Domestic Silkworms, Wild Silkworms, Chicken Eggs, Duck Eggs.

Major agricultural products (7 items): 1. Rice, 2. Sweet Potatoes, 3. Sugarcane, 4. Peanuts, 5. Bananas, 6. Hogs, 7. Chickens.

The calculation of diversity index B is based on 7 products, the sum of whose squares comprises more than 98% of the 118 products' squares. The reasoning is seen in the following equations.

$$\text{Diversity Index A} = \frac{1}{\sum\limits_{i=1}^{118} \left(\dfrac{y_i}{Y}\right)^2}$$

$$\text{Diversity Index B} = \frac{1}{\sum\limits_{i=1}^{7} \left(\dfrac{y_i}{Y}\right)^2}$$

$$\sum_{i=1}^{7} \left(\frac{y_i}{Y}\right)^2 < \sum_{i=1}^{118} \left(\frac{y_i}{Y}\right)^2 = \sum_{i=1}^{7} \left(\frac{y_i}{Y}\right)^2 + \sum_{i=1}^{118} \left(\frac{y_i}{Y}\right)^2$$

but

$$\sum_{i=1}^{7} \left(\frac{y_i}{Y}\right)^2 \doteq \sum_{i=1}^{118} \left(\frac{y_i}{Y}\right)^2$$

The proportions of $\sum\limits_{i=1}^{7}\left(\dfrac{y_i}{Y}\right)^2 \Big/ \sum\limits_{i=1}^{118}\left(\dfrac{y_i}{Y}\right)^2$ are shown below.

Year	$\dfrac{\sum\limits_{i=1}^{7}\left(\frac{y_i}{Y}\right)^2}{\sum\limits_{i=1}^{118}\left(\frac{y_i}{Y}\right)^2}$ (%)	Year	$\dfrac{\sum\limits_{i=1}^{7}\left(\frac{y_i}{Y}\right)^2}{\sum\limits_{i=1}^{118}\left(\frac{y_i}{Y}\right)^2}$ (%)
1952	99.60	1962	99.50
1953	99.80	1963	99.33
1954	99.71	1964	99.17
1955	99.42	1965	99.09
1956	99.53	1966	99.08
1957	99.49	1967	98.97
1958	99.37	1968	98.75
1959	99.30	1969	98.43
1960	99.92	1970	98.12
1961	99.56	1971	98.12

3.   T.H. Lee, "Impact of Land Reform on the Farm Economy Structure" (Taipei: Joint Commission on Rural Reconstruction, March 1969; mimeo.).

4.   Yen-tien Chang, *Land Reform and Its Impact on Economic and Social Progress in Taiwan* (Taipei: National Taiwan University, 1965).

5.   Te Tsui Chang, *Long-Term Projections of Supply, Demand and Trade for Selected Agricultural Products in Taiwan* (Taipei: National Taiwan University, College of Agriculture, The Research Institute of Agricultural Economics, 1970).

6.   T.H. Lee, "Government Interference in the Rice Market," *Economic Essays,* Vol. 2 (Taipei: National Taiwan University, Graduate Institute of Economics, 1971).

7.   Te Tsui Chang, ibid.

8.   Te Tsui Chang, ibid.

PART II

4

Labor Absorption and Full Employment

Employment data from various sources seem to indicate that in the 1950s Taiwan had substantial unemployment, that the rate of unemployment declined during the mid 1960s, and that by 1971 the economy had reached full employment. *But where, how, and why was labor absorbed?* This chapter tries to answer these questions. It is hoped that this study will illuminate the past labor absorption and methods of labor utilization which will be useful for other economies now embarking on a labor-intensive strategy.

The chapter contains three sections. In section one, a review and adjustment of the employment data, including unemployment rates, are presented. Labor data are known to be among the weakest of the various kinds of statistics in Taiwan. The available employment data series differ in definition, sampling and compilation techniques, and hence diverge from one another. Virtually none of the existing studies has attacked the problem posed by these diverse and confusing data series. Before we can use employment data properly, a review of various existing series is necessary and appropriate adjustments are called for.

In section two the question asked is: Where was labor absorbed? In order to answer this question, the period from 1954 to 1971 is divided into three sub-intervals: 1954–61, 1961–66, and 1966–71. Labor absorption is first observed at the agricultural and nonagricultural levels. Then the non-agricultural sector is broken down into seven major industries and further into 19 manufacturing sub-industries.

In order to answer how and why labor was absorbed, characteristics of labor absorption are studied in section three. Analyses are on (1) labor absorption, labor intensity and wage rates; (2) labor absorption and income distribution; and (3) labor absorption and capital expansion.

I.   Changes in Unemployment Rates

Available employment figures differ in definition, sampling and compilation techniques, which makes them diverge from one another.   Before we can use employment data properly, a review and adjustment are called for.   A review and adjustment of unemployment rates are presented in Appendix I. A reestimation of employment is presented in Appendix II. A brief report will be given in this section.

The existing unemployment data on a continuous basis are derived from Household Registration Statistics and the Labor Force Survey.   The unemployment figures in the former have been available since 1954; however, the figures before 1967 are inappropriate.   The reason is that for the period 1954–60,   the category of "jobless" includes both the unemployed and persons unwilling to work.   As a result, Household Registration Statistics show a huge amount of unemployment based on this faulty definition. From 1961 to 1966, unemployment was distinguished from the "jobless" category, but the rates of unemployment derived from this source were as low as 0.2% to 0.3%; these figures are inconsistent with the 1966 Census data.

The Labor Force Survey was initiated in 1963. This source of data needs adjustment in two respects. One pertains to the consistency of definition. (For example, the lower age limit of the unemployed was 12 in 1963–68; it was changed to 15 in 1968.) The other concerns the coverage of unemployment. The definition adopted by the Labor Force Survey tends to underestimate the level of unemployed. A minor adjustment is needed in this regard.

Two fragmentary sources of data are the Population Censuses (in 1956, 1966, and 1970) and the 1953 Unemployment Survey. However, the 1953 Unemployment Survey covered only part of the unemployed. It excluded first-job seekers, those aged 61 and over, and those aged 17 and below. As a result, it puts the unemployment rate for 1953 as low as 1.03%. In order to be definitionally appropriate and comparable to other years, some necessary adjustments have to be made based on these incomplete data.

The review and estimates of unemployment rates for 1953–71 are done as follows:

(1) The 1953 unemployment data are adjusted. To the adjusted data of the 1953 Unemployment Survey, 1956 Census and adjusted Labor Force Survey, figures of unemployed for 1954–55 and 1957–63 are interpolated.

(2) Because employment data were not available before 1963, figures for the number of those employed for 1954–63 are estimated to provide the denominator for unemployment rates.

The unemployment rates from various sources, some of which are adjusted or estimated, are presented in Fig. 4.1.

These rates give a general idea of the level of and changes in the rates of unemployment during the period from 1953 to 1980. The unemployment rate was high before 1965. It dropped rapidly between 1965 and 1968. By 1971, the unemployment rate had reached 3.36% according to the household registration statistics, and 3.01% according to the labor force survey in broad terms. Thus, if 3% is viewed as a criterion of full employment, it can be said that by 1971 the Taiwan economy had successfully reached the full employment level after a period of extensive labor absorption.

The adjusted time series of unemployment rates based on all sources and adjustments are presented in Table 4.1.

II. Where was Labor Absorbed?

As we have seen above, the unemployment rate decreased

Fig. 4.1   Unemployment Rate, 1953–1980

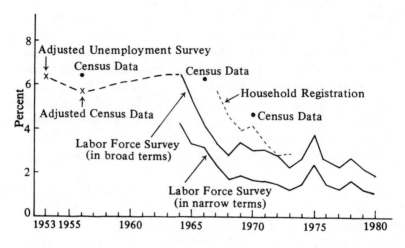

Note: The sharp increase in 1978 is mostly due to a change in sampling and
statistical methods, which are subject to a further revision.

from 6.29% to 3.01% from 1953 to 1971. During this period,
newcomers to the labor force totaled about 1.8 million persons,
who comprised 60% of total employment of 1953. During this
period, the economy was capable not only of absorbing those
newcomers, but also of absorbing a part of the originally
unemployed.   The total labor absorption during this period
was about 1.9 million persons. In this section, we would like
to ask this question: where was labor absorbed?

In order to answer this question, the period from 1954 to
1971 is divided into three sub-intervals: 1954–61, 1961–66,
and 1966–71. The main reasons for this division are two.
First, the years of division correspond to the years when
industrial surveys were conducted (four times in all); thus, the
survey reports can be used as basic data. Second, the division
of years corresponds to our purpose of analysis from an
economic point of view in that the 1950s had distinct
characteristics; 1961 was the very critical year of "the take-off"
(the reasons for which are discussed in Chapter 2); and 1966

roughly corresponds to the year when agricultural outmigration accelerated.

Table 4.1   Unemployment Rate (1953—1980)

Year	No. of Unemployed (1,000 persons)	Unemployment Rate (%)
1953	194	6.29
1954	188	6.02
1955	182	5.79
1956	176	5.63
1957	185	5.73
1958	194	5.88
1959	204	5.99
1960	213	6.12
1961	222	6.21
1962	231	6.32
1963	241	6.38
1964	250	6.40
1965	203	5.20
1966	161	4.15
1967	140	3.36
1968	120	2.76
1969	157	3.42
1970	142	3.01
1971	147	3.01
1972	141	2.77
1973	122	2.24
1974	150	2.66
1975	214	3.73
1976	153	2.63
1977	138	2.27
1978	173	2.69
1979	145	2.21
1980	137	2.05

Source and Note: See Appendix I, Table AI.4.

The decrease in the unemployment rate was due to two labor absorptive components, namely a reduction in the existing number of unemployed and a higher rate of absorption of newcomers. Newcomers are defined as the difference between the change in P and N, i.e., ($\Delta P - \Delta N$), where P is the population aged 15 and over, and N is the population aged 15 and over but not in labor force.

During the period 1951–61, the economy failed to absorb all the newcomers. As a result, the number of unemployed increased during this period. During the later two periods, 1961–66 and 1966–71, employment opportunities were successfully provided not only to absorb all the newcomers, but also a part of the unemployed. Thus, not only was the rate of unemployment reduced, but also the total number of unemployed.

Our major interest in this section is to ask where the labor force was actually absorbed. In order to answer this question, the absorption of labor will be examined from the following sector classification:

(1)   the agricultural and the nonagricultural sectors,
(2)   the eight major industries of the economy,
(3)   the manufacturing sub-industries.

1. Labor Absorption in Agricultural and Nonagricultural Sectors

The "critical minimum effort analysis" of Professors Ranis and Fei[1] contends that "Productivity in the agricultural sector must rise sufficiently so that a smaller fraction of the total population can support the entire economy with food and raw materials, thus enabling agricultural workers to be released; simultaneously, the industrial sector must expand sufficiently to provide employment opportunities for released workers." "If the combined forces of capital accumulation and innovation yield a rate of labor allocation in excess of the rate of population growth, the economy may be considered to be successful in the development effort in the sense that the center of gravity is continuously shifted towards the industrial sector." The

Table 4.2   Labor Absorption of Newcomers and Unemployed

(1,000 persons)

Period	Labor Absorption (Increment in Employment)	Increment in Population Aged 15 and Over	Increment in Population Aged 15 and Over but not in Labor Force	Newcomers	Change in Unemployed
	ΔL	ΔP	ΔN	$(\Delta P - \Delta N)$	ΔU
1954−61					
in persons	420	1,281	827	454	34
(in % of ΔL)	(100.0)			(108.1)	(8.1)
1961−66					
in persons	369	1,086	778	308	−61
(in % of ΔL)	(100.0)			(83.5)	(−16.5)
1966−71					
in persons	1,016	1,496	494	1,002	−14
(in % of ΔL)	(100.0)			(98.6)	(−1.4)

Source:
  1. Employment: 1954 and 1961 are based on the estimates in Appendix II. Data for 1966 and 1971, same as Appendix I, Table AI.2.
  2. Population aged 15 and over: 1954 and 1961 are based on the estimates given by Ministry of Interior in 1975. Data for 1966 and 1971, same as Appendix I, Table AI.2.
  3. Population aged 15 and over but not in labor force: 1954 and 1961 are estimates. Data for 1966 and 1971, same as Appendix I, Table AI.2.
  4. Unemployment: from Appendix I, Table AI.4.

Note:

i.e.

$$L \quad = \quad P \quad - \quad N \quad - \quad U$$

Employment = Population aged 15 and over − Population aged 15 and over but not in labor force − Unemployed

$$\Delta L \quad = \quad \Delta P - \Delta N \quad - \quad \Delta U$$

(Labor absorption) = Newcomers − Change in unemployed

condition of critical minimum effort is therefore given as this: the growth rate of nonagricultural labor is higher than that of the population.

The absorption of labor by the nonagricultural sector can be observed in Figure 4.2. The rate of labor absorption in the nonagricultural sector did not exceed the population growth rate before 1957. That is, no single year had reached the standard required by the critical minimum effort. But after 1957, not only was the condition satisfied every year, but the growth rate of nonagricultural employment far exceeded that of the population.

The growth of employment registered a higher rate after 1961, particularly for secondary industry. The higher speed of capital accumulation in the manufacturing sector caused a rapid increase in capital intensity in manufacturing after 1961. Real wages in manufacturing went up gradually during 1961– 71 and rose rapidly after 1971. This was due mainly to the fact that the Taiwan economy reached the "turning point" in 1968 and achieved full employment by 1971.

Fig. 4.2   Labor Absorption in the Nonagricultural Sector

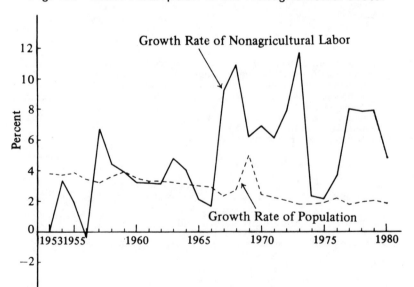

2. *Labor Absorption in the Eight Industries of the Economy*

In order to identify the particular industries which absorbed the most laborers, the nonagricultural sector is further broken down into seven major industries (for a total of eight, including agriculture). The relative weights of labor absorption show that during the three successive periods, the bulk of the labor force was absorbed by three industries: manufacturing, whole-sale and retail trade, and other business. For the period 1966—71, manufacturing accounted for 37.5% of labor absorption; wholesale and retail trade, 23.5%; and other business, 9.3%; together they accounted for 70.3% of total labor absorption. The contribution of these three industries was 66.1% in the period 1961—66 and 69.3% in 1954—61.

Thus, we know that during the two decades of 1954—71, manufacturing and its directly related industries accounted for more than two thirds of the economy's total labor absorption. Given this finding, we should like to ask which particular sub-industries in manufacturing absorbed the growing non-agricultural labor force and thus contributed to total labor absorption.

3. *Labor Absorption in the Manufacturing Sub-industries*

A decomposition of the manufacturing industry into 19 sub-industries makes it clear that the major labor absorbing sub-industries were: food processing, textiles & footwear and electrical machinery. The relative weights of labor absorption of these three industries were: 45.6% for the period 1954—61, 54.7% for the period 1961—66, and 48.0% for the period 1966—71; thus they accounted for about half of the labor absorption of the whole manufacturing industry. Labor absorption in the food processing industry registered the biggest share in the 1950s, but it ceased to be a labor absorbing industry after 1965. The share of absorption in the electrical machinery industry in the 1950s was rather insignificant; however, it increased drama-tically in the 1960s. The textile and footwear industries'

Table 4.3   Relative Weights of Labor Absorption in the Eight Industries of the Economy

Industry	Increment of Employment ΔL_j (Thousand persons)		
	1954−61	1961−66	1966−71
1. Agriculture	59	68	48
2. Mining	10	8	36
3. Manufacturing	106	88	381
4. Construction	23	19	142
5. Electricity, gas & water supply	5	4	6
6. Transportation	32	26	70
7. Wholesale and retail trade	78	66	239
8. Other business	107	90	94
The whole economy (ΔL)	420	369	1,016

Source: 1954, 1961: Based on the adjusted data (Table AII.5) in Appendix II.
   1966, 1971: Taiwan Provincial Labor Force Survey & Research Institute, *Quarterly Report on the Labor Force Survey in Taiwan, Republic of China,* various years.
Note: The subscript j refers to the jth industry.

contribution to labor absorption increased all throughout the three periods. In particular, the contribution during 1966−71 by the footwear industry to the expansion was notable.

In short, the above observations show us the following characteristics of labor absorption in Taiwan:

(1) The rapid outmigration of agricultural labor in the latest period was possible only because of the rapid labor absorption in the nonagricultural sector.

(2) During the period 1954−61, the economy failed to absorb all the newcomers. As a result, the number of unemployed increased during this period.

(3) During the later two periods, 1961−66 and 1966−71, employment opportunities were successfully provided not only

Relative Weight $\Delta L_j / \Delta L$ (%)			Industry
1954−61	1961−66	1966−71	
14.0	18.4	4.7	1. Agriculture
2.4	2.2	3.5	2. Mining
25.2	23.8	37.5	3. Manufacturing
5.5	5.1	14.0	4. Construction
			5. Electricity, gas & water
1.2	1.1	0.6	supply
7.6	7.1	6.9	6. Transportation
18.6	17.9	23.5	7. Wholesale and retail trade
25.5	24.4	9.3	8. Other business
100.0	100.0	100.0	The whole economy (ΔL)

to absorb all the newcomers but also a part of the unemployed.

(4) More than two thirds of the economy's total labor increment was absorbed into manufacturing and its directly related industries during 1954−71.

(5) Three sub-industries out of nineteen − food processing, textiles, and electrical machinery − accounted for about a half of the total labor absorbed by manufacturing.

(6) The food processing industry had a different pattern from the other two labor absorbing industries. Labor absorption in the food processing industry registered the biggest share in the 1950s, but it ceased to be a labor absorbing industry after 1965. During this latest period, the electrical machinery industry completely took the place of the food processing industry in labor absorption.

Table 4.4   Relative Weights of Labor Absorption in the
Manufacturing Sub-industries

Industry	Increment of Employment ΔL_j (Thousand persons)		
	1954−61	1961−66	1966−71
1. Food processing	29	30	−10
2. Textiles & footwear	25	32	142
Textiles	18	29	95
Footwear	7	3	47
3. Electrical machinery	8	19	74
4. All other sub-industries	74	67	223
Total manufacturing (ΔL)	136	148	429

Source: The Committee on Industrial and Commercial Censuses of Taiwan and
Fukien Area, Executive Yuan, *Industrial & Commercial Censuses of Taiwan and
Fukien Area, Republic of China,* various years.   Footwear includes tailoring
services.   All other sub-industries includes: beverages; tobacco; wood products
& furniture; paper & paper products; printing, publishing and allied industries;

III. Characteristics of Labor Absorption

Within the manufacturing industry, what kind of industries
absorbed most of the labor, and what kind of labor was mostly
absorbed?   And how did labor absorption affect income distribution?   Further, how was capital expansion related to labor
absorption?

In order to give some answers to these questions, the following relationships will be successively studied: (1) labor absorption, labor intensity and wage rates, (2) labor absorption and
income distribution, and (3) labor absorption and capital
expansion.

1.   Labor Absorption, Labor Intensity and Wage Rates

To examine what kind of industries within the manufactur-

Relative Weight $\Delta L_j / \Delta L$ (%)			Industry
1954–61	1961–66	1966–71	
21.3	20.3	−2.3	1. Food processing
18.4	21.6	33.1	2. Textiles & footwear
13.2	19.6	22.1	Textiles
5.2	2.0	11.0	Footwear
5.9	12.8	17.2	3. Electrical machinery
54.4	45.3	52.0	4. All other sub-industries
100.0	100.0	100.0	Total manufacturing (ΔL)

leather & its products; rubber products; chemicals & chemical products; products of petroleum and coal; nonmetallic mineral products; basic metal; metal products; machinery; transport equipment; and miscellaneous manufacturing industries.

Note: The subscript j refers to the jth industry.

ing industry absorbed most of the labor, the 19 sub-industries are ranked by labor intensity and wage rate. The labor intensity of industry j is defined as L_j / O_j where O_j is the value of output of industry j (including intermediate inputs) and L_j is the labor input in industry j.[2]

Based on data for the 19 sub-industries a study of the relationship between the speed of labor absorption $\Delta L_j / L_j$ and the level of labor intensity L_j / O_j was done respectively for the three periods. The inter-industry correlation indicates that during the first period (1954–61), $\Delta L_j / L_j$ and L_j / O_j were not correlated; during the second period (1961–66), the two had a negative correlation at the 5% significance level, i.e., the less labor-intensive industries had a faster labor absorption; and during the third period (1966–71), the two had a positive correlation at the 1% significance level, indicating that labor absorption in the labor-intensive industries became faster. It seems that during the late 1960s, the role of providing a high rate of labor absorption shifted from the less labor-intensive industries to the more labor-intensive industries, and that the rapid rate of labor absorption in the latest period was mainly due to labor absorption in the labor-intensive industries.

Table 4.5   Inter-industry Correlation Between Speed of Labor Absorption $\Delta L_j / L_j$ and Labor Intensity L_j / O_j

Period	Correlation Coefficient	The Years of L_j / O_j Observed	F-value
1954−61	−0.2860	(1954)	1.51
	−0.2860	(1961)	1.51
1961−66	−0.4772	(1961)	5.01*
	−0.4930	(1966)	5.46*
1966−71	−0.5789	(1966)	8.57**
	−0.6351	(1971)	11.49**

Source: The Committee on Industrial and Commercial Censuses of Taiwan and Fukien Area, Executive Yuan, *Industrial & Commercial Censuses of Taiwan and Fukien Area, Republic of China*, 1961, 1966, 1971.

Note:
  1. The inter-industry correlation is for 19 manufacturing sub-industries.
  2. $\Delta L_j / L_j$ is observed for each period and each industry.
  3. The correlation coefficient is Spearman's rank coefficient.
  4. * significant at 5% level; ** significant at 1% level.

Similarly, the relationship between the speed of labor absorption and wage rate shows the same pattern for the three periods. Wage rate of industry j. W_j / L_j is defined as compensation to employees W_j divided by number of employed L_j.

The observations show that during the first period, there was no obvious relation between the speed of labor absorption and the level of wage rate; during the second period, labor was more rapidly absorbed in the higher-wage industries; then the trend gradually changed, and during the third period the labor force was more rapidly absorbed by lower-wage industries where unskilled labor constitutes a relatively larger proportion. Generally, in the latest period the labor force was more rapidly absorbed into more labor-intensive and lower-productivity industries, which made the use of more unskilled labor possible.

Table 4.6   Inter-industry Correlation Between Speed of Labor Absorption $\triangle L_j / L_j$ and Wage Rate W_j / L_j

Period	Correlation Coefficient	The Years of W_j / L_j Observed	F-value
1954–61	0.2474	(1954)	1.11
	0.2702	(1961)	1.34
1961–66	0.5825	(1961)	8.73**
	0.3754	(1966)	2.78
1966–71	−0.5333	(1966)	6.76*
	−0.7860	(1971)	27.48**

Source: Same as Table 4.5.
Note:
  1. The inter-industry correlation is for 19 manufacturing sub-industries.
  2. $\triangle L_j / L_j$ is observed for each period and each industry.
  3. The correlation coefficient is Spearman's rank coefficient.
  4. * significant at 5% level; ** significant at 1% level.

One point we may note is that the greater use of unskilled labor in the latest period seems to have caused the wage rate of unskilled labor to increase more rapidly than that of skilled labor. Although wage statistics in Taiwan are far from being sufficient and accurate enough for the purpose of comparing the wages of skilled and unskilled labor, some observations can be made based on the indices of salaries and wages classified by staff and workers, and by male and female labor.

Table 4.7   Indices of Average Salaries and Wages

(1968 = 100)

Year	Manufacturing		Textiles	
	Staff	Worker	Staff	Worker
1968	100.0	100.0	100. 0	100.0
1969	112.2	110.8	119.6	122.2
1970	122.5	125.3	129.8	143.5
1971	136.3	137.0	134.2	159.0
1972	144.4	148.9	138.2	177.0

Source: Department of Statistics, Ministry of Economic Affairs, *Taiwan Industrial Production Statistics Monthly, Republic of China* (April 1973).

Table 4.8   Indices of Average Wages by Industry and Sex (1972)

(1964 = 100)

Industry	Male	Female
Manufacturing	203.2	203.0
Textiles	210.0	215.8
Electricity, Gas, Water & Sanitary Services	157.8	180.4
Transportation & Communication	225.2	262.9

Source: Department of Reconstruction, Taiwan Provincial Government, Republic of China, *Report of Taiwan Labour Statistics* (1973).

The statistics show that the wage rate of workers rose more rapidly than that of staff in the manufacturing and textile industries; and that the wages of female workers increased more than those of males in some industries. These phenomena deserve further attention.

If the ultimate purpose of economic development is the improvement of the general standard of living, then an increase in wages should be regarded as a direct and efficient means of achieving this purpose. In recent years real wage increases have been generally suppressed all over the world. This is because the rate of increase in wages has far exceeded the rate of increase in labor productivity, causing inflation. The ideal situation would be one in which real wages increased at the same rate as productivity.

In the 1950s, Taiwan's economy was still in a state of surplus labor. In such a situation, although the real wage may rise, the level of wages will, nonetheless, be kept at a subsistence level. The significance of achieving full employment is not only that jobs will be available for everyone, but also that the real wage can rise with increasing productivity, so that the fruits of economic development can be more evenly distributed to all participants.

The point at which real wages start to rise in accord with increases in labor productivity is called, by economists, the turning point. The turning point of the Taiwan economy is identified as the year 1968. Since then, real wages have been generally increasing at a rate even higher than labor productivity. In addition to this, the wage rate of manufacturing after 1968 went up much faster than that of other sectors, reflecting rapid industrialization (see Figure 4.3). This phenomenon provided a good stimulus for absorption of the labor force both from the pool of newcomers and from the agricultural sector. During the critical period of 1966–71, the labor force was quite rapidly absorbed by the lower wage industries in which unskilled labor constitutes a relatively large proportion of those employed. That is, the labor force was more rapidly absorbed into more labor-intensive and lower-productivity industries, making possible greater use of unskilled labor.

Table 4.9   Annual Growth Rate of Real Wages

(%)

Period	Agriculture	Manufacturing
1953–68	3.4	4.2
1968–78	7.9	10.8

Source: Council for Agricultural Planning and Development, Executive
Yuan; Manpower Planning Committee, Council for Economic Planning
and Development, Executive Yuan, *Statistics of Wages of Agriculture,
Taiwan District, the Republic of China, 1961-1979* (May 1980); Overall
Planning Department, Economic Planning Council, Executive Yuan,
*Adjusted Statistics of Wages of Manufacturing, Taiwan District, the
Republic of China, I. 1952–IV. 1976* (July 1977); Directorate-General
of Budget, Accounting and Statistics, Executive Yuan, *Yearbook of
Labour Statistics, Republic of China* (1980).

Note: The data are three-year moving averages.

Fig. 4.3   Indices of Real Wages (1952 = 100)

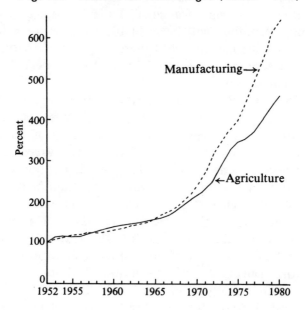

We also note that the increase of manufacturing real wages in the 1950s was trivial, only around 2% per year. However, it rose to around 5-6% in the 1960s. Furthermore, the increase in manufacturing real wages accelerated to become nearly 10% in the 1970s. Again, the wage rate for workers went up faster than that for staff in the later period.

2. Labor Absorption and Income Distribution

During the period 1964—72 in Taiwan, the income gap between farm and nonfarm families widened because farm income grew at a slower rate. However, in spite of the widening gap between sectors, income inequality on the national level was found to have decreased significantly. The question has often been raised as to how nationwide income inequality can be reduced as income inequality between farm and nonfarm families widens. It is found that the reduction in income inequality for the total economy was made possible because the reduction in income inequality within the nonfarm sector was more than enough to compensate for the adverse inter-sectoral change.[3] (see Chapter 6)

The family survey data show that during the period 1964—72, real per family income of the farm and nonfarm sectors had a considerable increase in every income bracket. The rate of increase in per family income was largest for the lowest income bracket and smallest for the highest income bracket within each sector. It also shows that the increase in the lower income groups in the nonfarm sector was much larger than that in the farm sector. For example, the lowest decile of the non-farm sector had a 153.5% increase of income, while the lowest decile of the farm sector had only a 64.2% increase.

In view of the higher growth rates of the incomes of the lower income family groups in the nonagricultural sector, we thus find additional support here for the notion that it was the relatively rapid rate of employment generation for members of the lower income groups initially, and the change in their wages in the later period, which were responsible for the good overall performance. During the period under observation,

Table 4.10   The Rate of Increase in Real Per Family Income by Each of the Ten Deciles (1964—1972)

(%)

Ten Equal Divisions of Family Number	Farm	Nonfarm	Whole Economy
The richest 10% of families	42.5	65.3	65.5
The 2nd 10% of families	46.5	103.2	88.0
The 3rd 10% of families	51.3	99.6	86.7
The 4th 10% of families	55.4	100.9	89.5
The 5th 10% of families	58.7	102.2	91.0
The 6th 10% of families	59.0	98.3	89.7
The 7th 10% of families	59.4	105.8	94.0
The 8th 10% of families	58.8	112.8	95.7
The 9th 10% of families	62.0	127.8	101.0
The poorest 10% of families	64.2	153.5	114.6

Source: DGBAS Data (Taipei City data are added to Taiwan Province data). The city of Taipei was part of Taiwan Province and included in the overall DGBAS surveys before 1968. Since 1968, Taipei has been reclassified as a Special Municipality and the available 1972 income distribution data are separated in two volumes, Taiwan Province and Taipei City. For comparability we have merged the two sets of data by adding, for each Taiwan Province income bracket, both the families and income of those residing in the city of Taipei.

Note: The calculation is based on the annual income of each sector in 1972 constant prices.

rapid labor absorption first eliminated unemployment. Newcomers and originally unemployed individuals were absorbed mainly by the nonagricultural sector and particularly in the light manufacturing industries. Unskilled labor was efficiently utilized.   As the economy grew, unskilled labor became relatively more scarce in terms of the reduction in its excess supply. Thus, the wage rate of unskilled labor rose more rapidly than that of skilled labor.   Undoubtedly, the rapid absorption of unskilled labor at low opportunity costs contributed substantially to the rise in relative incomes of the lower income families in the nonfarm sector.

3.   Labor Absorption and Capital Expansion

In this section, labor absorption is examined in relation to capital expansion and technological change. This is an inquiry from the production side, or technology side. Here output is viewed to be determined by a certain amount of production factors at a certain level of technology, and hence output is a dependent variable of factors and technology.

The basic concern is about capital formation (ΔK), which is a complementary factor to labor absorption at a given K/L ratio; and about technological change $\Delta(K/L)$, which is a competitive factor with labor absorption at a given K. Technically, the amount of L is determined once K and K/L are determined. Namely,

$$L = f(K, K/L)$$

That is, in order to have employment L realized, there must be a certain amount of capital to associate with labor at a given level of technology. In order to identify capital formation and technological change in each industry in each period, and their effects on labor absorption, let us view L in the form of

$$L = \frac{K}{K/L} \; (= f\,(K, K/L))$$

We obtain the following relationship:

$$dL = \frac{1}{K/L}\, dK - \frac{K}{(K/L)^2}\, d(K/L) \ldots\ldots\ldots (1)$$

The first term of the right hand side in Equation (1) will be referred to as "the complementary effect" and the second term, "the substitution effect." Namely, labor absorption is the algebraic sum of the two effects.

In Fig. 4.4, theoretically the move from R to S can be explained in two ways. One is from R to T and then from T to S; the other is from R to U and then from U to S. The move from R to T is caused by an increase in capital of ΔK^* at a given technology $(K/L)_1$, which generates the complementary effect under the former technology, B + A. Then, the move from T to S with a change in technology from $(K/L)_1$ to $(K/L)_2$ generates the substitution effect of capital deepening,

−A. The actual labor absorption ΔL^*, is the sum of the positive complementary effect $(B + A)$ and the negative substitution effect $(−A)$. Thus, $\Delta L^* = (B + A) + (−A) = B$

Fig. 4.4   Labor Absorption Due to Changes in Capital and Technology

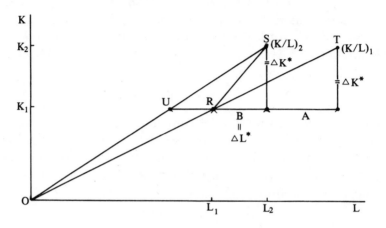

That is, with the original technology of OR, the complementary effect of the capital increment ΔK^* on labor absorption is $(B+A)$.   However, due to the change in technology from $(K/L)_1$ to $(K/L)_2$, the negative substitution effect $(−A)$ is generated.   And the realized labor absorption is the algebraic sum of the positive complementary effect $(B + A)$ and the negative substitution effect $(−A)$.   We know that other things being equal, the bigger the increase in capital and the smaller the technological advancement, the greater the observed labor absorption will be.

We have shown that two thirds of total labor absorption was accounted for by manufacturing and its related industries, and that among them the three sub-industries absorbed half of manufacturing's contribution during the past period. Questions asked here are these:

Fig. 4.5 Capital Increase, Technology Change, and Labor Absorption of the Three Labor Absorbing Industries (1954 — 1971)

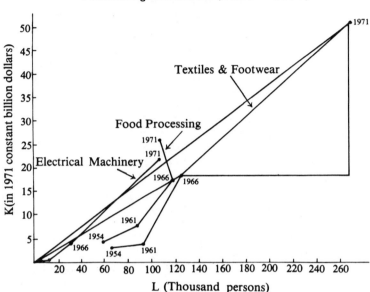

How was this labor absorption related to the capital increase and technological change? How large was the complementary effect under the former technology and how large was the substitution effect of capital deepening?

In order to answer these questions, the complementary effect (B+A), and the substitution effect (−A), will be calculated separately for each industry during each period. The findings as can be seen in Table 4.11 are as follows:

(1) The complementary effect under the former technology was greatest for each industry during the second period (1961–66) because of a large increase in the amount of capital. However, the substitution effect was also the greatest because capital deepening was occurring at its most rapid pace. As a result, total labor absorption in this period was not very impressive as compared with the latest period.

Table 4.11   Complementary Effect and Substitution Effects

(1,000 persons)

Industry	Complementary Effect Under the Former Technology (A+B)			Substitution Effect Due to Capital Deepening (−A)		
	1954 ~61	1961 ~66	1966 ~71	1954 ~61	1961 ~66	1966 ~71
Food processing	44	115	58	−(15)	−85	−68
Textiles & footwear	17	334	216	−(−8)	−302	−74
Electrical machinery	9	125	131	−(1)	−106	−57
All other sub-industries	42	787	517	−(−32)	−720	−294
Manufacturing Total	116	1,224	916	−(−20)	−1,076	−487

Source: Same as Table 4.4.

(2) During the latest period (1966−71), the complementary effect was large because of the enormous increase in the amount of capital. On the other hand, capital deepening was relatively insignificant, and thus the substitution effect was rather small. As a result, the amount of labor absorption observed was largest during this period.

(3) Only the food industry followed a different pattern. The increase in capital in relation to labor during the period 1966−71 was so rapid that the marginal capital/labor ratio had a negative slope. There was no labor absorption, only labor release. The negative substitution effect caused by the technological change (capital deepening) exceeded the complementary effect under the former technology.

(4) The labor absorption in other industries taken together followed the same pattern as textiles and electrical machinery, but the degree of labor absorption was smaller.

IV. Conclusions

In the 1950s, the Taiwan economy was still in a state of

Observed Labor Absorption			Industry
$B = (A + B) + (-A) = \Delta L^*$			
1954	1961	1966	
~ 61	~ 66	~ 71	
29	30	-10	Food processing
25	32	142	Textiles & footwear
8	19	74	Electrical machinery
74	67	223	All other sub-industries
136	148	429	Manufacturing Total

surplus labor; however, the economy had reached full employment by 1971. During this period, newcomers to the labor force totaled about 1.8 million persons, who comprised 60% of total employment of 1953. The total labor absorption during this period was about 1.9 million persons, absorbing not only those newcomers, but also of a part of the originally unemployed. The growth of employment registered a higher rate after 1961, particularly for secondary industry. Real wages in manufacturing went up gradually during 1961–71 and rose rapidly after 1971. This was due mainly to the fact that the Taiwan economy reached the "turning point" in 1968 and achieved full employment by 1971.

During 1954–71, manufacturing and its directly related industries accounted for more than two thirds of the economy's total labor absorption. Out of 19 sub-industries, three sub-industries – food processing, textiles, and electrical machinery – accounted for about half of the manufacturing labor absorption. The food processing industry registered the biggest share of labor absorption in the 1950s, but it ceased to be a labor absorbing industry after 1965. After that the electrical machinery industry completely took the place of the food processing industry in labor absorption.

In the latest period, the labor force was more rapidly absorbed into more labor-intensive and lower-productivity industries, which made the use of more unskilled labor possible on the one hand, while it made the wage rate of unskilled labor increase more rapidly than that of skilled labor on the other. The rapid absorption of unskilled labor at low opportunity costs contributed substantially to the rise in relative incomes of lower income families in the nonfarm sector.

We may conclude with two points as the essential factors contributing to the past labor absorption and economic development in Taiwan's case. *They are industrialization and labor intensiveness.* That is, the success of labor absorption and growth was possible firstly because of the rapid industrialization, and secondly because of the relatively labor-intensive development.

Industrialization caused the economy to depart from agriculturally-oriented production, which is by nature less productive than manufacturing and also incapable of absorbing more labor. Industrialization made the economy move to an "improved" status where average productivity of the whole economy, and labor-absorbing capacity, are higher than before because manufacturing occupies a bigger share. Thus, the larger weight of the nonagricultural sector could be considered as one of the most essential factors for labor absorption and economic growth.

Secondly, the labor intensive development was important in the sense that it played the following roles during the course of development:

(1) The labor intensive development made it possible to absorb more labor.

(2) From the production side, light industries made the production of manufacturing goods possible due to their relatively simple technologies and their requirement for less capital.

(3) From the demand side, labor-intensive output made competition in the world market possible because of the higher

labor content at relatively lower labor cost. The role of exports in Taiwan's economic development can be identified in this context.

Exports were a factor that made labor-intensive industrialization successful. The opportunity for export was crucial in that exports broadened the market to provide more productive opportunities; at the same time, exports made it possible to earn the foreign exchange necessary for imports of materials and equipment needed for production. This will be elaborated in Chapter 7.

NOTES

1. G. Ranis and J. C. H. Fei, "Innovation, Capital Accumulation, and Economic Development," *American Economic Review,* Vol. 53 (June 1963), p. 283; see also idem, *Development of the Labor Surplus Economy: Theory and Policy* (Homewood, Ill.: Richard D. Irwin, 1964).

2. Hal B. Lary proposed to use value added per worker to assess capital intensity for the capital data scarce developing countries for the following reasons (Hal B. Lary, *Imports of Manufactures from Less-Developed Countries,* New York, 1968). Value added can be high because the industry incurs user costs of a large amount of physical capital, or pays rents for the use of natural resources. Among industries differences in value added are closely associated with the average amount of physical capital of all sorts. Since neither capital data nor value added data at an industry level for this early period are available in Taiwan, here we use output per worker to represent capital intensity, i.e., the reciprocal of output per worker to indicate labor intensity.

3. John. C.H. Fei, Gustav Ranis, and Shirley W.Y. Kuo, *Growth with Equity: The Taiwan Case* (London: Oxford University Press, 1979).

5
Female Participation in Economic Development

Female labor force has played a significant role in the process of economic development in Taiwan. In the following, we examine the utilization and changes in patterns of employment of the island's female labor force from 1964 to 1980. The factors we try to look into are:

1. Percentage of female employment in total employment
2. Female labor force participation rate by age group and education
3. Female employment by industry and occupation group
4. Female higher education

I. Percentage of Female Employment in Total Employment

Female employment has comprised more than 30% of total employment since 1968. It comprised 33% of total employment in 1980 after hitting its peak of 35% in 1973. The highest percentages have been observed for age groups 15-19 and 20-24. The relative shares in employment for these two groups in 1980 were 52% and 55% respectively. This is mostly due to causes from two sides. From the demand side, the rapid expansion in labor-intensive industry provided many job opportunities. From the supply side, high participation rate together with the expansion of the female population aged 15 and over, especially the 15-24 group, provided ample labor supply. As a result, the active female participation greatly contributed to speedy economic growth.

Table 5.1   Percentage of Female Employment to
Total Employment by Age

(%)

Year	Total	15-19	20-24	25-34	35-44	45-54	55-64	Over 65
1964	28	43		23	24	19	18	12
1968	30	48	47	26	25	19	13	12
1972	32	50	52	24	27	22	14	13
1973	35	50	53	29	31	24	14	13
1974	34	49	51	27	30	25	15	10
1975	33	49	51	27	28	23	15	11
1980	33	52	55	30	29	23	16	11

Source: Directorate-General of Budget, Accounting and Statistics, Executive Yuan,
 Yearbook of Labour Statistics, 1980.

II. Female Labor Force Participation Rate by Age Group and Education

The female labor force participation rate increased from 34% in 1964 to 39% in 1980.[1] The highest participation rate, 42%, was observed for the peak year of the business cycle, 1973. Age groups 15-19 and 20-24 have a higher participation rate; however, their pattern of change is different. For the 15-19 age group, the participation rate was kept high (more than 50%) up until 1974; however, it gradually declined to 43% in 1980, mainly because of an increase in female higher education for this age group. For age group 20-24, the participation rate has been continuously increasing, from 43% in 1965 to 58% in 1980. It is interesting to note that during the period of 1964 to 1980, all age groups except that of over 65 had a rapid increase in female participation rate as can be seen in the following.

Age group	Female participation rate increase during 1965-1980
25-29	from 29% to 42%
30-34	from 28% to 40%
35-39	from 30% to 43%
40-44	from 30% to 43%
45-49	from 29% to 39%
50-54	from 23% to 31%
55-59	from 13% to 23%
60-64	from 6% to 13%

With respect to educational levels, females in the graduate of junior high vocational school group had the most rapid rates of growth of participation in the labor force. The junior high school group came next. The only reduction in participation rate was found among the senior high school group up to 1974. This was partly due to the sharp increase in the number of female graduates who decided to pursue higher education, and partly due to the absence of vocational training in school. However, after 1974, the participation rate of the senior high school group increased. A higher female participation rate was observed in the category of junior college, university, and graduate school graduates. This rate has been rising in recent years, reaching 55.3% in 1980. The advancing educational level of females in the labor force is not only a notable sociological factor, but also an important factor for improving female income and thus reducing income inequality.

III. Female Employment by Industry and Occupation Group

1. Female Employment by Industry

Because of rapid industrialization, Taiwan's economic structure changed appreciably over the past three decades. This change was accompanied by a substantial structural change in employment. Employment in agriculture decreased from 51.4% of total employment in 1952 to 19.5% in 1980, while employment in the industrial sector increased from 20.4% to

Table 5.2   Female Labor Force Participation Rate by Age

(%)

Year	Total	15-19	20-24	25-29	30-34	35-39
1964	34	49		32		
1965	31	53	43	29	28	30
1970	36	51	48	32	35	38
1971	35	52	48	32	33	38
1972	37	54	50	32	35	39
1973	42	54	55	40	42	46
1974	40	52	55	37	38	44
1975	39	49	54	35	37	41
1980	39	43	58	42	40	43

Source: 1964-70: Yen Hwa "The Female Labor Force of Taiwan: Tapping a New
Resource", *Conference on Population and Economic Development in Taiwan*
(The Institute of Economics, Academia Sinica, 1976).
1971–75: Overall Planning Department, Council for Economic Planning and
Development, Executive Yuan, *Manpower Utilization in Taiwan,* 1976.

Table 5.3   Female Labor Force Participation Rate by Education

(%)

Year	Illiterate	Self-Educated	Primary School	Junior High School	Junior Vocational School
1964	27.3	32.0	41.3	23.2	22.4
1968	23.8	34.3	43.5	41.3	43.8
1972	26.0	37.7	45.1	39.5	49.6
1973	30.1	45.2	49.4	42.9	54.2
1974	28.8	50.5	47.0	43.8	51.4
1980	19.1	36.9	36.8	50.8	

Source: Taiwan Provincial Labor Force Survey & Research Institute, *Quarterly
Report on the Labor Force Survey in Taiwan,* various years; Directorate-General

40-44	45-49	50-54	55-59	60-64	Over 65	Year
35		28		8	2	1964
30	29	23	13	6	2	1965
37	33	24	15	6	1	1970
37	33	24	13	3	1	1971
39	35	27	18	5	1	1972
46	40	29	19	6	2	1973
48	42	32	20	7	1	1974
42	39	29	22	8	2	1975
43	39	31	23	13	2	1980

1980: Directorate-General of Budget, Accounting and Statistics, Executive Yuan, *Monthly Bulletin of Labor Statistics — Special Topic: Supplementary Studies on Special Problem of Labor Force Survey,* July 1981.

Senior High School	Senior Vocational School	Normal School	College, University, and Graduate School	Year
32.1	41.3	60.9	38.0	1964
26.4	37.7	66.7	33.5	1968
26.3	42.7	68.2	40.9	1972
28.3	48.0	67.0	44.8	1973
27.3	48.4	62.9	43.4	1974
31.8	50.3		55.3	1980

of Budget, Accounting and Statistics, Executive Yuan, *Monthly Bulletin of Labor Statistics, Republic of China* , November 1980.

42.4% during the same period.

The ratio of employed female workers in agriculture to total female employment decreased much more rapidly, from 52.5% in 1965 to 16.5% in 1980. In the same period, there was a great increase in the number of employed women in secondary industry, which in 1980 comprised 43.7% of all employed female workers compared to 18.2% in 1965. Female employment in tertiary industry was 39.8% of total female employment in 1980, compared to 29.3% in 1965.

The changes in the manufacturing labor structure give a view of the kind of labor being absorbed. As shown in Table 5.5, from 1966 to 1980 manufacturing industry employment gained a much higher percentage of younger persons. The proportion of those 30 years and older decreased from 47.3% in 1966 to 36.7% in 1972, and then increased to 38.2% in 1980. Meanwhile, the group of persons 15-24 years of age increased from 38.5% to 51.6% over those years, but decreased to 43.2% in 1980. Manufacturing originally had a large proportion of young females. The rapid absorption of young females grew during the 1960s. In 1972, female workers under 24 years of age accounted for 74.2% of all female workers, although the proportion had changed to 63.8% by 1980.

Table 5.4   Female Employment by Industry

(%)

Year	Total	Primary Industry	Secondary Industry	Tertiary Industry
1965	100.0	52.5	18.2	29.3
1970	100.0	40.6	23.7	35.7
1975	100.0	31.2	34.3	34.5
1980	100.0	16.5	43.7	39.8

Source: Taiwan Provincial Labor Force Survey and Research Institute, *Quarterly Report on the Labor Force Survey in Taiwan, Republic of China,* various years; Directorate-General of Budget, Accounting and Statistics, Executive Yuan, *Monthly Bulletin of Labor Statistics, Republic of China,* November 1980.

Table 5.5   Manufacturing Labor Classified by Age and Sex

(%)

	Year	Total Manufacturing Labor	Age		
			15-24	25-29	30 and over
Total	1966	100.0	38.5	14.2	47.3
	1972	100.0	51.6	11.7	36.7
	1980	100.0	43.2	18.6	38.2
Male	1966	100.0	29.0	15.9	55.1
	1972	100.0	38.2	15.6	46.2
	1980	100.0	29.3	22.8	47.9
Female	1966	100.0	65.9	9.4	24.7
	1972	100.0	74.2	5.2	20.6
	1980	100.0	63.8	12.4	23.8

Source: Taiwan Provincial Labor Force Survey and Research Institute, *Quarterly Report on the Labor Force Survey in Taiwan, Republic of China,* October 1966 and October. 1972; Directorate-General of Budget, Accounting and Statistics, Executive Yuan, *Monthly Bulletin of Labor Statistics, Republic of China,* November 1980.

2. Female Employment by Occupation

Occupational groupings indicate the quality or technical level of the female labor force. In 1965, 52.5% of employed women were in agriculture, 17.2% were physical laborers, and 10.3% were sales workers. In the next fifteen years the percentage of female farm workers dropped year by year, until by 1980 they comprised 16.5% of all employed women workers; at the same time, the percentage of production workers and equipment operators reached 39.3%. Professional, technical and related workers (those holding jobs which required a higher educational level) increased from 4.4% in 1965 to 6.8% in 1980. Both clerical workers and sales workers recorded an increase in their shares of total employment. Only administrative, executive and managerial workers dropped, from 0.9%

to 0.1%.

Table 5.6   Female Employment by Occupation Group

(%)

Year	Total	Professional Technical & Related Personnel	Administrative Executive & Managerial Personnel	Clerical Workers
1965	100.0	4.4	0.9	5.6
1970	100.0	4.5	0.8	6.8
1975	100.0	5.8	0.5	11.4
1980	100.0	6.8	0.1	18.0

Source: Same as Table 5.4.

IV. Female Higher Education

Education was of major concern to the government, and a great deal was spent on it. The expenditure for education, science, and culture consistently accounted for more than 13% of the budget at all levels of government during 1954–68, increasing to 15% by 1980. Because of the government's emphasis on education, enrollment in the 6-11 age group reached 96% in 1961 and 99.8% in 1980, up from 80% in 1951. The proportion of primary school graduates who went on to junior high school increased from 32% in 1951 to 51% in 1961 and 96% in 1980. The proportion of junior high school graduates going on to senior high school remained around 62% during the thirty-year period. As a high-quality labor force is a necessary condition for effective labor absorption, the government's emphasis on upgrading education contributed in part to labor absorption.

Sales Workers	Service Workers	Farm Workers	Workers in Production, Operators and Others	Year
10.3	9.1	52.5	17.2	1965
14.8	8.4	40.3	24.4	1970
11.5	6.7	31.2	32.9	1975
11.3	8.0	16.5	39.3	1980

Extensive education generally leads to a higher income. Accordingly, providing equal opportunity for education is an efficient way to achieve a more equal income distribution. Although there is no way to ensure a completely equal education for everyone because of differences in teachers, facilities, and so on, two important government policies in the present education system of the Republic of China have made higher education equally accessible to rich and poor alike. The first policy is a low tuition system: Average tuition is US$100 a year at public colleges and US$300 at private colleges. The second policy is a unified entrance examination system, by which each student has a fair opportunity for competition. With no discrimination between rich and poor, it is possible for a larger proportion of students from low-income families to be admitted to better colleges.

Female higher education can be observed through the percentage of female enrollment in colleges as shown in Table

Table 5.7   Female College Students as Percentage
of Total Students by Field

(%)

Year	% of Female College Students in Total College Students	Hu- manities	Edu- cation	Fine Art	Law
1964	29	46	37	25	18
1965	31	48	41	26	23
1970	36	65	52	31	32
1975	37	71	50	52	33
1979	40	76	54	64	37

Source: Directorate-General of Budget, Accounting and Statistics, Executive Yuan, *Statistical Abstract of the Republic of China*, 1980.

5.7.   Female college students comprised 29% of the total in 1964, but increased to 40% in 1979. The high percentage of female college students in the humanities and fine arts is understandable.   However, one thing very impressive is that female college students in medical science comprise 55% of all medical science students, although about a half of them are students in the science of nursing.   The percentage in social science is also high, 62% in 1979.

Social Science	Natural Science	Engi- neering	Medical Science	Agricul- ture	Year
39	22	2	24	20	1964
41	22	2	27	20	1965
51	25	3	46	19	1970
55	20	3	51	18	1975
62	27	5	55	23	1979

From the above description, we understand that female employment played a significant role in Taiwan's economic development. A substantial increase in the female participation was possible because the economy has been growing rapidly to provide job opportunities, and higher educational opportunity has been provided to females. In turn, the active participation of relatively qualified females enabled the economy to grow faster.

NOTES

1. By international developing country standards, rates of participation
    in economic activities by women in Southeast and East Asia were
    relatively high. The rates in the East and Southeast Asian countries
    do not appear to differ markedly from those in Western or Latin
    American countries, and they are much higher than in the Arab
    countries and the Indian sub-continent.

Annex Table   Labour Force Participation Rates for Females in Urban
               Areas, East and Southeast Asian Countries Compared
               with Other Regions, 1970 (Ages 15+)

(%)

	Rate 1970	Rate 1980		Rate 1970	Rate 1980
East and Southeast Asian Countries			South Asian/Moslem Countries		
Republic of Korea	26.3		India (1971)	10.6	
Hong Kong	42.8[1]	45.4[4]	Pakistan	3.9[3]	3.5[5]
Singapore	29.5	44.2	Bangladesh (1974)	5.4	
Philippines	33.7		Morocco (1971)	17.3	
Indonesia	25.5[1]	27.7			
Western Countries			Latin America		
Japan	47.7	44.0[2]	Nicaragua (1971)	30.4	
Australia	38.6	44.7	El Salvador	40.8	
U.S.A. (14+)	41.4		Ecuador (1974)	25.4	
France (17+)		42.6[2]			

Source: Gavin W. Jones, "Economic Growth and Changing Female Employment
         Structure in the Cities of Southeast and East Asia" (paper read at the Conference
         on Women in the Urban and Industrial Workforce in Southeast and East Asia,
         Manila, November 1982).

Notes:
   1. 1971;   2. 1975;   3. Ages 10+;   4. 1976;   5. 1974-75.

6
Income Distribution

Economists have traditionally focused their attention more on the functional distribution of income related to the determination of factor prices and factor shares. While the family distribution of income has by no means been totally neglected, it is probably fair to say that it has been viewed more as a descriptive device and, until quite recently, not integrated with the main body of analytical economics. However, the real objective of distributive justice is more usefully conceived of as accelerating the development of poorer groups in society rather than in terms of relative share of factor incomes. A grouping of households according to the family income provides more insight into the nature of income distribution.

As is widely known, raising national income and thus improving the standard of living is one of the most important goals of economic development. If economic growth leads to an inequality of income distribution and an ever-widening gap between the rich and the poor, not only will the general public be precluded from sharing the fruits of economic development, but social unrest and urban crisis will ensue. The ultimate objective of each country's efforts is, therefore, more equal distribution of income. According to the findings of Professor Simon Kuznets' classical study,[1] the relationship between a country's growth and its income distribution usually makes it difficult to achieve the twin goals of equity and growth at an early stage of development. However, in the studies of Professor Chenery et. al.,[2] and Fei, Ranis and Kuo,[3] the Republic of China is identified as one country which has been able to make considerable achievements in narrowing

93

the income gap while undergoing rapid economic growth. Professor Kuznets in his recent study of Taiwan also indicates that "despite the rapid shifts in the production and use structure, there is no evidence of widening inequality in the sharing of gains from growth among various groups of households in the population."[4]

In general, the prime stimulant inducing a deterioration in income distribution during the process of industrialization and urbanization is that nonfarm family income and urban family income grow much faster than farm family income and rural family income. The higher productivity in the modern sector causes the gap between the modern and traditional sectors to widen. That gap appears necessary in development, for it provides the incentive to drive the economy toward modernization. In modern ethics that link social justice to equity, however, a more equitable distribution is advocated.

The main purpose of this chapter is to first clarify the status and changes of family income distribution in Taiwan for the period 1953–80, and second, examine the characteristics of industrialization and income distribution during the period 1966–80. Section I clarifies the status and changes of income distribution. In section II an attempt is made to decompose national income according to classifications of income recipients by group. The group classifications are based on farm and nonfarm family income and on the degree of urbanization — measured by rural, semiurban and most urban residence. Thus, changes in the inequality of income over time can be analyzed in relation to industrialization and urbanization. In section III, causes of reduction in income inequality are traced from the farm and nonfarm family income decomposition. In section IV, income disparities are examined through different degrees of urbanization.

I.   Status and Changes of Income Distribution, 1953–1980

The first estimate of family income distribution for the Taiwan area was made for the year 1953 by Professor Kowie Chang of National Taiwan University.[5]   The data of 1959–

60 and 1961 are also available in another study by Professor Chang.[6]   These data do have some deficiencies as pointed out by Professor Simon Kuznets[7]: for example, a wider difference with the national income data than those found in official family income data of later years; and they were based on very small samples.   However, due to lack of other data, the Chang data are presented in Table 6.1.

The first official estimate of family income distribution was made by the Directorate-General of Budget, Accounting and Statistics, Executive Yuan for the year 1964.[8]   Since then the pertinent data have been available for every other year from 1964 to 1970, and every year from 1970 on.

Another source of information on family income distribution is the income tax data of the Ministry of Finance.   Income tax data by this source is available after 1970.   However, the MOF data only include the incomes of taxpayers, who comprise only a portion of the total number of families.   In addition, the compilation of this source of data generally gives only a simple distribution picture.   In Table 6.1, based on DGBAS data and Chang's data, changes in income distribution for the period 1953–80 are presented according to various indicators: the Gini coefficient, income shares, and the ratio of the income share of richest 20% to that of poorest 20%.

For the income distribution of the early period, Chang's data show that the Gini coefficient, the ratio of income share of richest 20% to that of poorest 20% etc., were all much bigger in 1953 than in 1964.   Although the quality of the data in 1953 may not be comparable to that of DGBAS data, it may well be concluded that the income distribution in Taiwan improved during the period 1953–64.   For the period 1964–80, the Gini coefficient dropped from 0.360 to 0.303.   The income share of the richest 20% of families decreased from 41.1% to 36.8%, while the income share of the poorest 20% of families increased from 7.7% to 8.8%.   Accordingly, the ratio of the income share of the richest 20% to that of the poorest decreased from 5.34 to 4.18.   All these indicate first that the income distribution in the Taiwan area has been more even than in many other developing countries, e.g., compared

Table 6.1   Income Distribution of Taiwan Area
(1953—1980)

Item	1953	1959—60	1961	1964
Income share of the richest 20% of families	61.4	51.0	52.0	41.1
Income share of the second richest 20% of families	18.2	19.7	19.8	22.0
Income share of the third richest 20% of families	9.1	13.9	14.0	16.6
Income share of the fourth richest 20% of families	8.3	9.7	9.7	12.6
Income share of the poorest 20% of families	3.0	5.7	4.5	7.7
Gini coefficient	0.558	0.440	0.461	0.360
Per family income (NT$1,000) (1976 constant price)	39.0	54.7	59.4	67.4
Per capita GNP (NT$1,000) (1976 constant price)	11.1	14.2	14.9	18.1
The ratio of the income share of richest 20% to that of poorest 20%	20.47	8.95	11.56	5.34

Source: 1953: Kowie Chang, "An Estimate of Taiwan Personal Income Distribution in 1953—Pareto's Formula Discussed and Applied," *Journal of Social Science,* Vol. 7, P. 260 (National Taiwan University, Aug., 1956).
1959-61: Kowie Chang, "Report on Pilot Study of Personal Income and Consumption in Taiwan," (Prepared under the sponsorship of a working group of National Income Statistics, Directorate-General of Budget, Accounting and Statistics, Executive Yuan) P.23, Table A. and pp. 25-26, Table C.

1966	1968	1970	1972	1974	1976	1978	1980
41.5	41.4	38.7	38.6	38.6	37.3	37.2	36.8
22.0	22.3	22.5	22.5	22.1	22.7	22.7	22.8
16.2	16.3	17.1	17.1	17.0	17.5	17.5	17.7
12.4	12.2	13.3	13.2	13.5	13.6	13.7	13.9
7.9	7.8	8.4	8.6	8.8	8.9	8.9	8.8
0.358	0.362	0.321	0.318	0.319	0.307	0.306	0.303
74.1	80.5	85.8	104.1	109.0	127.4	153.5	173.4
20.8	23.8	27.7	34.1	37.5	42.6	51.3	56.9
5.25	5.31	4.61	4.49	4.39	4.19	4.18	4.18

1964-80: Directorate-General of Budget, Accounting & Statistics, Executive Yuan, Republic of China, *Report on the Survey of Personal Income Distribution in Taiwan Area, Republic of China,* 1980; Department of Budget, Accounting & Statistics, Taiwan Provincial Government, Republic of China, *Report on the Survey of Family Income & Expenditure, Taiwan Province, Republic of China,* various years, (includes Taipei & Kaohsiung Cities); Directorate-General of Budget, Accounting & Statistics, Executive Yuan, *National Income of the Republic of China,* 1981.

with those countries raised by Chenery, Ahluwalia, Bell, Duloy, and Jolly;[9] second that there has been a favorable change in the nationwide income distribution during the whole period under observation; and third that the improvement in income distribution was faster in the period 1953–64 than in the period 1964–80.

During the period 1964–80, the real per family income showed a considerable increase in every income bracket. The rate of increase in the per family income was the greatest for the lowest income bracket and the smallest for the highest income bracket. The growth rates of the five income brackets are shown in Table 6.2.

Table 6.2   Changes in the Real Family Income

(in 1976 prices; %)

Five Equal Divisions of Family Numbers	Rate of Increase During 1964–80
The richest 20% of families	112
The 2nd richest 20% of families	147
The 3rd richest 20% of families	151
The 4th richest 20% of families	158
The poorest 20% of families	165

Source: Department of Budget, Accounting & Statistics, Taiwan Provincial Government, *Report on The Survey of Family Income & Expenditure, Taiwan Province, Republic of China,* Volume 1, Summary Analysis (1980), pp. 21-22, pp, 138-139.

II. The Decomposition Equation by Group

In order to trace changes in income distribution associated with industrialization and urbanization, the decomposition equation should separately identify the intra-group and inter-group effects that contribute to overall income inequality. For this purpose, it helps if the inequality indicator of the whole economy can be explained in relation to such measures as the proportions of farm and nonfarm families, the relative incomes of the two groups, and the indicators of income inequality within the two groups.   As an inequality indicator, the coefficient of variation is convenient for this purpose. The decomposition equation based on the coefficient of variation developed by Fei, Ranis and Kuo will be used in this chapter.[10]

From the statistical definition of variance, it can be readily shown that:

(1) $V_w = h_1 V_1 + \cdots + h_n V_n$

$$+ h_1 (y_1 - y_w)^2 + \cdots + h_n (y_n - y_w)^2$$

where the notations stand for,

> V = variance
> h = family fraction of a group
> y = per-family income
> w = whole economy
> $1, \cdots n$ = group number

The coefficients of variation (I) are defined as follows:

$$I_w = \sqrt{V_w} / y_w \ , \quad I_1 = \sqrt{V_1} / y_1 \ , \quad I_n = \sqrt{V_n} / y_n$$

Substituting these definitions in Equation (1) gives:

(2) $I_w^2 = h_1 \left(\dfrac{y_1}{y_w} \right)^2 I_1^2 + \cdots + h_n \left(\dfrac{y_n}{y_w} \right)^2 I_n^2$

$$+ h_1 \left(\frac{y_1}{y_w} - 1 \right)^2 + \cdots + h_n \left(\frac{y_n}{y_w} - 1 \right)^2$$

Equation (2) is a general form of the group decomposition based on the coefficient of variation.   This equation contains three parameters: the share of the number of families h_j, income disparity among groups y_j / y_w, and income distribution within a group I_j. However, since y_w is the mean income of the whole economy, it is the weighted average weighted by

family share h_j: $y_w = \sum_{j=1}^{n} h_j y_j$. Because the object of this analysis
is to assess the separate effects on I_w of the variation of the group
family shares, the group coefficients of variation, and the group
income disparities, it is not convenient to include the variable h_j
in the expression of income disparities. In other words, when
y_j/y_w is used to show the income disparities, h_j will enter into
the definition of income disparities, and this is not appropriate.
In order to avoid the inclusion of family share in the definition
of income disparity between groups, we will use an indicator
of income disparity Z_j, which is based on a simple average
of the mean incomes of all groups, $\overline{y}$.
Namely,

$$Z_j = \frac{y_j}{\overline{y}}$$

where $\qquad \overline{y} = \sum_{j=1}^{n} y_j/n$

That is, Z_j expresses an individual group mean as a parity of
the simple arithmetic average of the mean incomes of all groups.
Then:

$$(3) \quad \frac{y_j}{y_w} = \frac{Z_j \left(\sum_{j=1}^{n} Z_j \right)}{n \left(\sum_{j=1}^{n} h_j Z_j \right)} = F^j (Z_j, h_j) \quad (j = 1, \cdots n)$$

Equation (3) shows that $\dfrac{y_1}{y_w}$, $\cdots$, $\dfrac{y_n}{y_w}$ are functions of Z_1,
$\cdots$, Z_n, h_1, $\cdots$, h_n. When the $\dfrac{y_j}{y_w}$'s in Equation (3)
are substituted in Equation (2), we have

$$(4) \quad I_w = f (I_1, \cdots, I_j, \cdots, I_n; h_1, \cdots, h_j, \cdots, h_n;$$
$$Z_1, \cdots, Z_j, \cdots, Z_n)$$

That is, I_w is a function of I_j, h_j and Z_j. I_j is the coefficient of variation for the group j; h_j is the family share of the group j; Z_j is the income disparity of the group j.

Treating these variables as a function of time t, I_w can be differentiated with respect to time. $\dfrac{dI_w}{dt}$ explains the overall change in terms of group changes by within-group effect and between-group effect as follows.

$$\text{Overall change} \doteq \text{Within-group effect} + \text{Between-group effect}$$

$$(5)\quad \frac{dI_w}{dt} = \sum_{j=1}^{n} \frac{\partial I_w}{\partial I_j} \frac{dI_j}{dt} + \left(\sum_{j=1}^{n} \frac{\partial I_w}{\partial h_j} \frac{dh_j}{dt} + \sum_{j=1}^{n} \frac{\partial I_w}{\partial Z_j} \frac{dZ_j}{dt} \right)$$

$$\text{(family weight effect)} \qquad \text{(income disparity effect)}$$

Within-group effect measures that part of the overall change that is due to the change in income distribution within a group. Between-group effect is composed of family weight effect and income disparity effect. Family weight effect measures that part of the overall change that is due to the change in the family fraction. Income disparity effect measures that part of the overall change that is due to the change in income disparity among groups.

III. Farm Income and Nonfarm Income Inequalities

During the period 1964–79 in the Taiwan area, the income gap between farm and nonfarm families widened because nonfarm income grew at a higher rate. However, the income inequality as measured by the whole economy decreased considerably. A question is often raised as to how overall income inequality can be reduced in such a dynamic economy where a structural change has been occurring at such a rapid pace. In order to identify the basic causes, the decomposition equation (5) is applied to decompose the causes of reduction

Table 6.3 Causes of Reduction in Income Inequality — Farm and Nonfarm Group Case (1964 — 1979)

	Within-Group Effect	Between-Group Effect	
Total Effect $\sum\limits_{j}$		Family Weight Effect	Income Disparity Effect
	$\sum\limits_{j} \dfrac{\partial I_w}{\partial I_j} \dfrac{dI_j}{dt}$	$\sum\limits_{j} \dfrac{\partial I_w}{\partial h_j} \dfrac{dh_j}{dt}$	$\sum\limits_{j} \dfrac{\partial I_w}{\partial Z_j} \dfrac{dZ_j}{dt}$
−0.1742	−0.2089	0.0347	
(%) (−100.0)	(−119.9)	(19.9)	
		0.0050	0.0297
		(2.9)	(17.0)
Farm group	−0.0185	0.0670	0.0164
	(−8.9)		
Nonfarm group	−0.1904	−0.0620	0.0133
	(−91.1)		

Source: Calculations are based on DGBAS data. See also Note 17.

Note: Figures in parentheses under each effect are % of the total effects. Positive coefficients represent effects which act to increase income inequality, and negative coefficients represent effects which act to decrease income inequality.

in inequality for the period 1964–79. The results obtained show the following facts:

1) The favorable factor contributing to the reduction in income inequality was mainly the reduction in internal inequality within both the farm and nonfarm groups. The contribution of each group to the total within-group inequality reduction was 9% and 91% respectively.

2) The change in the weights of farm and nonfarm family numbers and the widening of the income gap between the two sectors adversely affected the distribution of income. However, the rate of adverse effects combined was not very large, only comprising 20% of the total change.

3) The decomposition of the causes shows that the

essential cause of the reduction in income inequality in the
Taiwan area was the reduction in income inequality within
the nonfarm group. That is, the reduction in income inequality
for the total economy was made possible because the reduction
within the nonfarm group was more than enough to compensate
for the adverse between-group effect.

We have seen that the narrowing inequality within the
nonfarm group was the most influential factor causing the
reduction in nationwide income inequality. Given this finding,
we shall explore further the changes in the nonagricultural
income.

A characteristic of Taiwan's farm family income is that
it contains a quite big portion of nonagricultural income.
The portion of nonagricultural income in farm income was
34.1% in 1966 and increased to 72.7% in 1979.[11] Table 6.4
shows the detail of its composition by different farm income
levels. We note that the lower income families had smaller
shares of nonagricultural income in 1966, but a bigger share
of nonagricultural income became an important source of farm
family income in 1979. It also shows that about 99% of nonfarm income is from nonagricultural activities; thus, agricultural
income in nonfarm income is negligible.

During the period 1966–79, per family income of both
farm and nonfarm groups showed a considerable increase in
every income bracket.   However, nonagricultural income
was the major source of the increase in farm family income.
Nonagricultural income per farm family income grew 988%,
while agricultural income per farm family only grew 111%
(at current prices) over this period.   Thus, the 409% growth
rate of per farm family income was completely attributable to the growth of nonagricultural income in the farm
family.

In view of the higher growth rates of incomes of the lower
income family groups from nonagricultural activities, we
thus find support for the notion that it was the relatively rapid
rate of employment generation for members of the lower
income groups initially, and the change in their wages in the
later period, which were responsible for the good overall per-

Table 6.4   Sources of Farm and Nonfarm Incomes

(%)

Ten Equal Divisions of Family Numbers	1966		Nonfarm Family
	Farm Family		
	% of Agri. Income in Total Farm Family Income	% of Nonagri. Income in Total Farm Family Income	% of Nonagri. Income in Total Nonfarm Family Income
The richest 10% of families	67.6	32.4	98.2
The 2nd richest 10% of families	70.2	29.8	97.7
The 3rd richest 10% of families	70.1	29.9	97.8
The 4th richest 10% of families	68.5	31.5	98.3
The 5th richest 10% of families	65.5	34.5	97.6
The 6th richest 10% of families	64.3	35.7	98.2
The 7th richest 10% of families	61.0	39.0	97.6
The 8th richest 10% of families	57.3	42.7	97.0
The 9th richest 10% of families	55.3	44.7	97.2
The poorest 10% of families	54.7	45.3	97.1
Total	65.9	34.1	97.8

Source: Department of Budget, Accounting & Statistics, Taiwan Provincial Government, *Report on the Survey of Family Income & Expenditure, Taiwan Province, Republic of China,* 1966, 1979.

| 1979 | | | |
| Farm Family | | Nonfarm Family | |
% of Agri. Income in Total Farm Family Income	% of Nonagri. Income in Total Farm Family Income	% of Nonagri. Income in Total Nonfarm Family Income	Ten Equal Divisions of Family Numbers
24.4	75.6	99.2	The richest 10% of families
27.9	72.1	99.0	The 2nd richest 10% of families
26.8	73.2	98.5	The 3rd richest 10% of families
25.5	74.5	98.5	The 4th richest 10% of families
27.5	72.5	98.7	The 5th richest 10% of families
25.8	74.2	98.3	The 6th richest 10% of families
28.9	71.1	98.3	The 7th richest 10% of families
32.9	67.1	97.8	The 8th richest 10% of families
31.4	68.6	97.3	The 9th richest 10% of families
33.7	66.3	97.6	The poorest 10% of families
27.3	72.7	98.6	Total

formance.   During the period under observation, rapid labor absorption first eliminated unemployment.   Newcomers and originally unemployed individuals were absorbed mainly by the nonagricultural sector and particularly by the light manufacturing industries.

Unskilled labor was efficiently utilized.   As the economy grew, unskilled labor became relatively more scarce in terms of the reduction in its excess supply.   Thus, the wage rate of unskilled labor rose more rapidly than that of skilled labor. Undoubtedly, the rapid absorption of unskilled labor at low opportunity costs contributed substantially to the rise in relative incomes of the lower income families in both the farm and nonfarm groups.

Judging from the composition of factor income, we know that the wage income showed an increasing share during the past two decades.   The share of wage income in the national income increased from 40.8% in 1951 to 60.6% in 1979. The share of property income dropped accordingly.   That is, the share of wage income increased at an annual rate of 1.4%, while the share of property income decreased at an annual rate of 1.4%.   The composition and status of the employed underwent a gradual change as the advancement of society and improvement of economic organization occurred.

A formula similar to system (6) in Chapter 7 can be applied to trace the amount of value added and labor earning by each source of final demand. The results of calculations for these purposes are respectively as follows: The generation of value added and labor income is closely related to labor utilization. It is observed that in 1961, value added induced by exports comprised 12.2% of the total national income, and it increased to 34.8% in 1976.   The same tendency is observed for labor earning.   Labor earning due to exports grew from 9.7% in 1961 to 36.1% in 1976.   Here we find the importance of exports in terms of the economic growth and income distribution in Taiwan.   At the same time the decentralization of economic development contributed to this process and was one of the essential factors contributing to the reduction of income inequality.   This part will be examined in the following section.

IV. Income Distribution Associated with Urbanization

1. A Classification of Groups by Different Degrees of Urbanization

The speed of urbanization in the Taiwan area was tremendously high over the last three decades. In 1952, the urban population accounted for 48% of the total population, the number of urban centers with populations of 50,000 or more was twelve, and the development of the Taipei metropolitan area was in its initial phase. By 1980, the urban population had risen to 70% of the total, the number of urban centers had increased to seventy-three, and the development of metropolitan areas had extended to all the major cities and their surrounding communities.[12]

In almost all studies concerned with urbanization, the whole Taiwan area is classified conventionally into seven sectors, or more recently into four sectors (i.e., Northern, Central, Southern and Eastern Regions) based on location. This kind of classification, however, does not embody the precise characteristics of urbanization, nor is it suitable for examining the relationship between urbanization and income distribution. What is necessary is some type of classification able to both illustrate the characteristics of urbanization and provide information on income distribution broken down by different degrees of urbanization. The smallest units in terms of location which can be compiled independently in a time series of income distribution are prefectures and cities.[13] Faced with this constraint, in the classification used here prefectures and cities are the smallest units. This usage, moreover, allows us to employ some important economic indicators that accord with different degrees of urbanization.

The characteristics of urbanization will be represented by the following cluster of six indicators: job opportunities, wage rates, government expenditures, capital intensity, degree of industrialization, and population densities. These six indicators are further measured by the following twelve indicators: non-agricultural employment/population, nonagricultural employment/area, value added/area, total wages/area, nonagricultural value added/nonagricultural employment, nonagricultural value added/area, nonagricultural wages/nonagricultural employment, nonagricultural wages/area, government expenditures/area, nonagricultural capital stock/nonagricultural employment, value of nonagricultural output/total output, and population/area. Based on this cluster of indicators, the 21 prefectures and cities in the Taiwan area are classified into four categories, from the most urban to the least urban, as shown in Table 6.5.

The classification procedure may need some explanation. Table 6.5 consists of three parts, upper, middle and bottom. In the upper part of Table 6.5, the 12 indicators are listed in ascending order. No *a priori* divider exists for dividing these figures into four urban groups. What we have done for the division is based on the following principles: (1) smaller figures represent less-urban groups; and (2) if many prefectures' data are rather concentrated in a certain range, we use that range to indicate a group.

In the middle part of the table, each of the 12 indicators is denoted by number, running from 1 to 12. For example, 1 stands for nonagri. labor/population; 2 stands for nonagri. labor/area; 3 stands for value added/area and so on. The range of each one of the 12 indicators in the upper part is represented by each urban group in the middle part of the table. With this simple transformation, we can easily mark a cross based on the statistical data of each prefecture or city in the corresponding cell in the lower part of the table. For example, statistical data show that indicator 1 (nonagri. labor/population) in Taipei is 43%, and we know from the upper part of the table that the figure 43% belongs to the most urban category. Therefore, Taipei city has a cross for indicator 1 in the most urban category. Likewise, statistical data show that indicator 2 (nonagri. labor/area) in Taipei is 2,901 persons/ sq.km, and we know from the upper part of the table that it belongs to the most urban category. Therefore, Taipei city has a cross for indicator 2 in the most urban category. All the 21 x 12 crosses in the table are made in this way. It is interesting to know that indicators of urbanization are closely interrelated so as to enable them to provide a clear-cut classification, even though twelve indicators are used at one time.

According to this cluster of indicators, Taipei is clearly the most urbanized area. Located in the second urban category are four cities: Keelung, Taichung, Tainan, and Kaohsiung. Taipei prefecture, Taoyuan prefecture (both bordering on Taipei city) and Changhwa prefecture (bordering on Taichung) constitute the third urbanized area. The remaining prefectures all fall into the least urbanized category. The evident characteristics found in all urbanized areas are: higher employment rate, higher family income, higher productivity, larger government expenditure, greater capital intensity, and higher share of industrial products. The characteristics of rural areas are just the opposite.

There is a very close relationship between the agriculture — nonagriculture and rural-urban dichotomies. Consequently, some conclusions are relevant to both industrialization and urbanization.

2. Income Distribution by Degree of Urbanization

After 21 prefectures and cities are classified into four groups by different degrees of urbanization, we can examine the status and changes of income distribution within groups and income disparities among groups. In Table 6.6, four groups' income distributions are measured by both the Gini coefficient and the coefficient of variation. It is interesting to note that income distribution within the more urban groups was not necessarily less equal than within the less urban groups. Also, excepting the third urban group in 1972–76, all groups in all periods showed improved income distribution within groups.

Income disparities among groups are illustrated in terms of the ratio of per-family income in each group to the per-family income in the most urban group. The most urban group had in each period the highest per-family income. The gap among groups widened in 1966–72, but narrowed thereafter as the third and fourth groups began to catch up. Particularly, the improvement in the third urban group is noteworthy in that

Table 6.5   Classification of Urbanization

Upper part: Different degrees of urbanization shown by 12 indicators

	4th Urban
I. Job opportunities	
1 = Nonagri. labor/Population (%)	4.5 – 14.5
2 = Nonagri. labor/Area (Person/Sq. Km.)	5 – 68
II. Earnings	
3 = Value added/Area (NT$1,000/Sq. Km.)	567 – 3,794
4 = Salaries & wages/Area (NT$1,000/Sq. Km.)	328 – 2,021
5 = Nonagri. value added/Nonagri. labor (NT$1,000/Person)	12.5 – 23.3
6 = Nonagri. value added/Area (NT$1,000/Sq. Km.)	93 – 1,255
7 = Nonagri. salaries & wages/Nonagri. labor (NT$1,000/Person)	10.0 – 17.8
8 = Nonagri. salaries & wages/Area (NT$1,000/Sq. Km.)	65 – 975
III. Government expenditures	
9 = Gov't expenditure/Area (NT$1,000/Sq. Km.)	64 – 333
IV. Capital Intensity	
10 = Nonagri. capital/Nonagri. labor (NT$1,000/Person)	44 – 113
V. Degree of industrialization	
11 = Nonagri. products/Total products (%)	52.9 – 73.7
VI. Population density	
12 = Population/Area (Persons/Sq. Km.)	73 – 466

3rd Urban	2nd Urban	Most Urban
14.6 − 17.5	17.6 − 26.4	43
92 − 121	486 − 2,027	2,901
5,199 − 7,789	28,685 − 96,298	108,068
3,004 − 4,538	18,561 − 60,984	68,098
23.8 − 23.9	26.1 − 32.7	55
2,186 − 3,251	13,637 − 66,252	160,078
17.9 − 18.2	18.7 − 22.8	29
1,664 − 2,510	9,674 − 46,149	83,546
362 − 1,032	2,311 − 7,500	15,626
114 − 119	130 − 395	667
79.3 − 86.6	91.3 − 95.4	98.9
613 − 997	2,486 − 2,859	6,760 − 7,664

Table 6.5   Classification of Urbanization

(continued)

Middle part: Transformation of the upper part	4th Urban 1 2 3 4 5 6 7 8 9 10 11 12

Bottom part: Matching statistical data of each prefecture or city with each indicator

Taipei City

Keelung City
Taichung City
Tainan City
Kaohsiung City

Taipei Prefecture
Taoyuan Prefecture
Changhwa Prefecture   x   x

Yilan Prefecture   x x x x x x x x x x x x
Hsinchu Prefecture   x x x x x x x x x x x
Miaoli Prefecture   x x x x x x x x x x x x
Taichung Prefecture   x x x x x x x x x x x
Nantou Prefecture   x x x x x x x x x x x x
Yunlin Prefecture   x x x x x x x x x x x
Chiayi Prefecture   x x x x x x x x x x x x
Tainan Prefecture   x x x x x x x x x x x x
Kaohsiung Prefecture   x x x x x x x x x x x x
Pingtung Prefecture   x x x x x x x x x x x x
Taitung Prefecture   x x x x x x x x x x x x
Hualien Prefecture   x x x x x x x x x x x x
Penghu Prefecture   x x   x x x x   x x

Source:
(1) Population and Area are from *Statistical Abstract of the Republic of China*, DGBAS, 1972.
(2) Value Added and Salaries & Wages are from *Report on the Survey of Family Income & Expenditure in Taiwan Province* (Taiwan: Taiwan Provincial Government, Bureau of Accounting & Statistics 1971), and *Report on the Survey of Family Income and Expenditure and Personal Income Distribution of Taipei City* (Taipei: Taipei City Government, Bureau of Budget, Accounting and Statistics 1971).
(3) Nonagri. Labor, Nonagri. Value Added, Nonagri. Salaries & Wages, Non-

3rd Urban	2nd Urban	Most Urban
1 2 3 4 5 6 7 8 9 10 11 12	1 2 3 4 5 6 7 8 9 10 11 12	1 2 3 4 5 6 7 8 9 10 11 12

```
                                                          x x x x x x x x x x x x

                    x        x x x x x x x x x   x
                             x x x x x x x x x x x x
                             x x x x x x x x x x x x
                             x x x x x x x x x x                              x

  x x x   x   x x      x   x        x   x        x x
x x x x x x x x   x x                        x
  x x x x   x x x x x

                    x

                    x

                        x




  x x        x   x
```

agri. Capital, and Nonagri. Products are from *Industrial & Commercial Censuses of Taiwan and Fukien Area, Republic of China* (Taipei: The Committee on Industrial and Commercial Censuses of Taiwan and Fukien Area, Executive Yuan, 1971).

(4) Gov't Expenditure is from *Annual Report of Financial Statistics of Taiwan Province* (Taiwan: Taiwan Provincial Government, Department of Finance 1973) and *Yearbook of Financial Statistics of the Republic of China* (Taipei: Ministry of Finance, Department of Statistics 1973).

(5) Agri. Products is from *Taiwan Agricultural Yearbook* (Taiwan: Provincial Government of Taiwan, Department of Agriculture & Forestry 1972).

Note: All of these data are based on 1971 data.

Table 6.6   Income Distribution by Four Urban Groups (1966—1980)

Variable and Group	Notation	1966
1. Gini coefficient		
Total gini	G	0.3237
Most urban	G_1	0.3146
Second urban	G_2	0.3066
Third urban	G_3	0.2855
Fourth urban	G_4	0.3309
2. Coefficient of variation		
Total coefficient	I	0.6610
Most urban	I_1	0.6405
Second urban	I_2	0.6380
Third urban	I_3	0.5695
Fourth urban	I_4	0.6760
3. Sectoral family income parity		
Most urban	y_1/y_1	1.00
Second urban	y_2/y_1	0.96
Third urban	y_3/y_1	0.79
Fourth urban	y_4/y_1	0.81
4. Share of the number of families		
Most urban	h_1	0.2122
Second urban	h_2	0.0952
Third urban	h_3	0.1283
Fourth urban	h_4	0.5643

Source: Calculated from the original questionnaire of the DGBAS surveys.

1972	1976	1980	Variable and Group
			1. Gini coefficient
0.3018	0.3000	0.2822	Total gini
0.3052	0.2584	0.2772	Most urban
0.2776	0.2714	0.2527	Second urban
0.2541	0.2821	0.2735	Third urban
0.2825	0.2751	0.2719	Fourth urban
			2. Coefficient of variation
0.6290	0.5878	0.5397	Total coefficient
0.6406	0.5397	0.5228	Most urban
0.5499	0.5508	0.4796	Second urban
0.4930	0.6140	0.5155	Third urban
0.6737	0.5598	0.5196	Fourth urban
			3. Sectoral family income parity
1.00	1.00	1.00	Most urban
0.83	0.81	0.84	Second urban
0.72	0.80	0.88	Third urban
0.61	0.67	0.67	Fourth urban
			4. Share of the number of families
0.2195	0.1518	0.1505	Most urban
0.1431	0.1593	0.1629	Second urban
0.1851	0.2236	0.2500	Third urban
0.4523	0.4653	0.4366	Fourth urban

its per-family income exceeded the per family income of the second urban group in 1980. During this period, however, the third urban group reflected an exceptionally adverse movement of income distribution. The group showed greater inequality in 1976 than in 1972, although it had improved again by 1980.

Migration rates appear related to parity changes. Throughout the three periods in-migration into the third urban region took place, with the rate of in-migration accelerating in 1972 and maintaining the fastest pace thereafter. As a result, the ratio of families in the third urban region increased continuously.

3. Effects of Changes in Group Distribution on Changes in the Whole Economy

In order to examine the effects of changes in group distribution on changes in the whole economy, the decomposition equation by group, Equation (5) of this chapter will be used. The results of our calculations are presented in Table 6.7. Positive figures represent adverse changes that act to increase income inequality, while negative figures represent the favorable changes that act to reduce income inequality. The figures in parentheses indicate the percentage composition of the within-group effect by respective group. Observations are based on the three periods respectively. The changes in the coefficients of variation for the whole economy were negative for all the three periods, indicating that there was an overall reduction in income inequality.

The following within- and between-group effects are observed:

1) The reduction in internal inequality within each of the four groups contributed most to the reduction in income inequality throughout the three periods. The rates of contribution to the reduction in income inequality of the total economy in the three periods were 182%, 42% and 108%, respectively.

2) The reduction in within-group inequality compensated for the adverse between-group effect in the first period and thus

significantly contributed to the reduction of income inequality for the whole economy.

3) The fourth urban group made the greatest contribution to the within-group effect in the first period; the most urban group replaced it in the second period; and the third urban group in the third period. The only contrary finding was when the third urban group in the second period registered an adverse intra-effect of 186%, it was compensated for by a favorable change in the most urban group.

4) The income disparity effect acted adversely on the overall income distribution in the first period. It then acted favorably in the second period as per family income in less urban groups increased relatively faster. Combining the family-weight effect and the income-disparity effect, the total adverse contribution produced by the between-group effect was 82% in the first period. However, it became favorable in the second period.

5) The change in the weights of family numbers had a moderately favorable effect on the reduction of income inequality in the first period; however, this effect became negligible in the second and third periods.

In summary, the between-group income gap widened only during the first period when the economy was in pre-full employment status. During this period, within-group inequality was reduced more than enough to compensate for the adverse between-group effect, thereby improving overall income distribution. After the economy reached full employment, even during the course of speedy industrialization and urbanization, no significant adverse income disparity effect was observed.

The fundamental reasons for the continual reduction in within-group income inequality were analogous to those observed for the changes in farm and nonfarm family incomes. First, the rapid rate of new job opportunities leading to full employment in 1971 provided unskilled labor with job opportunities. Newcomers and unemployed individuals were mainly absorbed by light manufacturing industries. Thus unskilled labor was efficiently used. As the economy grew further unskilled labor became relatively scarce, inducing a faster wage

Table 6.7 Sources of the Reduction in Income Inequality
Explained by Sectoral Changes in the Four
Sectors, 1966–1980

Sector	Total Effect	Within-Group Effect $\sum_j \dfrac{\partial I_w}{\partial I_j} \dfrac{dI_j}{dt}$
1966–72		
All sectors change in the coefficient of variation	−0.0333 (−100)	−0.0607 (−182)
Most urban		0.00003 (0)
Second urban		−0.0118 (−19)
Third urban		−0.0088 (−15)
Fourth urban		−0.0401 (−66)
1972–76		
All sectors change in the coefficient of variation	−0.0297 (−100)	−0.0126 (−42)
Most urban		−0.0318 (−253)
Second urban		0.0001 (1)
Third urban		0.0234 (186)
Fourth urban		−0.0043 (−34)
1976–80		
All sectors change in the coefficient of variation	−0.0505 (−100)	−0.0547 (−108)
Most urban		−0.0039 (−7)
Second urban		−0.0115 (−21)
Third urban		−0.0266 (−49)
Fourth urban		−0.0127 (−23)

Between-Group Effect	Family Weight Effect $\sum_j \dfrac{\partial I_w}{\partial h_j} \dfrac{dh_j}{dt}$	+	Income Disparity Effect $\sum_j \dfrac{\partial I_w}{\partial Z_j} \dfrac{dZ_j}{dt}$	Sector
				1966–72
0.0274	−0.0077		0.0351	All sectors change
(82)	(−23)		(105)	in the coefficent
				of variation
	−0.0018		0.0174	Most urban
	−0.0177		−0.0006	Second urban
	−0.0234		−0.0013	Third urban
	0.0352		0.0196	Fourth urban
				1972–76
−0.0171	0.0001		−0.0172	All sectors change
(−58)	(0)		(−58)	in the coefficient
				of variation
	0.0154		−0.0065	Most urban
	−0.0059		−0.0005	Second urban
	−0.0134		−0.0009	Third urban
	0.0040		−0.0093	Fourth urban
				1976–80
0.0042	−0.0003		0.0045	All sectors change
(8)	(−1)		(9)	in the coefficient
				of variation
	0.0003		−0.0031	Most urban
	−0.0012		0.000001	Second urban
	−0.0074		0.0025	Third urban
	0.0080		0.0051	Fourth urban

Table 6.7   Sources of the Reduction in Income Inequality
Explained by Sectoral Changes in the Four
Sectors, 1966—1980

(continued)

Sector	Total Effect	Within-Group Effect $$\sum_j \frac{\partial I_w}{\partial I_j} \frac{dI_j}{dt}$$
1966—80		
All sectors change in the coefficient of variation	−0.1173 (−100)	−0.1246 (−106)
Most urban		−0.0297 (−24)
Second urban		−0.0217 (−17)
Third urban		−0.0103 (−8)
Fourth urban		−0.0629 (−51)

Source: Same as Table 6.6. See also Note 17 at the end of this chapter.
Notes:
  1. Positive coefficients represent effects which act to increase income inequality;
     negative coefficients represent effects which act to reduce income inequality.

rate increase for unskilled labor than for skilled labor. Thus
rapid absorption of unskilled labor contributed substantially
to the rise in relative incomes of lower income families, both
urban and rural.

Second, an increasing share of off-farm income in the total
income received by farm families impeded ever-widening
income gaps between groups. During the 1966—79 period,
while per family income in both the farm and nonfarm sectors
showed a considerable increase in all income brackets, nonagricultural income was the major source of increased farm-family
income. Undoubtedly, rapid labor absorption and industrial
decentralization were essential factors contributing to the

Between- Group Effect	=	Family Weight Effect	+	Income Disparity Effect	Sector
		$\sum_j \dfrac{\partial I_w}{\partial h_j} \dfrac{dh_j}{dt}$		$\sum_j \dfrac{\partial I_w}{\partial Z_j} \dfrac{dZ_j}{dt}$	
					1966–80
0.0073		−0.0112		0.0185	All sectors change
(6)		(−10)		(16)	in the coefficient
					of variation
		0.0171		0.0044	Most urban
		−0.0229		−0.0009	Second urban
		−0.0417		0.0004	Third urban
		0.0363		0.0146	Fourth urban

2. Figures in parentheses refer to percentages.
3. The reductions in income inequality presented in this table are the total effect calculated from Equation (5), but not a direct deduction of the coefficient of variation. The two results have a negligible difference.

reduction of income inequality.

4.   Urbanization and Standard of Living

In recent years, it has been recognized that the traditional measure of national economic progress, the growth rates of GNP and per capita income, cannot alone measure real human welfare. As development strategies have shifted their emphasis toward addressing social goals, there has been a growing concern about the achievement of equity not only in terms of money income, but also in terms of social welfare. Social indicators are designed to measure national welfare in a systematic and comprehensive way. Social indicators often incorporate some popular welfare goals relating to environment, health, education, leisure, and so on. Here, we will discuss some of these social and economic criteria in two parts. First, we will observe the improvement of living standards over time, after which we will compare differences in living standards existing among our four urban sectors.

(1) Improvement of Living Standards Over Time

Table 6.8 shows clearly improvements in living standards over time in terms of advances made in education, sanitation, transportation and communication, and housing.

Although some education was available to the people of Taiwan when the island was under Japanese occupation, it was usually limited to the primary level. Advanced education was rare and almost always limited to medical science. After Taiwan was restored to Chinese sovereignty, the government of the Republic of China made efforts to promote education. Not only was a large portion of government money spent on education, but equal opportunity for education was also emphasized. As a result, the level and rate of education increased greatly.

The literacy rate of persons 6 years and older increased from 45% in 1946 to 89.3% in 1979. Over the same period, the percentage of school-age children in primary schools increased from 78.6% to 99.7%. In 1968, nine years of education was made compulsory. Over the 1966–79 period, the percentage of junior high-age youth (12–14 years old) in junior high schools increased from 48.3% to 91.1%; the percentage of senior high-age youth (15-17 years old) in senior high and vocational schools increased from 28.3% to 52.3%; and the percentage of junior college- and university-age youth (18–21 years old) in colleges and universities increased from 11.3% to 27.5%. The promotion of education on the island greatly contributed to the rapid growth of the economy by providing higher-quality labor for advanced production.

The crude death rate and life expectancy are considered

Table 6.8   Quality of Life Indicators

Item		
1. Education		1979
Literacy rate (of population 6 years old and older) (percent)	45.0 (1946)	89.3
Percentage of school age children (6-11) in primary schools	78.6 (1946)	99.7
Percentage of junior high age youths (12-14) in junior high schools	48.3 (1966)	91.1
Percentage of senior high age youths (15-17) in senior high and vocational schools	28.3 (1966)	52.3
Percentage of junior college and university age youths (18-21) in junior colleges and universities	11.3 (1966)	27.5
2. Sanitation	1952	1980
Crude death rate (per 1,000)	9.9	4.8
Life expectancy (years)	58.6	70.8
Per capita daily calorie intake	2,078	2,812
Per capita daily protein intake (grams)	49	78
3. Transportation and Communications	1952	1980
Automobiles (per 1,000 households)	5	52
Motorcycles (per 1,000 households)	1	785
Telephones (per 1,000 households)	20	517
Correspondence posted per capita	7	52
4. Housing	1949	1980
Percentage of households served with electric lighting	33.0	99.7
Percentage of households served with piped water	14.4	66.9
Living space per head (square meters)	4.6	17.9
Dwellings investment/GNP (percent)	1.0 (1952)	4.5

Source: Council for Economic Planning and Development, Executive Yuan, *Economic Development, Taiwan, Republic of China* (July 1977 and May 1980); Manpower Planning Committee, Council for Economic Planning and Development, Executive Yuan, *Social Welfare Indicators, Republic of China* (1980); Directorate-General of Budget, Accounting and Statistics, Executive Yuan, *Statistical Abstract* (1980); Directorate-General of Budget, Accounting and Statistics, Executive Yuan, *National Income of the Republic of China* (1980).

to be two typical indicators of the level of sanitation. The crude death rate in Taiwan decreased from 9.9 per thousand in 1952 to 4.8 per thousand in 1980, and life expectancy increased from 58.6 years to 70.8 years over the same period. During the same years, the per capita daily calorie intake increased from 2,078 calories to 2,812 calories, and per capita protein intake increased from 49 grams to 78 grams.

Transportation in Taiwan has become increasingly problematic because of Taiwan's land-scarce, population-dense character. Particularly in the 1960s, the speed of industrialization greatly exceeded the rate of highway and harbor construction. However, transportation construction was intensified during 1974–78 through the implementation of the "ten major projects". Transportation has been greatly facilitated since then, although the situation is still far from satisfactory. The number of automobiles, motorcycles, and telephones also increased rapidly as the economy grew.

Housing construction during the past three decades has been quite successful. About 90% of the houses in Taipei City and 80% of the houses in Taiwan Province were built after World War II. Living space per head increased from 4.6 square meters in 1949 to 17.9 square meters in 1980. The share of dwelling investment in the GNP increased from 1% in 1952 to 4.5% in 1980. One particular welfare item, the wide-scale diffusion of public utilities, increased in scope far more than what can be measured in terms of money income. For example, the percentage of houses equipped with electric lighting grew from 33% in 1949 to 99.7% in 1980. In sum, it is obvious that industrialization and urbanization have brought in their wake significant social welfare benefits.

(2) Inequalities in Living Standards Among Groups

Table 6.9 offers comparisons of sanitation and education over time and place. It should be noted that in both the past and at present, living conditions expressed in terms of death rate, life expectancy, medical personnel, literacy rate, and the percentage of school age children in primary schools were better in the more urbanized areas. However, it is interesting to note that the gaps shown by these indicators among different urban sectors are not as wide as family income differentials. Furthermore, the gaps were generally narrower in 1979 than in previous years. Finally, the gaps in the most fundamental human concerns, viz., life expectancy and primary education, were almost nonexistent by 1980.

The pattern of consumption in the past clearly reflects Engel's Law. The proportion of expenditures on daily necessities, i.e., food, beverages, tobacco, clothing and footware, decreased from 67.5% in 1951 to 48.4% in 1979 for the overall economy. The more urban groups consumed a smaller proportion of those daily necessities throughout the entire period.

The higher standard of living in the more urban regions is reflected in the more extensive use of modern facilities. The gaps between urban and rural families differ in degree by items of consumption. Very small gaps can be found for the ownership of such items as televisions, refrigerators, gas stoves and electric cookers. For example, the number of refrigerators per thousand families in the four sectors is, respectively, 969, 964, 955 and 898; and televisions, 1,045, 1,032, 1,039, and 994. Relatively larger gaps can be found for such items as air conditioners, enamel baths, flush toilets, and pianos. The number of those items owned by the fourth urban group per thousand families comprised roughly half of what was owned in the most urban sector in 1980. For example, the number of flush toilets per one thousand families in each of the four groups is, respectively, 1,062, 952, 800, and 529. However, we should note that the prevalence of those items in the fourth urban group has risen rapidly during the past few years. Motorcycles showed a reverse pattern as automobile ownership increased in the more urban regions.

Above we have seen many of the benefits that urbanization has brought to the economy and to individual families: higher per family income, higher employment rate, higher productivity, and higher standard of living. However, urbanization has exerted a negative impact as well. For example, the incidence of fires, crimes, automobile accidents, transportation expendi-

Table 6.9   A Comparison of Sanitation and Education
Among Groups Over Time

Region	Death Rate (0/00)		Life Expectancy (years)		Medical Personnel (per 10,000 population)	
	1961	1979	1964	1979	1964	1979
Most urban	4.6	3.7	70.1	72.2	30.7	52.1
2nd urban	5.6	4.2	67.3	71.9	16.9	29.9
3rd urban	7.1	4.3	66.9	72.6	6.8	18.1
4th urban	7.2	5.4	66.0	70.8	7.5	15.4
Average	6.6	4.7	66.5	70.7	10.8	22.9

Source: Department of Civil Affairs, Taiwan Provincial Government, *Household Registration Statistics of Taiwan*, 1959–1961; Ministry of Interior, *Taiwan Demographic Fact Book, Republic of China*, 1971.   Ministry of Interior, *Taiwan-Fukien Demographic Fact Book, Republic of China*, 1979; Directorate-General of Budget, Accounting and Statistics, Executive Yuan, *Statistical*

tures, and level of dust fall are all higher in the more urban sectors.   The net gain from urbanization, therefore, should be measured after these necessary costs of urbanization are subtracted.   Needless to say this calculation is not an easy task.

There perhaps exists a point at which urbanization's positive and negative effects are equal.   Before an urban region has reached this point, the existence of the positive net gain from urbanization may attract people to in-migrate.   As a result, the figures will show a positive migration rate. After this point is passed, however, the negative net gain from urbanization may induce people to out-migrate.   In Taiwan, between 1966 and 1972 the in-migration rate into the most urban sector, Taipei, was substantial.   It began to decline in 1972, approached zero in 1976, and became negative thereafter. The same pattern can be observed for the second urban region. After 1970, in-migration into the third urban region rose at an accelerating rate, as this sector replaced the first two. The fourth urban region

Percentage of School Age Children in Primary Schools		Literacy Rate (%)		Region
1964	1979	1971	1979	
98.8	99.8	92.1	94.1	Most urban
97.9	99.8	89.1	91.4	2nd urban
95.9	99.8	83.9	88.5	3rd urban
96.6	99.6	84.5	87.7	4th urban
96.8	99.7	86.0	89.3	Average

Abstract, 1979; Department of Health, Taiwan Provincial Government, *Health Statistical Abstract, Taiwan Province,* 1964; National Health Administration, Taiwan Provincial Health Department, Taipei City Health Department, *Health Statistics-General Health Statistics,* 1979.

showed a continuously negative rate of migration.

We have witnessed the rather small gaps among different urban groups in terms of the most basic needs, such as primary education, life expectancy, and possesion of refrigerators and televisions. When we also bring the ill effects of urbanization into our calculation, the superiority of the more urban regions must be diminished to some extent; the gaps among groups therefore, may be even smaller than the statistics indicate.

5. Demographic Change and Income Distribution

The unique demographic change in Taiwan and its special relevance to the reduction in income inequality among regions was emphasized by Professor Simon Kuznets in his recent study.[14] According to Professor Kuznets, marked declines in fertility without an introduction of deliberate population control policies in free societies represent significant economically

Table 6.10   A Comparison of the Percentage of Consumption of Daily Necessities Among Groups Over Time

Year	Region	Percentage of Consumption of Daily Necessities in Family Consumption
1951	Average	67.5
1961	Average	64.2
1970	Most urban	50.6
	2nd urban	54.8
	3rd urban	57.6
	4th urban	60.1
	Average	56.7
1976	Most urban	46.2
	2nd urban	51.6
	3rd urban	52.7
	4th urban	58.0
	Average	53.3
1979	Most urban	43.2
	2nd urban	46.7
	3rd urban	47.9
	4th urban	52.4
	Average	48.4

Source: Directorate-General of Budget, Accounting and Statistics, Executive Yuan, *National Income of the Republic of China,* 1980; Department of Budget, Accounting and Statistics, Taiwan Provincial Government, *Report on the Survey of Family Income and Expenditure, Taiwan Province,* 1970, 1976 and 1979; Bureau of Budget, Accounting and Statistics, Taipei Municipal Government, *Report on the Survey of Family Income and Expenditure and Personal Income Distribution of Taipei Municipality,* 1970, 1976 and 1979; Bureau of Budget, Accounting and Statistics, Kaohsiung Municipality Government, *Report on the Survey of Family Income and Expenditure of Kaohsiung Municipality,* 1979.

Note: Daily necessities include food,beverages, tobacco, clothing & footwear.

Table 6.11   A Comparison of Consumer Durables Among Sectors (1980)

(per 1,000 households)

Item	Most Urban	2nd Urban	3rd Urban	4th Urban	Average for the Economy
1. Televisions	1,045	1,032	1,039	994	1,019
2. Refrigerators	969	964	955	898	934
3. Air conditioners	434	200	187	62	172
4. Electric fans	2,001	2,020	1,988	1,775	1,902
5. Washing machines	808	723	703	537	650
6. Telephones	792	639	544	359	516
7. Gas stoves	991	986	982	997	990
8. Electric cookers	1,029	990	996	950	980
9. Exhaust fans	579	545	524	299	437
10. Vacuum cleaners	86	60	44	19	42
11. Flush toilets	1,062	952	800	529	747
12. Enamel baths	928	757	693	416	618
13. Sewing machines	404	494	506	579	521
14. Cameras	488	314	314	159	273
15. Video cameras	16	15	12	6	11
16. Video cassettes	44	25	19	13	20
17. Pianos	87	69	35	30	46
18. Hi-Fi stereo sets	347	260	291	208	258
19. Recorders	627	436	492	353	443
20. Sedan vehicles	93	59	53	35	52
21. Motorcycles	396	873	665	949	783
22. Newspapers	857	618	660	445	589
23. Magazines	156	108	104	75	100

Source: Department of Budget, Accounting and Statistics, Taiwan Provincial Government, *Report on the Survey of Family Income and Expenditure, Taiwan Province*, 1980; Bureau of Budget, Accounting and Statistics, Taipei Municipal Government, *Report on the Survey of Family Income and Expenditure and Personal Income Distribution of Taipei Municipality*, 1980; Bureau of Budget, Accounting and Statistics, Kaohsiung Municipality Government, *Report on the Survey of Family Income and Expenditure of Kaohsiung Municipality*, 1980.

Table 6.12   Negative Impact of Urbanization

(per 10,000 population)

Region	Fires		Automobile Accidents		Average Family Transportation Expenditure (NT$)	
	1976	1979	1976	1979	1976	1979
Most urban	6.5	5.5	5.9	8.4	3,104	4,368
2nd urban	2.1	3.4	3.0	3.0	1,246	1,901
3rd urban	0.9	2.8	5.9	7.2	1,726	2,472
4th urban	1.2	1.8	7.8	9.8	1,013	1,445
Average	1.9	2.7	6.4	8.0	1,527	2,227

Source: Housing and Urban Development Department, Council for Economic Planning and Development, Executive Yuan, *Urban and Regional Development Statistics, Republic of China,* 1976 and 1980.

Table 6.13   Rate of Migration (by Four Urban Regions)

(%)

Region	1961	1966	1968	1970	1971	1972
Most urban	1.81	1.66	2.50	2.78	1.50	1.83
2nd urban	1.15	1.64	1.64	2.01	1.63	1.26
3rd urban	0.24	0.62	0.04	1.28	1.02	0.88
4th urban	−0.43	−0.61	−0.95	−0.53	−0.92	−0.98
Taiwan area	0.11	0.17	−0.01	0.59	0.14	0.08

Source: Department of Civil Affairs, Taiwan Provincial Government, *Household Registration Statistics of Taiwan,* 1959–1961; Department of Civil Affairs, Taiwan Provincial Government, *Taiwan Demographic Fact Book, Republic of China,* 1966; Ministry of Interior, *Taiwan Demographic Fact Book, Republic of*

Crimes		Dust Fall (Ton/km^2 /month)		Region
1976	1979	1976	1979	
50.1	59.3	20.2	9.3	Most urban
39.5	47.7	8.9	13.1	2nd urban
20.8	20.2	8.5	12.5	3rd urban
19.0	21.3	7.7	9.9	4th urban
26.4	29.8	9.9	11.0	Average

1973	1974	1975	1976	1977	1978	1979	Region
1.26	0.58	0.40	0.10	0.33	0.04	−0.16	Most urban
1.02	0.97	0.70	0.03	−0.04	−0.21	0.18	2nd urban
1.20	1.49	1.63	1.88	2.24	2.08	2.10	3rd urban
−1.19	−1.20	−1.02	−1.11	−0.94	−1.15	−1.18	4th urban
−0.05	−0.07	−0.00	−0.11	0.09	−0.09	−0.04	Taiwan area

China. 1968, 1970–1973; Ministry of Interior, *Taiwan-Fukien Demographic Fact Book, Republic of China*, 1974–1979; Directorate-General of Budget, Accounting and Statistics, Executive Yuan, *Statistical Abstract*, 1976–1979.

rational responses of the population to changes in economic and social conditions that favor fewer children and greater investment in their education and training. As he says: "Hence, such wide diffusion of fertility reduction is a significant index of the extent to which the revised view on children and their future prospects has spread, and thus an index of the spread of the positive contributions of economic growth in their distribution among the population."[15]   Also, "Wide diffusion of fertility reduction among all strata of the population prevents or minimizes the inequality effects of uneven diffusion, which in the past of many currently developed countries meant a gradual and slow spread of the pattern from the higher income brackets to the lower."

Prefessor Kuznets found that the fertility rate in Taiwan declined sharply over a two-decade span, dropping from 6.7 per thousand in 1951–53 to 3.4 per thousand in 1971–73. This decline is almost as great as the decline that occurred in the currently developed countries over a century of economic growth. Professor Kuznets also demonstrated that the proportional decline in fertility was as large in the rural townships as in the urban townships and cities. The initial relative discrepancy in fertility between the rural and urban populations, narrow proportionally to begin with, remained unchanged, while the absolute differences shrank sharply. Further, this rapid reduction in fertility occurred before the perceptive element of inequality in incidence of childbearing and in the implications for income inequalities was introduced. The widespread reduction in fertility, reflecting increasing confidence of the population in the advantages of a smaller but better brought-up and educated next generation, suggests that the effects of, and gains from, a technologically advancing economy have also been widespread. Thus, Professor Kuznets concludes: "a major factor in the high growth rate sustained over the long span and the marked structural shifts that were accomplished, possibly without widening income inequality, was the forward movement in Taiwan's demographic transition to modern population patterns."[16]

As we have seen above, the specific characteristic of the

Taiwan economy was a more equitable income distribution amidst rapid industrialization and urbanization. The narrowing inequality within the nonfarm group was the most influential factor causing the reduction in nationwide income inequality. The rapid absorption of labor force contributed substantially to the rise in relative incomes of the lower income families, both urban and rural. Industrialization and urbanization have brought in their wake significant welfare benefits: higher per family income, higher employment rate, higher productivity, and higher standard of living. The gaps between the four urban sectors in the most basic needs, such as primary education, life expectancy, and possession of refrigerators and televisions, have been rather small. The welfare gap is probably even smaller when the "bads" associated with urbanization are also considered.

NOTES

1. Simon Kuznets, "Economic Growth and Income Inequality," *American Economic Review,* Vol. 45, No. 1, 1955, pp. 1-28; idem, "Quantitative Aspects of the Economic Growth of Nations: VIII, Distribution of Income by Size," *Economic Development and Cultural Change,* Vol. 11, No. 2, 1963, pp. 1-80.

2. H.B. Chenery, M.S. Ahluwalia, C.L.G. Bell, J.H. Duloy, and R. Jolly, *Redistribution with Growth* (London: Oxford University Press, 1974).

3. John C.H. Fei, Gustav Ranis, and Shirley W.Y. Kuo, *Growth with Equity: The Taiwan Case* (London: Oxford University Press, 1979).

4. Simon Kuznets, "Growth and Structural Shifts," in Walter Galenson ed., *Economic Growth and Structural Change in Taiwan, The Postwar Experience of the Republic of China* (Cornell University Press, 1979).

5. Kowie Chang, "An Estimate of Taiwan Personal Income Distribution in 1953—Pareto's Formula Discussed and Applied," *Journal of Social Science,* Vol.7 (Taipei: National Taiwan University, 1956).

6. Kowie Chang, "Report on Pilot Study of Personal Income and Consumption in Taiwan" (Prepared under the sponsorship of working

group of National Income Statistics, Directorate-General of Budget, Accounting and Statistics, Executive Yuan).

7. Simon Kuznets, "Growth and Structural Shifts," in Walter Galenson ed., *Economic Growth and Structural Change in Taiwan, The Postwar Experience of the Republic of China* (Cornell University Press, 1979).

8. Directorate-General of Budget, Accounting and Statistics, Executive Yuan, Republic of China, *Report on the Survey of Family Income and Expenditure and Study of Personal Income Distribution in Taiwan* (1964).

9. H.B. Chenery, M.S. Ahluwalia, C.L.G. Bell, J.H. Duloy, and R. Jolly, *Redistribution with Growth* (London: Oxford University Press, 1974).

10. John C.H. Fei, Gustav Ranis, and Shirley W.Y. Kuo, *Growth with Equity: The Taiwan Case* (London: Oxford University Press, 1979).

11. In the DGBAS family survey, a farm family refers to a family the head of which is registered as a farmer; accordingly, the farm family income includes all incomes received by the farm family: both incomes from agricultural and nonagricultural activities.

12. Housing and Urban Development Department, Council for Economic Planning and Development, Executive Yuan, *Urban and Regional Development Statistics, Republic of China,* 1981; *Urban Growth and the Planning of Urban and Regional Development in Taiwan, Republic of China,* December 1981.

13. Another set of classifications by smaller units like towns and villages may bring out more clearly the underlying characteristics of urbanization. But its usefulness for economic analysis is limited because not even the information on value added is available in this classification.

14. Simon Kuznets, "Growth and Structural Shifts," in Walter Galenson ed., *Economic Growth and Structural Change in Taiwan, The Postwar Experience of the Republic of China* (Cornell University Press, 1979).

15. ditto, ibid.

16. ditto, ibid.

17. Calculations of $\partial I_w / \partial I_j$, $\partial I_w / \partial h_j$, and $\partial I_w / \partial Z_j$ are done as follows: The magnitudes of the beginning and ending years of the period under observation are first calculated, and then averaged.

PART III

7

Effects of Exports on Growth and Employment

With exports of US$22.6 billion and imports of US$21.2 billion, the Republic of China was the 20th largest trading country in the world and the 8th largest trading partner of the United States in 1981. Causes of successful development in Taiwan have been many. Foreign trade, however, is considered the decisive factor in the very fruitful development process.

The purpose of this chapter is to examine the effects of exports on growth and employment in Taiwan. The chapter contains four sections. Section I provides a historical review of exports and imports. Section II provides a decomposition equation which will be used for appraising the contribution of exports to growth and employment. Sections III and IV analyze the effects of exports on growth and employment, and make a quantitative appraisal. Causes of the successful trade-oriented development in terms of government policies, however, will be discussed in Chapter 14.

I. Historical Review of Exports and Imports

1. Initial Conditions

In the prewar period, Taiwan's trade was mainly with Japan. By trading agricultural products, mainly rice and sugar, for manufactured consumer goods, mainly textiles, Taiwan maintained a considerable trade surplus prior to 1944. This ready market, however, was cut off after Taiwan ceased to be a Japanese colony in 1945.

During the period of 1946—48, mainland China was in a state of war and had a very rapid inflation that spread to Taiwan. With the movement of the Chinese central government to Taiwan in 1949, the economic relationship with the mainland came to an end and Taiwan became an independent economy. The postwar economic development of Taiwan had some advantages and disadvantages at the outset.

On the positive side, first, the initial condition of the infrastructure in Taiwan was relatively advanced at the starting point. The infrastructure, including electric power generation, railways, education, and medical care, was more advanced around 1951 than that of other Asian countries excluding Japan.[1] The accumulation of past investment was one of the important factors contributing to the subsequent development of the Taiwan economy.

Second, agricultural development was already comparatively successful in Taiwan before World War II. By 1937, the productivity of agriculture was already high. Agricultural production was characterized by an appropriate technology relying on modern inputs (a new rice variety and widespread use of chemical fertilizer), irrigation and drainage, which generated high productivity.[2]

Third, the influx of a substantial volume of talented officials, managers and entrepreneurs from the mainland provided good human resources in addition to what originally existed on the island. Thus, by the time most of the production of agriculture and industry had recovered to prewar levels in 1951, Taiwan was in possession of an unusually good physical and institutional infrastructure, especially in agriculture, as well as a well-educated human resource base.

On the other hand, general conditions were such that population was excessive relative to existing economic resources. The rate of population growth was a high 3.5% per annum, and the need for national defense made budget deficits almost unavoidable. These posed a serious threat to the stability of the economy of Taiwan and even to the maintenance of the status quo.

2. High Dependence on Trade

In analyzing the role of foreign trade, we should, first of all, emphasize its quantitative importance in an open economy. The growth rates of both exports and imports have been much higher than the growth rates of GNP in the past three decades. As a result, the shares of exports and imports in the GNP increased, respectively, from 8.6% and 14.8% in 1952 to 49% and 46% in 1981. Furthermore, the role of foreign trade has reflected the natural evolution of the transition growth of the economy as manifested by the commodity content of imports and exports as well as by the natural selection of trading partners consistent with comparative advantages.   With the transformation of the economic structure, the composition of exports has shown a marked change.   Exports of agricultural

Table 7.1   Growth Rate and Share of Trade

(in 1976 constant prices; %)

Period	Growth Rate of GNP	Growth Rate of Exports	Share of Exports in GNP	Growth Rate of Imports	Share of Imports in GNP
1952–1961	7.5	8.2	8.6 (1952)	5.3	14.8 (1952)
1961–1971	10.2	22.9	11.2 (1961)	17.0	18.5 (1961)
1971–1981	8.8	13.5	31.4 (1971)	11.6	28.2 (1971)
			48.7 (1981)		45.7 (1981)

Source: Directorate-General of Budget, Accounting & Statistics, Executive Yuan, *National Income of the Republic of China* (1981). Department of Statistics, Ministry of Finance, *Monthly Statistics of Exports and Imports, the Republic of China*, No. 153 (1982).

products decreased from 92% in 1952 to 8% in 1981, while exports of industrial products increased from 8% to 92%. In 1952, rice and sugar accounted for 74% of total exports; however, speedy industrialization in the 1960s brought this share down to 3% in 1970. Imports have been a prerequisite for exports. The main imports were raw materials and machinery and equipment, comprising more than 90% of the total. The processing character of the economy is obvious.

3. Trading Partners

Due to historical and geographical reasons, Japan was formerly the major market for Taiwan exports. Exports to the U.S. increased rapidly, however, and replaced Japan as the largest market after 1967. In 1981, exports to the U.S. amounted to US$8.2 billion and imports, to US$4.8 billion. Exports to Japan in 1981 were US$2.5 billion and imports were US$5.9 billion. In 1953, the U.S. market absorbed only 4.2% of Taiwan's total exports. This share increased to 21.9% in 1961, then to a high of 41.7% in 1971, but decreased to 36.1% in 1981. ROC exports to the U.S. grew at an annual rate of 33.1% in 1954–81. This probably provided the most important stimulus to the rapid economic growth in Taiwan over the past three decades.

ROC imports from the U.S. also showed an accelerating trend. If we divide 1956–81 into five periods, the average growth rates of imports from the U.S. were 4.7% (1956–60), 10.7% (1961–65), 17.3% (1966–70), 39.1% (1971–75), and 20% (1976–81). Imports from the U.S. were US$131 million in 1961, but increased to US$4,766 million in 1981.

Using 1971 as the demarcation year to divide the period 1961–1981 into two periods, we find that the growth rate of total exports was faster in the second period than in the first. Also, we find that exports to the United States grew much faster than exports to other destinations in the first period, which encouraged a government policy of diversifying the destinations. The success of this policy is shown by the reduction in growth rate of exports to the U.S. from 35.0% in the

Table 7.2   Trade Between ROC and USA
(1953—1981)

Year	ROC Exports to the U.S.		ROC Imports from the U.S.		Trade Balance (US$ million)
	Value (US$ million)	Share of Total Exports (%)	Value (US$ million)	Share of Total Imports (%)	
1953	5.3	4.2	74.1	38.7	−68.8
1960	18.9	11.5	113.1	38.1	−94.2
1961	42.8	21.9	130.8	40.6	−88.0
1966	115.9	21.6	166.3	26.7	−50.4
1971	859.2	41.7	408.2	22.1	+451.0
1976	3,038.7	37.2	1,797.5	23.7	+1,241.2
1981	8,163.1	36.1	4,765.7	22.5	+3,397.4

Source: Council for Economic Planning and Development, Executive Yuan, *Taiwan Statistical Data Book* (1981).

Table 7.3   Growth Rate of Exports by Destination

(in current prices; %)

Period	Total	U.S.	Japan	Europe	Others
1961−71	26.6	35.0	15.8	29.3	25.1
1971−81	27.1	25.2	26.0	30.3	28.3
1961−81	26.8	30.0	20.8	29.8	26.7

Source: Department of Statistics, Ministry of Finance, *Monthly Statistics of Exports and Imports, the Republic of China* (February 1982).

first period to 25.2% in the second, with a concomitant increase in the growth rate of exports to Japan from 15.8% to 26.0%, and to Europe from 29.3% to 30.3%. This diversification of export markets transformed the export structure as shown in

Table 7.4. On the other hand, growth rates of imports revealed a different pattern. Imports from the U.S. increased at a rate of 12.0% in the first period, and then climbed to 27.9% in the second. The growth rate of imports from Japan remained at about 23%, and imports from Europe increased from 20.7% to 25.9%.

Table 7.4   Structure of Exports by Destination

(%)

Year	U.S.	Japan	Europe	Others
1961	21.9	29.0	8.0	41.1
1971	41.7	11.9	9.9	36.5
1981	36.1	11.0	12.7	40.2

Source: Same as Table 7.3.

Table 7.5   Growth Rate of Imports by Import Origin

(in current prices; %)

Period	Total	U.S.	Japan	Europe	Others
1961–71	19.1	12.0	23.6	20.7	20.9
1971–81	27.7	27.9	21.8	25.9	35.4
1961–81	23.3	19.7	22.7	23.3	28.0

Source: Same as Table 7.3.

4. Structure of Exports and Imports

The rapid growth of Taiwan's exports was led by manufacturing. Manufactured exports accounted for about 33% of total manufacturing production in 1980. The past success of manufacturing development in Taiwan was characterized by product cycles of food processing, textiles, and then electrical machinery as leading industries. As an extension of agriculture,

the food processing industry was the most important manufacturing sub-industry in the early period.   In 1952, food
processing comprised 44% of manufacturing production and
94% of manufacturing exports; however, its share of production
decreased to 12%, and its share of exports to 7% in 1980.

The textile industry expanded its share of exports from
1% to 25% over the same period.   The most rapid expansion
in both production and exports in the 1960s, however, took
place in electronics.   Thus, in 1980 exports of textiles and
electronics amounted to US$8.2 billion, comprising 50.4% of
total exports.

Major markets for textiles and electrical machinery were
the United States, Europe, Hong Kong and Japan. The exports
of textiles to these countries and areas comprised 63.7% of total
textile exports in 1976 and 65.2% in 1980, and the exports
of electrical machinery to these four destinations comprised
78.8% of total electrical exports in 1976 and 67.5% in 1980.
However, during this period, the market share of the United
States was decreasing while Europe's share was increasing.
The market share of Hong Kong and Japan did not change
much.   For example, over 1976–80, textile exports to the U.S.
decreased from 33.3% to 31.5% of total exports and exports
of electrical machinery dropped from 54.8% to 40.5%, while
the share of textile exports to Europe increased from 10.9%
to 12.4% and the share of electrical machinery grew from 8.6%
to 10.6%.

The expansion of the European market was a result of a
concerted effort by government and entrepreneurs to diversify
markets, which was urgently required for the following reasons:
a big trade surplus with the United States, too much concentra-
tion on the U.S. market, and more severe import restrictions
in the U.S.   For trade expansion, among other things, more
trade liaison offices were set up in several European countries,
and six branches of European Banks and two liaison offices
were established in Taipei from 1980 to 1982.

Taiwan imported mainly capital goods, particularly
machinery and equipment, from Europe.   The major imports
from the United States were machinery & tools, chemicals

& pharmaceuticals, transportation equipment, and agricultural products (soybeans, wheat and raw cotton).

In the early period (1961–1971) we can see a triangular trading structure in which Taiwan imported much of its needed producer goods from Japan while exporting its labor-intensive manufactures to the U.S. market. However, this triangle was modified in the 1971–1981 period as Taiwan's productive capacity advanced, allowing more exports to the European and Japanese markets, while the island relied increasingly on the U.S. as a source of needed agricultural imports.

II. Decomposition of Demand Expansion

1. Importance of Demand

The traditional theory of production emphasizes the technological relationship between factors and output. Output is determined by the available quantities of factors and the level of technology; factors determine output, but not vice versa. This theory is based on Say's Law, which says "supply creates its own demand." Thus, according to traditional theory, the amount of output produced is simply determined by factor availability and technology; and the amount of output that is technically producible is equivalent tautologically to the amount of output that will be produced.

However, since the publication of Keynes' General Theory, and the Great Depression of the 1930s, we have become fully aware that Say's Law does not always hold true and that the production function alone cannot determine the amount of output realized, mainly because the size of demand is a decisive factor as well.

Since demand is one of the two determinants of production, we should take a closer look at sources of demand, which in this paper will be disaggregated into four categories: 1) domestic demand expansion, 2) export expansion, 3) import substitution, and 4) changes in technology.

2. Sources of Demand Decomposition

The pioneering works on sources of demand decomposition were done by Chenery (1960)[3] and Chenery, Shishido and Watanabe (CSW, 1962).[4]   Recently, subsequent modifications were proposed by Syrquin (1976)[5] and Balassa (1976)[6] with regard to the definition of import substitution.

One common characteristic of all these decompositions is that they begin with a basic demand-supply material balance and attempt to attribute changes in the structure of production or in a particular expansion to various sources of demand. Yet each model has its particular characteristics, which can be categorized as follows:

First, the observations are either based on the concept of "the deviation from a proportional growth path," or on "the change in the amount" of each sector's production over a certain period. Since some sectors in the economy grow faster than average and others grow slower, the observation of the deviation from a proportional growth path of individual sectors will assess the structural change of the economy. On the other hand, the observation of the change in the amount of individual sectors will trace out the magnitude of growth. The Chenery, CSW and Syrquin models are all studies of the deviation from a proportional growth path, while Balassa's study is of the change in the amount.

Second, the methods used can be classified into direct and total. The direct method only measures the direct contribution of a particular sector without using inverse matrices of input-output tables, while the total method takes care of both direct and indirect effects by utilization of inverse matrices of input-output tables. The direct method is relevant in assessing the effects of various incentive policies on individual sectors, but is unable to separate intermediate goods into those for domestic use and those for export. The total method, on the other hand, is considered to be a relevant measure of the contribution of export expansion and import substitution to economic growth, since it takes care of the total effective demand for the products of various sectors induced by given changes in final demand.   The above cited models, except Chenery (1960), are based on the total method.

Third, the new formulas proposed by Syrquin and Balassa are intended to refine the definition of import substitution. What Syrquin wants to identify by import substitution is the amount of imports substituted for by domestic production, supposing that there is no change in the technology of production.   In Balassa's formulation import substitution is actually measured by the deviation of the increase in imports from the expected increase in imports, which are supposed to increase at the same rate as national income.

In this chapter, a model of sources of demand decomposition is constructed.   It is based on the concept of "changes in the amount" of the total method, and on Syrquin's definition of import substitution.   That is, what we measure is the difference in magnitude, i.e., the increment of production over two periods, ΔX.   The model is based on input-output analysis. Also we define import substitution as the part relating only to "the changes in imports that are replaced by domestic production," and exclude "changes in imports which are due to technology change."   Accordingly, this latter part is added to the changes caused by technology change.   The model is shown below.

For the decomposition model, the following notations will be used.

n   = the number of sectors; n=58 in this model

X   = domestic production, column vector (nx1)

A   = input coefficients, matrix (nxn)

A^d = domestically produced input coefficients, matrix (nxn)

A^m = imported input coefficients, matrix (nxn)

C   = private plus government consumption, column vector (nx1)

B   = gross investment (private + government investment), column vector (nx1)

$\hat{U}_c$ = the proportion of total consumption supplied from domestic production, diagonal matrix (nxn)

$\hat{U}_B$ = the proportion of total investment supplied from domestic production, diagonal matrix (nxn)

U_{ijw} = the proportion of intermediate input i supplied from domestic production j

E   = exports, column vector (nx1)

M^w = imports of intermediate goods, column vector (nx1)

M^f = imports of final demand, column vector (nx1)

R^d = inverse matrix $(I-A^d)^{-1}$, matrix (nxn)

$\tilde{A}^m$ = import matrix of intermediate goods assuming technology did not change, matrix (nxn)

1   = first period

2   = second period

The supply-demand balance equation of the input-output system can be shown as:

(1) $X = A^d X + A^m X + C + B + E - M^w - M^f$

  (where $A^m X = M^w$)

In domestic terms,

(2) $X = A^d X + \hat{U}_c C + \hat{U}_b B + E$ [7]

i.e.

$$
\begin{bmatrix} X_1 \\ X_2 \\ \cdot \\ \cdot \\ \cdot \\ X_n \end{bmatrix} = \begin{bmatrix} a_{11}^d & a_{12}^d & \cdots & a_{1n}^d \\ a_{21}^d & a_{22}^d & & a_{2n}^d \\ \cdot & & & \cdot \\ \cdot & & & \cdot \\ \cdot & & & \cdot \\ a_{n1}^d & a_{n2}^d & \cdots & a_{nn}^d \end{bmatrix} \begin{bmatrix} X_1 \\ X_2 \\ \cdot \\ \cdot \\ \cdot \\ X_n \end{bmatrix} + \begin{bmatrix} U_{1c} & 0 & \cdots & 0 \\ 0 & U_{2c} & & 0 \\ \cdot & & & \cdot \\ \cdot & & & \cdot \\ 0 & 0 & \cdots & U_{nc} \end{bmatrix} \begin{bmatrix} C_1 \\ C_2 \\ \cdot \\ \cdot \\ \cdot \\ C_n \end{bmatrix}
$$

$$
+ \begin{bmatrix} U_{1b} & 0 & \cdots & 0 \\ 0 & U_{2b} & & 0 \\ \cdot & & & \cdot \\ \cdot & & & \cdot \\ 0 & 0 & \cdots & U_{nb} \end{bmatrix} \begin{bmatrix} b_1 \\ b_2 \\ \cdot \\ \cdot \\ \cdot \\ b_n \end{bmatrix} + \begin{bmatrix} e_1 \\ e_2 \\ \cdot \\ \cdot \\ \cdot \\ e_n \end{bmatrix}
$$

Solving (2) for X, we have

(3) $X = (I-A^d)^{-1} (\hat{U}_c C + \hat{U}_b B + E)$

$X = R^d (\hat{U}_c C + \hat{U}_b B + E)$

Based on this equation, the change in output of each and every sector over the two periods can be decomposed as seen in Equation (4). (For the mathematics of the decomposition of ΔX, see Appendix III).

Equation (4) takes the magnitudes of the first period, C_1, B_1, W_1, and X_1 as weights. In this regard, if we call this equation the Laspeyres version, ΔX can alternatively be decomposed into the Paasche version which uses the magnitudes of the second period, C_2, B_2, W_2, and X_2, as weights. This Paasche version is shown in Equation (4)'.

(4) $\Delta X =$

$\quad R_2^d \hat{U}_c^2 \Delta C$ Consumption expansion with fixed import structure ⎤

$\quad + R_2^d \hat{U}_b^2 \Delta B$ Investment expansion with fixed import structure ⎦ Domestic Expansion

$\quad + R_2^d \Delta E$ Export expansion   Export Expansion

$\quad + R_2^d \Delta \hat{U}_c C_1$ Import substitution of consumption goods ⎤

$\quad + R_2^d \Delta \hat{U}_b B_1$ Import substitution of investment goods   Import Substitution

$\quad + R_2^d [\Delta U_{ijw} \overset{*}{a}_{ij1}] X_1$ Import substitution of intermediate goods ⎦

$\quad + R_2^d [U_{ijw}^2 \overset{**}{\Delta a}_{ij}] X_1$ Change in I-O coefficients   Change in I-O Coefficients

(4)' $\Delta X = R_1^d (\hat{U}_c^1 \Delta C + \hat{U}_b^1 \Delta B + \Delta E)$

$\qquad + R_1^d \left\{ \Delta \hat{U}_c C_2 + \Delta \hat{U}_b B_2 + [\Delta U_{ijw} a_{ij2}] X_2 \right\}$

$\qquad + R_1^d [U_{ijw}^1 \Delta a_{ij}] X_2$

---

* $[\Delta U_{ijw} a_{ij1}]$ is a matrix whose typical element is $\Delta U_{ijw} a_{ij1}$.

** $[U_{ijw}^2 \Delta a_{ij}]$ is a matrix whose typical element is $U_{ijw}^2 \Delta a_{ij}$.

Since the numerical results of the Laspeyres and Paasche versions will be somewhat different, we have calculated both the Laspeyres and Paasche versions. All results reported in this chapter are averages of these two versions.[8]

In the present study, the calculation of sources of demand expansion are based on five input-output tables, 1956, 1961, 1966, 1971 and 1976, which are reclassified into 58 comparable sectors and deflated into terms of consistent constant domestic prices. Among them, 1961, 1966 and 1971 are based on original tables, while the tables of 1956 and 1976 are extended by the extrapolation, respectively, of tables for 1961 and 1971, with constant domestic prices.

Since value added (V) is the product of the value added ratio (v) and gross output (X) (i.e. since $V = vX$), we have

$$\text{(A)} \qquad \Delta V = v \cdot \Delta X + \Delta v \cdot X$$

Once the output increment (ΔX) is decomposed, the increment of value added (ΔV) can be decomposed as well. Since the level of employment (L) is the product of output (X) and the labor coefficient (ℓ) (i.e. since $L = \ell X$), we have

$$\text{(B)} \qquad \Delta L = \ell \cdot \Delta X + \Delta \ell \cdot X$$

Thus, the expansion of employment (ΔL) can be decomposed once ΔX is decomposed. In the following two sections, Equations (A) and (B) will be used for the assessment of the contribution of export expansion to economic growth and employment.

III. Contribution of Exports to Growth — A Quantitative Appraisal

1. An Aggregate Analysis — Contribution of Exports to Gross Output

What are the sources of growth that have propelled Taiwan's industrialization?   How much have exports contributed to rapid growth?   In order to deal with these questions, this section analyzes the sources of growth of gross output and value added for the period 1956–1976.

The calculations are based on the amount of change over a period in order to measure the absolute contributions of each source to output expansion in that particular period. A "total method," which utilizes an inverse matrix of an input output table, is used to account for all the direct and indirect contributions by each source and sector.

Sources of growth are average figures based on Equations (4) and (4)' for each of the 58 sectors and for each period. The sum of the results of the 58 sectors calculated from each source provides the aggregate of each source for the total economy. These are shown in Table 7.6.

Table 7.6   Contribution of Exports to Output Expansion

(%)

Period	Output Expansion Due to Domestic Expansion	Output Expansion Due to Export Expansion	Output Expansion Due to Import Substitution	Output Expansion Due to Changes in I-O Coefficient
1956–61	61.6	22.5	7.7	8.2
1961–66	63.2	35.0	0.5	1.3
1966–71	51.4	45.9	5.7	−3.0
1971–76	34.7	67.7	−2.4	—

Source: Calculation based on the Input-Output data consistently deflated to 1971 constant domestic prices.

Notes: Calculated from the 1971 constant domestic price I-0 data for 1956, 1961, 1966, 1971 & 1976. All estimates of total contributions are arithmetic averages of the estimates derived by Laspeyres and Paasche versions. The estimates for 1961–71 in Tables 7.8, 7.9, 7.10 are obtained by the chain measures of decompositions for the two periods, 1961–66 and 1966–71.

It is very impressive to note that export expansion as a source of output expansion has been becoming increasingly important. In the early period, 1956–61, the contribution of export expansion to output growth was 22.5%; it then rapidly increased, to 35.0% in 1961–66, 45.9% in 1966–71, and 67.7% in 1971–76. It is evident that after the 1960s, export expansion was a decisive factor in rapid growth, and in the 1970s its importance even outweighed domestic expansion. Import substitution was trivial, although it did register a slight contribution in the 1950s.

2. Sources of Manufacturing Growth

It may be of interest to examine closely the sources of growth of manufacturing, since it has been the leading sector. In order to examine their characteristics, the sub-sectors of manufacturing are grouped into three classes in this section:

(1) Four group classifications by trade pattern: export competing, export-import competing, import competing, and non-import competing.

(2) Two categories: labor absorbing manufacturing and other than labor absorbing manufacturing.

(3) Seven category classifications.

(1) Decomposition for Four Trade Pattern Categories

The definitions and the contents of export competing, export-import competing, import competing and non-import competing manufacturing industries in this chapter are given in Table 7.7.

It is interesting to observe the following results from Table 7.8:

(a) Manufacturing expansion was led by export expansion. After the 1960s, the contribution of export expansion outweighed that of domestic expansion.[9]

(b) The contribution of export expansion was greatest in the export competing category throughout the whole period,

Table 7.7   Manufacturing Industries by the Four Group Classification

Ratio of Exports in Domestic Production / Ratio of Imports in Domestic Use	More Than 10%	Less Than 10%
	Export-import Competing	Import Competing
More than 10%	3, 8, 19, 20, 22, 24, 30, 31, 33, 34, 35, 40, 41, 42, 43, 44, 45, 46, 47, 48, 49.	5, 9, 11, 21, 29, 32, 36, 37.
	Export Competing	Non-import Competing
Less than 10%	6, 13, 14, 16, 23, 25, 26, 27, 28, 38, 39.	1, 2, 4, 7, 10, 12, 15, 17, 18.

Source: Same as Table 7.6.
Notes:
  1. The ratios are based on 1971 data.
  2. The industries represented by the above numbers are given in Appendix IV.

1956–76. Export expansion in export-import competing and import competing categories was also very high. This result indicates that there was a close relationship between exports and imports in Taiwan; in other words, Taiwan's economy was highly oriented toward processing.

(c) The contribution of export expansion has been increasing rapidly over time for each and every category, illustrating Taiwan's increasingly high dependence on exports.

(d) A significant contribution made by import substitution was observed for the import competing and export-import competing categories in the first period. Although the contribution by import substitution in the import competing category has been decreasing, it has always been positive.

Table 7.8 Sources of Manufacturing Output Growth
(by Trade Pattern)

(%)

Period and Item	Domestic Demand Expansion	Export Expan- sion	Import Substitu- tion	Change in I-O Coefficients
1956—61				
Export competing	50.4	43.0	2.5	4.1
Export-import competing	46.2	24.3	23.4	6.1
Import competing	43.9	23.2	29.2	3.7
Non-import competing	92.5	3.4	1.1	3.0
Manufacturing total	44.3	36.3	13.2	6.2
1961—71				
Export competing	35.6	67.1	1.6	−4.3
Export-import competing	38.4	53.1	4.8	3.7
Import competing	37.3	36.0	17.7	9.0
Non-import competing	91.0	13.9	1.4	−6.3
Manufacturing total	36.9	51.5	7.6	4.0
1971—76				
Export competing	11.2	91.0	−2.2	−
Export-import competing	23.9	76.3	−0.2	−
Import competing	10.3	81.4	8.3	−
Non-import competing	82.1	19.6	−1.7	−
Manufacturing total	19.8	80.6	−0.4	−

Source: See Table 7.6.
Note: See Note on Table 7.6.

(2) Decomposition for Labor-Absorbing Categories

Labor-absorbing manufacturing sub-industries are those that ranked in the top tenth in the absorption of labor, either in terms of amount (1971) or growth rate (1966—1971).

The contribution of export expansion in labor-absorbing manufacturing showed different patterns before and after 1961. That is, for labor-absorbing manufacturing before 1961, the

Table 7.9   Sources of Manufacturing Output Growth
(by Degree of Labor Absorption)

(%)

Period and Item	Domestic Demand Expansion	Export Expansion	Import Substitution	Change in I-O Coefficients
1956–61				
Labor-absorbing				
manufacturing	52.0	27.9	14.3	5.8
Other manufacturing	39.2	41.8	12.6	6.4
Manufacturing total	44.3	36.3	13.2	6.2
1961–71				
Labor-absorbing				
manufacturing	32.8	58.4	5.1	3.7
Other manufacturing	42.4	42.3	10.8	4.5
Manufacturing total	36.9	51.5	7.6	4.0
1971–76				
Labor-absorbing				
manufacturing	16.5	82.7	0.8	—
Other manufacturing	26.6	76.1	−2.7	—
Manufacturing total	19.8	80.6	−0.4	—

Source: See Table 7.6.
Notes:
  1. See Note on Table 7.6.
  2. Labor-absorbing manufacturing: (14,19,20,22,25,26,27,28,30,31,39,
     41,44,45,46,47,48,49)
     Other than L-A manufacturing: (13,15,16,17,18,21,23,24,29,32,33,34,
     35,36,37,38,40,42,43)
     Manufacturing total: (13-49)
  3. The industries represented by the above numbers are given in Appendix IV.

contribution of export expansion to growth was smaller when
compared to other manufacturing, and the situation reversed
after 1961. In other words, labor absorbing industries came to
have a bigger export expansion effect. The largest export
expansion effect was found in textiles and electrical machinery
throughout the period, 1961–76.

We also note that the contribution made by import substitution to the labor-absorbing category declined more rapidly, and that changes in I-O coefficients of the two categories did not differ very much.

(3) Decomposition for Seven Manufacturing Categories

The exclusive classification in Table 7.10 contains seven categories that add up to the manufacturing total. Interesting results are observed as follows:

(a) The greatest export expansion contribution was made by the food processing industry in the first period, 1956—61. However, the first place shifted to textiles during 1961—71 and 1971—76.

(b) The increase in the contribution by export expansion to electrical machinery was very significant, as it was to final goods.

(c) In the import substitution period of 1956—61, a large share of import substitution was observed in the category of steel, iron and their products; intermediate goods; and electrical machinery. However, the degree of contribution by import substitution has been decreasing even in these industries. In particular, for the categories of machinery and intermediate goods, a negative import substitution was observed in 1971—76. This seems to indicate that the speed of secondary import substitution was not fast enough to meet the increasing requirement in the 1970s.

3. Import Content in Domestic Demand and Export

We know that the final demand (domestic final demand plus export) can be traced to two sources: domestic content and import content. The domestic content is the value added in the domestic economy, which constitutes the GDP (Gross Domestic Product). The domestic content is composed of three components: labor earnings, capital earnings, and indirect taxes.

Import content refers to the amount or proportion of

Table 7.10   Sources of Manufacturing Output Growth
(by Industry Group)

(%)

Period and Item	Domestic Demand Expansion	Export Expansion	Import Substitution	Change in I-O Coefficients
1956–61				
Food processing	40.9	54.0	4.6	0.5
Textiles	56.0	37.4	0.6	6.0
Steel, iron, and their products	3.8	41.4	41.9	12.9
Electrical machinery	54.5	23.4	21.5	0.6
Machinery	67.3	17.6	13.0	2.1
Intermediate goods	34.7	28.4	27.9	9.0
Final goods	62.5	17.3	8.0	12.2
Manufacturing	44.3	36.3	13.2	6.2
1961–71				
Food processing	65.9	28.0	2.0	4.1
Textiles	24.4	64.7	8.0	2.9
Steel, iron, and their products	43.1	49.6	10.9	−3.6
Electrical machinery	24.7	65.3	7.2	2.8
Machinery	54.7	30.8	9.0	5.5
Intermediate goods	43.1	42.1	8.1	6.7
Final goods	24.9	60.6	8.9	5.6
Manufacturing	36.9	51.5	7.6	4.0
1971–76				
Food processing	65.9	37.7	−3.6	—
Textiles	−12.2	103.8	8.4	—
Steel, iron, and their products	27.8	66.1	6.1	—
Electrical machinery	16.7	82.8	0.5	—
Machinery	52.0	58.5	−10.5	—
Intermediate goods	57.0	57.2	−14.2	—
Final goods	12.4	89.0	−1.4	—
Manufacturing	19.8	80.6	−0.4	—

Source: See Table 7.6.
Note: See Note on Table 7.6, and Note 10.

imported intermediate goods that are contained in final demand. The amount of import content is the amount of imported goods that is used in producing goods to satisfy domestic final demand and exports. The portion of import content is the portion of imported intermediate goods that is used in one dollar value of final product (domestic final demand and export). Thus, import content itself is not a component of the GDP. It plays an instrumental role, however, in that imported materials and intermediate goods are important components in various production processes. In this sense, an appropriate import is necessarily required for production as well as for the generation of domestic value added and economic growth.

In this regard, we seek to study the status and change in import content over time as classified into import content in domestic final demand and exports, and as classified by industry.

This is calculated according to the Equation system (5)

$$
\left.
\begin{aligned}
M^d &= \hat{m}\ (I - A^d)^{-1}\ F^d \\
M^E &= \hat{m}\ (I - A^d)^{-1}\ E \\
M^{Ek} &= \hat{m}\ (I - A^d)^{-1}\ E_k
\end{aligned}
\right\} \quad \cdots\cdots\cdots\cdots (5)
$$

where each symbol stands for:

M = the induced amount of import used for each source of final demand, column vector

m = the portion of imported intermediate goods used in one dollar value of production, i.e., import coefficient, diagonal matrix

$(I - A^d)^{-1}$ = inverse matrix of domestic I-O coefficient

F^d = domestic final demand (including consumption and investment), column vector

d = domestic; $\wedge$ = diagonal matrix

E = export

k = area or country of destination, e.g.,
   US = United States
    e = Europe

The results show that in 1961, 77% of imported inter-mediate goods were used in the production of domestic final demand and only 23% for exports. However, in 1976 the situation changed drastically: 63% of imported intermediate goods were used in the production of exports, and exports of manufactures alone used 60% of the imported intermediates. Import content in exports to the U.S. grew most rapidly between 1961–76, from 5% to 28%.

The share of import content in exports grew at a rapid rate due to a high rate of export expansion. At the same time, a rapid rate of export expansion was only possible because of a rapid increase in imported intermediate goods. In the above sections, we have emphasized the importance of export opportunities to production, i.e., the importance of the market side. But on the production side, the import of intermediates was no less important. That is, were the imports not available, the economy may not have grown as it did in the past; the opportunity to export was crucial because exports broadened the market to provide more productive opportunities and at the same time earned foreign exchange necessary for the import of materials and equipment needed for processing production.

IV. Contribution of Trade to Employment – A Quantitative Appraisal

One of the most important features of the Republic of China's economic development was the achievement of full employment by 1971. In order to identify the contribution of exports to employment, sources of employment growth, which are decomposed in Section II, will be used. Since the employment data in an I-O classification is only available after 1961, and also because rapid labor absorption occurred after 1961, the decomposition of employment growth will be carried out only for 1961–76.

1. Creation of Job Opportunities – Employment Expansion

In the period 1961–76, employment in Taiwan increased

by 2.3 million persons, which was equivalent to 60% of the 1961 employment. This was a remarkable increase. But why and how were those job opportunities created?

The creation of job opportunities is closely connected with two essential factors. One is an advancement of labor productivity, and the other, an expansion of output markets. In the production of a given quantity, an advancement in labor productivity will reduce the number of laborers required. If labor productivity is kept unchanged, on the other hand, an expansion of output markets will, by increasing production opportunities, create more job opportunities. Therefore, the number of job opportunities a society can really create is actually dependent on the algebraic sum of the above two elements, namely, the number reduced by the advancement of labor productivity and the number increased by market expansion. At the same time, we know that an expansion of production opportunities is caused by 1) expansion of domestic demand, 2) expansion of exports, 3) expansion due to import substitution, and 4) change due to change in I-O coefficients. An increase in these components will increase production opportunities, and thus create job opportunities.

Causes of employment expansion are calculated in Table 7.11. The actual increments of employment during the three periods 1961–66, 1966–71, and 1971–76 were, respectively, 377 thousand, 1,015 thousand and 925 thousand. These increments were realized as the net results of employment release due to advancement in labor productivity and employment expansion due to output expansion. It is shown that the continuous advancement in labor productivity over the fifteen-year period produced a continuous labor release. During 1961–66, the advancement in labor productivity caused labor demand to decrease by 1,824 thousand persons. The demand decrease in 1966–71 was 1,339 thousand, and that in 1971–76 was 1,681 thousand. It is obvious that if the production opportunities had not been able to expand, the advancement of labor productivity would have carried in its wake large unemployment. In other words, in the course of increasing productivity, market expansion is a necessary condition for the

7.11 Causes of Employment Expansion: An Aggregate Observation, 1961—1976*

Period	Actual Increment of Employment	Employment Release Due to Advancement in Labor Productivity (with no expansion in output)	Employment Expansion Due to Output Expansion (with no increase in labor productivity)
Increase in employment (1,000 persons)			
1961—66	377	−1,824	2,201
1966—71	1,015	−1,339	2,354
1971—76	925	−1,681	2,606
Increase in employment in % of total increase (%)			
1961—66	100	−484	584
1966—71	100	−132	232
1971—76	100	−182	282

Source: Same as Table 7.6. * Based on Equation (B) on Page 148.

achievement and maintenance of full employment.

The increment of labor demand due to market expansion was crucial for employment expansion in all three periods. During 1961—66, market expansion (including domestic expansion, export expansion, import substitution, and change in I-O coefficients) induced labor demand to increase by 2,201 thousand. The increase in labor demand due to market expansion was 2,354 thousand in 1966—71, and in 1971—76 it was 2,606 thousand. It is evident that the additional job opportunities created by market expansion far exceeded the decrease of job opportunities caused by the advancement of productivity, thus generating a net increase in employment.

How, then, was the market expanded? From Table 7.12 we know that in the first period, domestic expansion and

Table 7.12   Causes of Employment Expansion: An Aggregate Observation, 1961—1976

Period	Employment Expansion Due to Output Expansion	Employment Expansion Due to Domestic Expansion	Employment Expansion Due to Export Expansion
(1,000 persons)			
1961—66	2,201	1,454	730
1966—71	2,354	1,503	1,048
1971—76	2,606	1,185	1,533
in % of total (%)			
1961—66	100	66	33 (100)
1966—71	100	64	45 (100)
1971—76	100	45	59 (100)

Source: Same as Table 7.6.

export expansion, respectively, accounted for 66% and 33% of the increment. The contribution to employment expansion due to domestic expansion was twice that due to export expansion in this early period. The contributions by import substitution and change in I-O coefficients were trivial. The importance of export expansion increased in the second period, and it increased further in the third period. The contribution to employment expansion by export expansion increased relatively in the second period. Thus export expansion was the decisive factor in bringing the economy to full employment in 1971. Furthermore, export expansion helped maintain this status after 1971. The increment of job opportunities due to export expansion in 1971—76 increased to account for 59% of total employment expansion, a very significant portion, out of

Employment Expansion Due to Exports to Developed Countries	Employment Expansion Due to Exports to Developing Countries	Change in Employment Due to Import Substitution	Change in Employment Due to Changes in I-O Coefficients	Period
402	328	−10	27	1961−66
786	262	−21	−176	1966−71
1,172	361	−112	−	1971−76
18 (55)	15 (45)	−1	2	1961−66
34 (75)	11 (25)	−1	−8	1966−71
45 (76)	14 (24)	−4	−	1971−76

which 45% was generated by export expansion to developed countries, and the remaining 14% by export expansion to developing countries.

The productivity advance in manufacturing was fastest, so the employment release due to productivity advancement in manufacturing was largest, throughout the period 1961−76. On the other hand, the creation of job opportunities in manufacturing through export expansion was greatest. During the second and third periods, especially, the employment gains due to export expansion in manufacturing were large enough to comprise 59% of total employment. Employment opportunities created by export expansion far exceeded reductions generated by the advancement in productivity, leading to employment increases that absorbed both newcomers and the originally unemployed labor force.

As to the agricultural sector in 1961–66, the increase in labor productivity reduced job opportunities by 44% of 1966 agricultural employment, while domestic expansion and export expansion, respectively, contributed 32% and 14% of 1966 agricultural employment.   Therefore, actual agricultural employment increased slightly. The same tendency was observed during 1966–71. In the period 1971–76, although the speed of advancement in agricultural labor productivity slowed to reduce job opportunities by only 7%, the positive contributions by both domestic expansion and export expansion were unable to compensate for that decrease. Consequently, agricultural employment decreased in terms of absolute amount.

Since productivity in the agricultural sector is lower than in the nonagricultural sector, the out-migration of agricultural labor to the nonagricultural sector increases the average productivity of the entire economy on the one hand, and raises the "per household income" of farmers on the other. Therefore, we consider the shift of the center of gravity away from agriculture to nonagriculture a beneficial movement.

In short, the successful absorption of 2.3 million laborers over the past 15 years can be attributed significantly to market expansion.   Particularly in the 1970s, the contribution of export expansion far exceeded the contribution of domestic expansion.

2. Labor Utilization by Export Businesses

In the above, I discussed how much export expansion contributed to the "increase" in employment over a given period of time. Here, I want to examine how much labor was "used" in export businesses at specific times.   Therefore, instead of calculating the increment of employment, the amount of labor utilization will be examined by the following equations:

$$
\left.
\begin{array}{l}
L^d = \hat{\ell}\,(I - A^d)^{-1}\,F^d \\[4pt]
L^E = \hat{\ell}\,(I - A^d)^{-1}\,E \\[4pt]
L^{E_k} = \hat{\ell}\,(I - A^d)^{-1}\,E_k
\end{array}
\right\} \quad \ldots\ldots\ldots\ldots\ldots\ldots\ldots \quad (6)
$$

where each symbol stands for:

L = the number of laborers, column vector

ℓ = labor coefficient, diagonal matrix

$(I - A^d)^{-1}$ = inverse matrix of domestic I-O coefficient

F^d = domestic final demand (including consumption and investment), column vector

d = domestic; $\wedge$ = diagonal matrix

E = export

k = area or country of destination

The calculations were done according to consistently recompiled I-O tables for four years in constant domestic prices. The allocation of labor utilization is shown in Table 7.13.

In Table 7.13, "direct employment" refers to the direct utilization of labor excluding the indirect effect by linkages. "Total employment" refers to the sum of direct and indirect employment that includes the indirect effect. Accordingly, the ratio of total employment to direct employment measures the relative size of indirect employment induced by a particular sector.

Characteristics of the allocation of labor utilization are as follows:

1) The labor force has been significantly utilized in export producing and related businesses. The number of workers so employed was 400 thousand in 1961, comprising 11.9% of that year's employment; it increased to 1,924 thousand, comprising 34.0%, in 1976. In other words, in 1976 export businesses provided 34% of all employment opportunities.

2) The indirect effect of the production of export goods has been bigger than that of domestic goods. In particular,

Table 7.13   Labor Utilization, Direct and Indirect (1961—1976)

Year	Labor Used by Total Final Demand	Labor Used by Domestic Final Demand	Labor Used by Total Exports
Employment (thousand persons)			
1961			
Direct + Indirect employment	3,353	2,953	400
Direct employment	1,920	1,739	181
1966			
Direct + Indirect employment	3,731	2,969	762
Direct employment	2,150	1,761	389
1971			
Direct + Indirect employment	4,746	3,523	1,223
Direct employment	2,923	2,241	682
1976			
Direct + Indirect employment	5,670	3,746	1,924
Direct employment	3,492	2,437	1,055
% of Direct + Indirect employment in total employment of the economy			
1961	100.0	88.1	11.9
1966	100.0	79.6	20.4
1971	100.0	74.2	25.8
1976	100.0	66.0	34.0

Source: Same as Table 7.6.

the production of exports to developing countries came to have a bigger indirect effect after 1966.

Table 7.14 is a more detailed presentation of Table 7.13. It depicts the allocation of labor utilization in the agricultural, manufacturing and service sectors. We note that in 1976

Labor Used by Exports to the Developed Countries	Labor Used by Exports to the Developing Countries	Year
		Employment (thousand persons)
		1961
238	162	Direct + Indirect employment
105	76	Direct employment
		1966
454	308	Direct + Indirect employment
240	149	Direct employment
		1971
836	387	Direct + Indirect employment
489	193	Direct employment
		1976
1,385	539	Direct + Indirect employment
771	284	Direct employment
7.1	4.8	1961
12.2	8.2	1966
17.6	8.2	1971
24.5	9.5	1976

export businesses provided 34% of all employment opportunities, out of which manufactured exports accounted for
18.2% of employment; manufactured exports to developed
countries alone provided 12.7% of employment. In economic
theory, and especially in pure theory, services are often treated
as "non-tradables." However, in reality, services are also

Table 7.14   Allocation of Labor Utilization
(1961—1976)

(%)

Year and Industry	Labor Used by Total Final Demand	Labor Used by Domestic Final Demand	Labor Used by Total Exports
1961			
Agriculture	47.3	42.4	4.9
Manufacturing	13.3	9.7	3.6
Services	39.4	36.0	3.4
Whole economy	100.0	88.1	11.9
1966			
Agriculture	44.0	35.9	8.1
Manufacturing	15.7	9.3	6.4
Services	40.3	34.4	5.9
Whole economy	100.0	79.6	20.4
1971			
Agriculture	35.7	29.3	6.4
Manufacturing	22.7	10.7	12.0
Services	41.6	34.2	7.4
Whole economy	100.0	74.2	25.8
1976			
Agriculture	29.6	24.3	5.3
Manufacturing	28.1	9.9	18.2
Services	42.3	31.8	10.5
Whole economy	100.0	66.0	34.0

Source: Same as Table 7.6.

exported indirectly. For example, employment opportunities provided by the exports of the services sector in 1976 reached as high as 10.5% of total employment. That is to say, in 1976, the export of services brought Taiwan's economy 600 thousand

Labor Used by Exports to the Developed Countries	Labor Used by Exports to the U.S.	Labor Used by Exports to the Developing Countries	Year and Industry
			1961
3.4	1.0	1.5	Agriculture
1.8	0.9	1.8	Manufacturing
1.9	0.7	1.5	Services
7.1	2.6	4.8	Whole economy
			1966
6.1	1.4	2.0	Agriculture
2.9	1.5	3.5	Manufacturing
3.2	1.2	2.7	Services
12.2	4.1	8.2	Whole economy
			1971
4.7	1.1	1.7	Agriculture
8.0	5.1	4.0	Manufacturing
4.9	2.9	2.5	Services
17.6	9.1	8.2	Whole economy
			1976
4.3	1.0	1.0	Agriculture
12.7	7.0	5.5	Manufacturing
7.5	4.0	3.0	Services
24.5	12.0	9.5	Whole economy

job opportunities, out of which transportation and warehousing, communications, wholesale and retail trade, and misc. services provided 100 thousand, 95 thousand, 291 thousand and 134 thousand employment opportunities, respectively.

In short, the maintenance of full employment in the ROC currently depends greatly on export businesses. Export businesses utilized 34% of total employment in 1976, among which the utilization of agricultural exports was 5.3%; manufacturing exports, 18.2%; and services, 10.5%. Quantified, they are 300 thousand, 1,030 thousand, and 600 thousand, respectively, for a total of 1,930 thousand employment opportunities.

3. Factor Intensity of Imports and Exports

Sources of growth decomposition for capital stock can be done only for the period 1961–71, because capital stock and investment data in input-output classification are available only for that period. The results show that changes in I-O coefficients had a negative contribution to the growth of capital as well as the growth of employment during 1961–71. This indicates the trend towards rising total factor productivity and factor saving technological change. It does not, however, provide any clue regarding the question of whether the primary factors have been allocated efficiently in line with Taiwan's factor endowments and comparative advantages. In order to shed some light on this question, the factor intensity of trade and trends in factor utilization are discussed in this section.

In the early 1950s, Taiwan had the typical characteristics of a labor surplus economy as defined by Lewis, Ranis and Fei.[11] It may, therefore, be safely assumed that Taiwan's comparative advantage, at least during those years, lay in labor-intensive rather than capital-intensive activities, although a country's comparative advantage is determined not only by factor endowment, but also by many other conditions. If this assumption is correct, then the allocative efficiency of Taiwan's industrialization can be assessed, although only partially, in terms of the factor intensity of trade.

Factor intensity of imports and exports is calculated as follows:

For the estimation of factor intensity of exports, the formulas used are:

$$K = \hat{k} (I-A^d)^{-1} E$$
$$L = \hat{\ell} (I-A^d)^{-1} E$$

$$\left. \right\} \quad \dots \dots \dots \dots \dots \dots \quad (7)$$

where k and ℓ are respectively capital coefficient and labor coefficient. A^d is the matrix of domestic input-output coefficients, and E, exports.

For the estimation of factor intensity of imports, the formulas used are:

$$K = \hat{k} (I-A^d - A^{cm})^{-1} M^{cm}$$
$$L = \hat{\ell} (I-A^d - A^{cm})^{-1} M^{cm}$$

$$\left. \right\} \quad \dots \dots \dots \dots \dots \quad (8)$$

where A^{cm} is the matrix of input-output coefficients of competitive imports, and M^{cm} is the column vector of the amount M^{cm}_j of competitive imports.

The total factor intensity in terms of K/L ratios in Table 7.15 was obtained by dividing the corresponding K and L according to formulas (7) and (8).

Table 7.15   Total Factor Intensity of Exports and Competitive Imports[12] (Capital/Labor Ratio including Direct and Indirect Effects)

(NT$1,000/person)

Year	Total Factor Intensity (Capital/Labor Ratio) of			
	Competitive Imports	Exports	Exports to Developed Countries	Exports to Developing Countries
1961	88.3	84.8	82.8	87.8
1966	98.9	88.5	80.2	100.7
1971	113.6	98.3	92.8	110.1

Source: Same as Table 7.6.

As can be seen from Table 7.15, the total capital intensity

shows the following:

1) The total capital intensity of competitive imports was always higher than that of exports: Taiwan's exports required less capital per worker than did Taiwan's import competing goods.   This result supports the Heckscher-Ohlin theorem: a country exports goods that make intensive use of its relatively abundant factor of production, in the ROC's case, it was labor. The exports being more labor-intensive than import replacements proved that the development in Taiwan was in accord with its comparative advantage.   This result was similar to that of Korea as found by Wontack Hong.[13]

2) Capital intensity of both exports and competitive imports increased during the period 1961 to 1971. The speed of increase was faster in 1966–71 than in 1961–66.

3) It is interesting to note that the capital intensity of exports to developed countries was always lower than to developing countries.   In other words, more labor-intensive commodities were exported to the developed countries.

Value added per worker is the sum of an industry's payments to all primary factors of production divided by its number of employees.   Hal B. Lary proposed to use this simple measurement of value added per worker to assess how much capital of all sorts the industry requires for the following reasons:[14]   Value added per worker can be high because the industry incurs user costs of a large amount of physical capital or pays rents for the use of natural resources.   It can be high because the   industry's workers are highly paid. Among industries differences in average pay are closely associated with the average amount of human capital as well as physical capital of all sorts.   Thus value added per worker is used as an indicator to measure capital intensity.

It is noted that the value added per worker in competitive inputs is higher than that in exports throughout the whole period.   Also, exports to developing countries, rather than to developed countries, had a higher per worker value added. We also note that over the fifteen-year period, the value added per worker more than doubled.   However, it is interesting that the value added per worker of exports to developing countries increased at the highest rate among all the categories. The above findings are consistent with the results obtained by the observation of capital/labor ratio. This also proves that the Heckscher-Ohlin theorem provides useful predictions about the composition of Taiwan's rapidly growing exports of manufactured goods.

Table 7.16   Value Added per Worker of Exports and Competitive Imports

(NT$1,000/person)

Year	Value Added per Worker of			
	Competitive Imports	Exports	Exports to Developed Countries	Exports to Developing Countries
1961	38.2	32.2	31.6	33.1
1966	65.6	43.7	39.4	50.1
1971	78.4	59.0	56.0	65.4
1976	82.1	68.6	65.3	77.1

Source: Same as Table 7.6.

In conclusion, this chapter found that export was a factor that made labor-intensive industrialization successful. The opportunity for exports was crucial in that exports broadened the market to provide more production opportunities and at the same time made it possible to earn the foreign exchange necessary to import material and equipment needed for production.

The contributions made by export expansion increased very rapidly after 1961 for the economy in general and for manufacturing in particular. Export expansion was the dominant source of manufacturing growth after the 1960s. Export expansion to developed countries was much faster than to developing countries. At the same time, in the production of exports, and particularly in exports to developed countries, relatively labor-intensive technology was used. Thus, the abundant labor force was efficiently utilized in labor-intensive industries, allowing the economy to reach full employment in 1971. This in turn contributed to more equitable income distribution, first by increasing the incomes of lower income groups and second by providing farmers with the opportunity to earn nonagricultural income. For the economy as a whole, export expansion was the truly essential factor contributing to rapid growth and successful labor absorption.

NOTES

1. Shirley W. Y. Kuo, "The Service Sector in Taiwan, 1952–1976." (paper read at the International Symposium on the Service Sector of the Economy, June 26-30, 1978, University of Puerto Rico, San Juan, Puerto Rico).

2. See, for example, Shigeru Ishikawa, *Economic Development in Asian Perspective,* (Tokyo: Kinokuniya Bookstore Co., Ltd., 1967).

3. H.B. Chenery, "Patterns of Industrial Growth," *American Economic Review,* Vol. 50 (September 1960).

4. H.B. Chenery, S. Shishido, and T. Watanabe, "The Pattern of Japanese Growth, 1914–1954," *Econometrica,* Vol. 30 (January 1962).

5. Moshe Syrquin, "Sources of Industrial Growth and Change: An Alternative Measure," (World Bank, 1976).

6. Bela Balassa, "Accounting for Economic Growth: The Case of Norway," (World Bank Development Research Center Discussion Paper No. 17, 1976).

7. The supply-demand balance equation of the input-output system can have two alternative measures, based respectively on R or R^d, where R is the inverse matrix $[I-A]^{-1}$, of which $A = A^d + A^m$. The decomposition of the sources based on R will overestimate the indirect effects, for it fails to take account of leakage through import. The calculation based on R^d provides an accurate result. For the Taiwan case, since complete import matrices are separately available from domestic production matrices, the most refined methodology which is based on R^d will be used.

8. In this chapter, the calculation of sources of demand expansion are based on five input-output tables, 1956, 1961, 1966, 1971 and

1976, which are reclassified into 58 comparable sectors and deflated into terms of consistent constant domestic prices. Among them, 1961, 1966 and 1971 are based on original tables, while the 1956 and 1976 tables are extension tables extrapolated from 1961 and 1971 tables in constant domestic prices.

The sector classifications of the original 1961, 1966 and 1971 tables are different and some definitions inconsistent. In order to construct a comparable consistent set of tables, the 1961 table was disaggregated into 58 sectors from its original 37 sectors, and the 1966 and 1971 tables were aggregated into 58 sectors from their original 76 sectors. The disaggregation of the 1961 table was based on the original questionnaires. Some recompilations and adjustments were made either for consistency of definition or for correction.

The input-output tables of the Taiwan economy value productions differently according to destination. Namely, exports and imports are valued in world prices, while goods for domestic uses are valued at protected domestic prices which are distorted due to protection by import restriction, tariffs and commodity taxes. Before the tables were deflated into constant domestic prices, exports and imports were inflated so as to be consistent with output for domestic use. For this purpose, rates of nominal protection based on domestic-world price comparisons at commodity levels were used. Thus, consistent tables were obtained. Finally, those consistent tables were deflated into terms of constant domestic prices. For the deflation of input-output tables, the author would like to acknowledge the advice given by Dr. L. Westphal and the late Professor T. Watanabe, and the financial support given by the World Bank. For the details of the reclassification, recompilation and deflation measures, see Shirley W. Y. Kuo, "Sources of Industrial Growth and Structural Change in Taiwan, ROC" (Mimeo, prepared under the auspices of the World Bank, 1977); idem, "Economic Growth and Structural Change in the Republic of China" (Mimeo, prepared under the auspices of the World Bank, 1979).

9.   The conclusion obtained by the present study basically differs from that obtained by Professors Kuo-shu Liang and Ching-ing Hou Liang. The contributions of export expansion to manufacturing expansion were much smaller by their assessment: 13.8%, 31.2%, and 20.9% for the periods 1960—65, 1965—70, and 1970—72, respectively (Kuo-shu Liang and Ching-ing Hou Liang, "Exports and Employment in Taiwan" in Institute of Economics, Academia Sinica, *Conference on Population and Economic Development in Taiwan,* Taipei, 1976). This is because their calculation is based on Chenery's 1960 decomposition formula while the calculation of the present study is based

on most recent Chenery decomposition formula of 1979. The probable underestimation of the contribution of export expansion in the Liangs' study may be due to its application of the direct method which is unable to separate intermediate goods into those for domestic use and those for exports, and treats all expansion of intermediate goods as domestic expansion.   Accordingly, it tends to overestimate the contribution of domestic expansion and underestimate the contribution of export expansion. The application of Chenery's 1979 formula, which is based on the total method (shown as Equations (4) and (4)' on page 147), enables us to separate intermediate goods into those for domestic use and those for exports. Accordingly, the overvaluation of the contribution by domestic expansion can be avoided and thus a much larger contribution of export expansion is obtained as shown in the text.

10. (1) Food processing: (13, 14, 15, 16, 17, 18, 19, 20); Textiles: (21, 22, 23, 24, 25); Steel, iron & their products: (40, 41); Electrical machinery: (45, 46, 47); Machinery: (44, 48); Intermediate goods: (26, 27, 29, 31, 32, 35, 36, 37, 38, 39, 42, 43); Final goods: (28, 30, 33, 34, 49); Manufacturing: (13-49).
    (2) The industries represented by the above numbers are given in Appendix IV.

11. Arthur Lewis, "Economic Development with Unlimited Supplies of Labor " (The Manchester School May 1954); G. Ranis and J. C. H. Fei, "A Theory of Economic Development," *American Economic Review,* Vol. 51 (September 1961).

12. Competitive imports and non-competitive imports are classified at commodity levels of four digit I-O classification. If imports of a commodity exceeded 90% of the total domestic use in the past and will exceed 90% of total domestic use in a certain period of the future, it is classified into non-competitive imports.

13. Wontack Hong, "Capital Accumulation, Factor Substitution, and the Changing Factor Intensity of Trade: The Case of Korea (1966–72)," in Wontack Hong and Anne O. Krueger ed., *Trade and Development in Korea* (Korea Development Institute, 1975).

14. Hal B. Lary, *Imports of Manufactures from Less-Developed Countries* (New York: NBER, 1968). Cited from Richard E. Caves and Ronald W. Jones, *World Trade and Payments, An Introduction* (1981).

8
The Basic Cause of Export Expansion —A Comparison of ROC, Japan, Korea and Hong Kong

We all know that the Republic of China, Japan, Korea and Hong Kong are all typical export-oriented countries. But was there any important factor that can be singled out as decisive in their rapid export expansion? And if there was, how important was this factor for the Taiwan economy as compared with the others? In order to answer these questions, the basic causes of export expansion will be studied for those four countries for the rapid export expansion period, 1965–1970.

Those years can be identified as a critical period of export expansion for the Taiwan economy. During this period, exports grew at an annual rate of 40.8%. At the same time, agriculturally oriented exports were superseded by industrial expansion. The share of food processing in exports decreased from 51.5% to 18.6%, while the share of miscellaneous manufactured[1] exports (mostly textiles) increased from 33.3% to 57.6%, growing at an annual rate of 61.4%; and the share of electronics and transportation equipment increased from 4.4% to 16.7%, growing at the highest rate of 102.9%.

It is interesting to compare the export performance of the ROC with Japan, Korea and Hong Kong for this particular period. During 1965–1970, Japanese exports grew at an annual rate of 29.1%. Japan's major exports, electronics, and machinery and equipment, comprised 86.0% of her total exports in 1965 and 88.1% in 1970. Korea, like the Republic of China, experienced tremendously high export growth during this period. Its annual growth rate for exports was 46.3% during 1965–1969. Miscellaneous manufacturing became the largest export category, comprising 66.8% in 1969. Although the share of electronics and transportation equipment was still low, these two categories grew at annual rates of 133.4% and 156.1%, respectively. Hong Kong's exports were largely in the miscellaneous export category, which comprised more than 80% of total exports and grew at an annual rate of 24.4%. Thus we can see that the exports of ROC, Korea and Hong Kong greatly depended on the miscellaneous exports category (mostly textiles) while Japanese exports were mainly electronics and transportation equipment during the rapid expansion period, 1965–1970.

The basic causes of export expansion can be decomposed into the following four categories: 1) increases in world trade, 2) changes in the commodity structure of world trade, 3) changes in area distribution of world trade, and 4) increases in the competitiveness of a country's exports.

In Table 8.1 these four effects are calculated for each of the four countries.[2] Each effect is expressed as a percentage of the value of each country's export expansion, ΔX. As can be seen in this table, increased competitiveness made decisive contributions in all four countries. Numerically, the extent of the contributions to total national export expansion resulting from increased competitiveness ranged from 48.9% (Hong Kong) to 78.0% (Korea). In the ROC, 72.7% of the export expansion during the period 1965–1970 was attributable to an increase in competitiveness.

An increase in the value of world trade ranked second, accounting for 26.2% (Korea) to 51.7% (Japan) of export expansion. It accounted for 30.6% of the export expansion of the Republic of China. Changes in commodity composition and changes in market distribution had negligible effects on export expansion except for Japan. For Japan's case, changes in commodity composition had a favorable effect, while changes in market distribution had an unfavorable effect.

In short, from a decomposition analysis, we find that the

Table 8.1   Comparison of Relative Competitiveness of
Exports Among ROC, Japan, Korea and
Hong Kong (1965–1970)

(%)

Item	ROC	Japan	Korea*	Hong Kong
1. Increase in value of world trade $$(\sum_i r X_{oi} - \sum_i X_{oi}) / \Delta X$$	30.6	51.7	26.2	50.2
2. Change in commodity composition $$(\sum_i r_i X_{oi} - \sum_i r X_{oi}) / \Delta X$$	−6.5	9.6	−2.7	5.4
3. Change in market distribution $$(\sum_i \sum_j r_{ij} X_{oij} - \sum_i r_i X_{oi}) / \Delta X$$	3.2	−22.8	−1.5	−4.4
4. Increase in competitiveness $$(\sum_i \sum_j X_{1ij} - \sum_i \sum_j r_{ij} X_{oij}) / \Delta X$$	72.7	61.5	78.0	48.9

Source: O.E.C.D., Trade by Commodities.
        United Nations, *Monthly Bulletin of Statistics,* March 1971.
Notes: * 1965–69; see Note 3.

basic factor contributing to the export expansion of these
four countries from 1965–70 was their increase in competitiveness in the world market. This increase in competitiveness
may have come from various factors. The important ones
were increase in productivity, advancement in quality, sales
of new products, rational international prices through domestic
price stability and/or favorable foreign exchange rates. This
chapter will not go into these details for the four countries.

Another important factor, increase in the value of world
trade, accounted for about half of the export expansion of
Japan and Hong Kong. However, it accounted for less than a
third in the case of the ROC and Korea. We know, therefore,

that advancement in competitiveness is still a very effective measure for future export expansion.

NOTES

1. Based on the SITC classification, miscellaneous manufacturing includes the 6th category (manufactured goods classified chiefly by material) and the 8th category (miscellaneous manufactured articles). The 6th category includes leather, manufactures of leather, rubber products, wood manufactures, paper and paperboard, textile yarn and thread, cotton fabrics, textile fabrics, made up textile products, lime, cement, iron and steel bars, and other mineral manufactures, etc.

2. The calculations are based on Tyszynski's formula. See H. Tyszynski, "World Trade in Manufactured Commodities, 1899– 1950," *Manchester School of Economic and Social Studies,* September 1951.

3. ΔX = An increment in export over the period under observation. Using the following notations,

    X_1 = Export of 1970*   . (* for the Korean case, 1969)
    X_0 = Export of 1965
    ΔX = Expansion of export during the period 1965–70 = $X_1 - X_0$
    r   = World trade in 1970/world trade in 1965
    i   = the number of SITC commodity classifications
    j   = the number of area classifications

    ΔX can be decomposed as follows.

    $$
    \begin{aligned}
    \Delta X &= X_1 - X_0 \\
    &= \sum_i X_{1i} - \sum_i X_{0i} \\
    &= \sum_i \sum_j X_{1ij} - \sum_i X_{0i} \\
    &= \left(\sum_i \sum_j X_{1ij} - \sum_i \sum_j r_{ij} X_{0ij} \right) \\
    &\quad + \left(\sum_i \sum_j r_{ij} X_{0ij} - \sum_i X_{0i} \right)
    \end{aligned}
    $$

$$\therefore \ \Delta X = (\sum_i \sum_j X_{1ij} - \sum_i \sum_j r_{ij} X_{oij})$$

$$+ (\sum_i \sum_j r_{ij} X_{oij} - \sum_i r_i X_{oi})$$

$$+ (\sum_i r_i X_{oi} - \sum_i X_{oi})$$

$$\Delta X = (\sum_i \sum_j X_{1ij} - \sum_i \sum_j r_{ij} X_{oij})$$
(4) reflects the effect of an increase in competitiveness on export expansion

$$+ (\sum_i \sum_j r_{ij} X_{oij} - \sum_i r_i X_{oi})$$
(3) reflects the effect of a change in market distribution

$$+ (\sum_i r_i X_{oi} - \sum_i r X_{oi})$$
(2) reflects the effect of a change in commodity composition

$$+ (\sum_i r X_{oi} - \sum_i X_{oi})$$
(1) reflects the effect of a change in the value of world trade

9

Cost-Price Changes Caused by External Shocks —The Case of 1973 Inflation

As the Taiwan economy had maintained a price stability for more than a decade, a sudden price rise in 1973 of 22.9% by a year average and 40.3% by end of year comparison, received serious attention. Being a small open economy, the Taiwan economy is easily affected by external shocks caused by changes in international prices and currencies. The price change in 1973 had a particularly complicated background.

First, the Taiwan economy had a large export surplus in 1972, so large as to comprise 8.2% of the GNP that year and to create a 37.9% increase in money supply. Second, the worldwide food shortage that started in late 1972 was severely affecting prices throughout the world. The United States was experiencing a record-breaking inflation rate[1] in the first quarter of 1973; in Japan, the inflation rate in March 1973 reached a 22.8%; inflation was spreading all over the world, to Germany, U.K., France .... and so on. Third, the sound international financial system collapsed after the Nixon shock in August 1971. The Smithsonian Agreement was reached in December 1971. By this Agreement, the U.S. dollar was devalued by 7.89% against gold, and the Japanese yen and Deutsche mark were revalued, respectively, by 16.88% and 13.56% against the U.S. dollar. Many other currencies also had their rates adjusted. A big U.S. trade deficit in 1972 made the U.S. dollar fall by 10% against SDR in February 12, 1973.

Table 9.1   Inflation Rates in 1973

(%)

Month in 1973	Changes in WPI (Percentage Increase Over Preceeding Month) (Percent Per Month)	Changes in WPI (Comparison with the Same Month of Previous Year) (Percent Per Annum)
Jan.	4.2	10.6
Feb.	2.6	12.8
Mar.	1.0	14.2
Apr.	−0.2	13.9
May	0.9	14.7
Jun.	2.0	17.1
Jul.	3.1	21.0
Aug.	4.5	24.8
Sep.	4.6	30.0
Oct.	4.3	35.2
Nov.	2.8	37.6
Dec.	4.6	40.3

Source: Directorate-General of Budget, Accounting and Statistics, Executive Yuan, *Commodity-Price Statistics Monthly, Taiwan Area, the Republic of China,* No. 139 (July 1982).

The Japanese yen started to float at that time. EEC currencies started to float together[2] on March 12, 1973 after another currency crisis which occurred early in that month.

As can be seen from this background, the 1973 inflation in Taiwan could be due to both demand pull and cost push. However, the cost push did not come from a domestic wage push, but from external shocks. This chapter tries to make a quantitative appraisal of the 1973 cost-price changes brought about by external shocks. External shocks will be examined in terms of major changes, namely, changes in foreign exchange rates and international prices.   For this purpose, a cost-price model, based on input-output relations, is constructed.

I.   A Cost-Price Model for the Taiwan Economy

In order to be able to relate the price changes in imported inputs to price changes in domestic outputs, a cost-price model based on input-output relations is constructed as follows:

1.   Characteristics of the Model

(1) The model consists of 75 simultaneous linear equations in order to be in accord with the number of industries in the 1969 I-O table compiled by CIECD.[3]

(2) Domestically produced and imported intermediate inputs are separately treated.

(3) Imported intermediate inputs are classified by three sources of origin: Japan, the United States, and other countries.

(4) Indirect taxes are divided into customs duties and other indirect taxes.   The tax rates are assumed to be constant during the period of observation.

2.   Basic Assumptions

(1) Since the exports from Taiwan comprised only a small share of the world market, international prices are assumed not to be affected by exports from Taiwan.

(2) The change in domestic prices is assumed not to have been affected by the change in international prices directly, but only through a change in production costs.

(3) Since 98% of Taiwan's petroleum was imported, it is assumed first, that there was no domestic oil production; second, that all oil consumption was imported; and third, that the price of oil was an exogenous variable which was completely determined by the world price.

(4) Value added is composed of wages (compensation of

labor), profits (compensation of capital) and indirect taxes other than custom duties.

(5) Since the import elasticity is close to zero,[4] tariffs are assumed to be all borne by the importers.

3. The Cost-Price Model

Under these assumptions, a cost-price model can be written in a matrix form as follows:

(1) $\quad A'P + M'_{Ja} P_f e_{Ja} + M'_{us} P_f e_{us} + M'_{oth} P_f e_{oth}$

$$+ M'_{Ja} T^m P_f e_{Ja} + M'_{us} T^m P_f e_{us}$$

$$+ M'_{oth} T^m P_f e_{oth} + TP + M_o + W + R = P$$

System (1) is a system composed of 75 simultaneous equations. The elements of each matrix are as follows:

$$A' = \left[a_{ij} \right]' = \begin{bmatrix} a_{11} & \cdots & a_{n1} \\ \vdots & & \vdots \\ a_{1n} & \cdots & a_{nn} \end{bmatrix}_{75 \times 75}$$

$$M'_{Ja} = \left[m_{ij\,Ja} \right]' = \begin{bmatrix} m_{11\,Ja} & \cdots & m_{n1\,Ja} \\ \vdots & & \vdots \\ m_{1n\,Ja} & \cdots & m_{nn\,Ja} \end{bmatrix}_{75 \times 75}$$

$$M'_{us} = \left[m_{ij\,us} \right]' = \begin{bmatrix} m_{11\,us} & \cdots & m_{n1\,us} \\ \vdots & & \vdots \\ m_{1n\,us} & \cdots & m_{nn\,us} \end{bmatrix}_{75 \times 75}$$

$$M'_{oth} = \left[m_{ij_{oth}}\right]' = \begin{bmatrix} m_{11_{oth}} & \cdots & m_{n1_{oth}} \\ \vdots & & \vdots \\ m_{1n_{oth}} & \cdots & m_{nn_{oth}} \end{bmatrix}_{75\times75}$$

$$P = \left[\frac{p_i}{p_i^*}\right] = \begin{bmatrix} \dfrac{p_1}{p_1^*} \\ \vdots \\ \dfrac{p_n}{p_n^*} \end{bmatrix}_{75\times1}$$

$$P_f\, e_{Ja} = \left[\frac{p_{if}\, e_{Ja}}{p_{if}^*\, e_{Ja}^*}\right] = \begin{bmatrix} \dfrac{p_{1f}\, e_{Ja}}{p_{1f}^*\, e_{Ja}^*} \\ \vdots \\ \dfrac{p_{nf}\, e_{Ja}}{p_{nf}^*\, e_{Ja}^*} \end{bmatrix}_{75\times1}$$

$$P_f\, e_{us} = \left[\frac{p_{if}\, e_{us}}{p_{if}^*\, e_{us}^*}\right] = \begin{bmatrix} \dfrac{p_{1f}\, e_{us}}{p_{1f}^*\, e_{us}^*} \\ \vdots \\ \dfrac{p_{nf}\, e_{us}}{p_{nf}^*\, e_{us}^*} \end{bmatrix}_{75\times1}$$

$$P_f\, e_{oth} \;=\; \left[\frac{p_{if}\, e_{oth}}{p_{if}^*\, e_{oth}^*} \right] \;=\; \left[\begin{array}{c} \dfrac{p_{1f}\, e_{oth}}{p_{1f}^*\, e_{oth}^*} \\[4pt] \cdot \\ \cdot \\ \dfrac{p_{nf}\, e_{oth}}{p_{nf}^*\, e_{oth}^*} \end{array} \right]_{75\times 1}$$

$$M_o \;=\; \left[m_{oj} \right] \;\frac{p_o}{p_o^*}\,(1+t_o)$$

$$=\; \left[\begin{array}{c} m_{o1} \\ \cdot \\ \cdot \\ m_{on} \end{array} \right]_{75\times 1} \frac{p_o}{p_o^*}\,(1+t_o)$$

$$T^m \;=\; \left[t_i^m \right] \;=\; \left[\begin{array}{ccc} t_1^m & \cdots & 0 \\ \cdot & & \cdot \\ \cdot & & \cdot \\ 0 & \cdots & t_n^m \end{array} \right]_{75\times 75}$$

$$T \;=\; \left[t_i \right] \;=\; \left[\begin{array}{ccc} t_1 & \cdots & 0 \\ \cdot & & \cdot \\ \cdot & & \cdot \\ 0 & \cdots & t_n \end{array} \right]_{75\times 75}$$

$$W \;=\; \left[s_i \right]\frac{w}{w^*} \;=\; \left[\begin{array}{c} s_1 \\ \cdot \\ \cdot \\ s_n \end{array} \right]_{75\times 1} \frac{w}{w^*}$$

$$R = \left[k_i \right] \frac{r}{r^*} = \begin{bmatrix} k_1 \\ . \\ . \\ . \\ k_n \end{bmatrix}_{75 \times 1} \frac{r}{r^*}$$

Each notation stands for:

a_{ij} = the value of domestically produced input i that is used in the production of one dollar's worth of output j

$m_{ij_{Ja}}$ = the value of imported input i from Japan, that is used in the production of one dollar's worth of output j

$m_{ij_{us}}$ = the value of imported input i from the U.S., that is used in the production of one dollar's worth of output j

$m_{ij_{oth}}$ = the value of imported input i from the other countries, that is used in the production of one dollar's worth of output j

$\dfrac{p_i}{p_i^*}$ = the price change of the domestically produced product i. p_i^* refers to the price in the base year, and p_i, the price in the calculation year.

$\dfrac{p_{if}}{p_{if}^*}$ = the change of the foreign price of the imported input i

$\dfrac{e_{Ja}}{e_{Ja}^*}$ = the change in the exchange rate of the Japanese yen against the N.T. dollar

$\dfrac{e_{us}}{e_{us}^*}$ = the change in the exchange rate of the U.S. dollar against the N.T. dollar

$\dfrac{e_{oth}}{e_{oth}^*}$ = the change in the exchange rate of the other currencies against the N.T. dollar

m_{oj} = the value of imported oil that is used in the production of one dollar's worth of output j

$\dfrac{p_o}{p_o^*}$ = the price change of oil in terms of the N.T. dollar

t_o = the tariff rate levied on the import of oil

$t_i^{\,m}$ = the average tariff rate levied on the imported input i

t_i = the average tax rate of indirect taxes other than tariffs levied on output i

s_i = the labor income share in one dollar's value of output i

k_i = the capital income share in one dollar's value of output i

$\dfrac{w}{w^*}$ = the change in wage rate

$\dfrac{r}{r^*}$ = the change in the rate of profit

The above system is a system of 75 equations with 75 unknowns. The unknowns are 75 domestic price changes, i.e., p_i/p_i^* ($i = 1, \ldots . 75$). Other than these 75 variables, all the others, including the change in oil price p_o/p_o^* , are exogenous variables in the system.

This model enables us to calculate the following items separately for the 75 sectors:

(1) The effect of changes in the exchange rate of the Japanese yen on production costs.

(2) The effect of changes in the exchange rate of the U.S.

dollar on production costs.

(3) The effect of changes in the exchange rate of the other currencies on production costs.

(4) The effect of changes in the Japanese yen, U.S. dollar, and other currencies on production costs.

(5) The effect of devaluation or revaluation of the New Taiwan dollar against other currencies on production costs.

(6) The effect of changes in international prices on production costs.

(7) The effect of adjustments in tariff rates on production costs.

(8) The effect of adjustments in indirect taxes other than tariffs on production costs.

(9) The effect of oil price adjustments on production costs.

Utilizing this cost-price model, the effects of changes in foreign exchange rates and international prices on domestic costs are assessed separately in the following sections.

II. Effects of Changes in Foreign Exchange Rates on Production Costs

1. Changes in Foreign Exchange Rates

In the two-year period right after the Smithsonian Agreement, the foreign exchange rates of major currencies changed significantly. Table 10.2 shows changes in the exchange rates of foreign currencies against the New Taiwan dollar from June 1971 to April 1973. June 1971 is chosen to represent the situation before the Nixon shock. April 1973 is chosen because it was right after the second devaluation of the U.S. dollar (by 10% against SDR in February 1973, following its first devaluation of 7.89% against gold in December 1971) and the resulting revaluation of the N.T. dollar by 5% against the U.S. dollar.

The exchange rates are calculated as a weighted average. The values of imports from and exports to 35 trading countries are used as weights. Since the figures in the table show changes in the exchange rates of foreign currencies against

Table 9.2   Changes in the Rates of Foreign Currencies Against
the N.T. Dollar (+ sign indicates an appreciation
of the foreign currency, i.e., a depreciation of the
N.T. dollar)

(%)

Area and Country	Changes Between June 1971 and April 1973	
	Weighted by Import Share	Weighted by Export Share
All foreign countries taken together	+ 13.72	+ 3.54
U.S. dollar	− 5.00	− 5.00
Japanese yen	+ 29.03	+ 29.03
All other countries	+ 2.36	+ 1.14

Source: Based on International Monetary Fund, *International Finance Statistics,*
and Chase Manhattan Bank, *International Finance.*
Note: 35 countries' export or import shares are used as weights.

the N.T. dollar, a positive figure means an appreciation of that
foreign currency, i.e., a depreciation of the N.T. dollar, while
a negative figure means a depreciation of that foreign currency,
i.e., an appreciation of the N.T. dollar. As can be seen from
Table 9.2, during the period from June 1971 to April 1973,
the foreign currencies taken together appreciated by 13.72%
for imports and 3.54% for exports. The appreciation of the
Japanese yen by 29.03% is noticeable. But how did these
changes in foreign currencies affect domestic production costs?
The model we have constructed above can be applied to assess
this effect.

2. *Effects of Changes in Foreign Currency Exchange Rates on
Production Costs*

Based on the model constructed above, effects of changes

in the exchange rates of foreign currencies on cost changes for the period from June 1971 to April 1973 are calculated separately for the 75 sectors. The results obtained for the 75 sectors are averaged in the 10 sectors as seen in Table 9.3. Here, two different cases are shown. First, the actual case: the N.T. dollar revalued by 5% against the U.S. dollar, and the yen and other currencies appreciated; and second, a hypothetical case of no revaluation of the N.T. dollar against the U.S. dollar. The effects on domestic cost increases by those changes are as follows:

The sectors affected most were, in order, durable consumer goods, machinery, transportation equipment, intermediate products II, intermediate products I, and non-durable consumer goods, with increases ranging from 3.31% to 8.57% in the actual case. If the N.T. dollar had not been revalued by 5% against the U.S. dollar, the cost rises would have been larger, ranging from 5.16% to 11.01% in these five sectors. Impacts on the other five sectors were much smaller. Evidently the effects on cost of the change in foreign exchange rates were concentrated on manufacturing, including intermediates. The cost rise in the whole economy was estimated to be 2.38%. If the N.T. dollar had not been revalued by 5% against the U.S. dollar, then the cost rise in the whole economy would have been 3.46%. It is also known that if the N.T. dollar had been revalued by 10%, then the cost rise would have been less, 1.32%.

In order to further examine the causes of cost rises, we will single out the effects of the change in the Japanese yen. We can see that even though the N.T. dollar was revalued by 5% against the U.S. dollar, the appreciation of the Japanese yen alone caused costs to rise by 1.83% for the economy as a whole, comprising 77% of the total cost increase by all currency changes. A sectoral observation makes it clear that the effects of the yen's relative appreciation or the N.T. dollar's relative depreciation were mainly on the cost rise in the categories of non-durable consumer goods, machinery, transportation equipment, and intermediate products II. In particular 82% of the cost change in intermediate products II was caused by the

Table 9.3   Effects of Changes in Foreign Exchange Rates on Costs of Production (Changes between June 1971 and April 1973)

(%)

Sector	Actual Situation: Changes Against the N.T. Dollar U.S. Dollar: −5% Japanese yen: 29.03% All Other Currencies: 2.36%	Hypothetical Case: The N.T. Dollar did not Revalue by 5%	Cost Changes Due Only to the Yen's Appreciation Against the N.T. Dollar by 29.03%
1. Agriculture, forestry & fishing	0.42	0.83	0.22
2. Processed foods	0.68	1.71	0.22
3. Tobacco, wine & other beverages	0.35	1.24	−0.12
4. Mining & energy	0.62	0.84	0.50
5. Construction materials	0.93	1.41	0.57
6A. Intermediate products I	3.31	5.16	1.90
6B. Intermediate products II	4.93	6.74	4.05
7. Non-durable consumer goods	3.10	4.47	2.36
8. Durable consumer goods	8.57	11.01	8.17
9. Machinery	7.44	9.44	6.84
10. Transportation equipment	5.76	7.38	5.30
Total Economy	2.38	3.46	1.83

Source: Based on the cost-price model, Equation (1).
Note: See Note 5.

relative appreciation of the yen. In other words, Taiwan's economic structure was such that when the N.T. dollar was devalued against the Japanese yen, the costs of production in intermediates and machinery would be greatly affected. Therefore, the value of the N.T. dollar against the yen should be paid special attention because of its implications for inflation.

III. Effects of Changes in Foreign Prices on Production Costs

A significant rise in international prices was observed beginning in the second half of 1972. In order to examine its effects on production costs, the same cost-price model (Equation 1) is applied for changes in international prices. The period of observation is May 1972 to May 1973. The results shown in Table 9.4 indicate that severe world inflation brought the Taiwan economy significant cost rises: for machinery, 11.47%, intermediate I, 8.38%, intermediate II, 7.35%, food processing, 6.77%, transportation equipment, 6.13%, and nondurable consumer goods, 5.00%. The weighted average cost rise in the whole economy caused by the change in foreign prices is estimated to have been 4.24%.

During approximately the same period (from January 1972 to April 1973), the major changes in the exchange rates of foreign currencies were: the Japanese yen appreciated by 17% against the U.S. dollar; all other currencies appreciated by 6% against the U.S. dollar; and the N.T. dollar appreciated by 5% against the U.S. dollar. The effects of these changes in exchange rates on cost rises are estimated in Table 9.4. The average cost rise was 0.82%. When these effects are added to the effects of changes in foreign prices, we obtain the combined effects of imported inflation, 5.06%, as shown in Table 9.4. It is noted that the rise in international prices was a dominant factor in the cost changes in early 1973.

In the above we have made a quantitative appraisal of the effects of changes in foreign prices and currencies on changes in the domestic cost-price. Naturally, what this estimation tells us is only how much cost-price in domestic products would be induced in theory. Furthermore, the theoretical model appli-

Table 9.4   The Combined Effects of Changes in Foreign Prices and Currencies — Imported Inflation

(%)

Sector	Effects of Changes in Foreign Currencies (From January 1972 to April 1973)	Effects of Changes in Foreign Prices (From March 1972 to March 1973)	Combined Effects of Foreign Prices and Currencies
1. Agriculture, forestry & fishing	0.08	1.79	1.87
2. Processed foods	−0.02	6.77	6.75
3. Tobacco, wine & other beverages	−0.10	1.39	1.29
4. Mining & energy	0.24	1.02	1.26
5. Construction materials	0.35	1.36	1.71
6A. Intermediate products I	1.18	8.38	9.56
6B. Intermediate products II	1.78	7.35	9.13
7. Non-durable consumer goods	1.09	5.00	6.09
8. Durable consumer goods	3.05	3.78	6.83
9. Machinery	2.81	11.47	14.28
10. Transportation equipment	2.15	6.13	8.28
Total Economy	0.82	4.24	5.06

Source: Based on the cost-price model, Equation (1).

Notes: From January 1972 to April 1973: The Japanese yen appreciated by 17% against the U.S. dollar; the N.T. dollar was revalued by 5% against the U.S. dollar; the other currencies appreciated by 6% against the U.S. dollar.

cable at the present time is such a model based on linear input-output relations, which is not a perfect representation of the real world. In addition, statistics used in the compilation of the input-output table and statistics of changes in international prices may not be sufficiently accurate. However, this appraisal at least serves to give us a rough idea about the absolute magnitude and relative degree of cost-push resulting from the external shocks of the inflation of early 1973.

Taking some time lag into account, the magnitude of the 5.06% cost-push, estimated for the period of March 1972 to March 1973, may be comparable to the actual annual inflation rates of 14.2% in March 1973, 13.9% in April, 14.7% in May, and 17.1% in June. This gives us the impression that cost-push from the external shocks accounted for about one third of the inflation that occurred during this period. We should note that this was before the oil crisis. In February 1973, the N.T. dollar was revalued by 5% against the U.S. dollar. The above estimation shows us that to have used exclusively a revaluation of the N.T. dollar as a means of preventing the cost-price change of that time would have been too drastic. However, a slightly larger revaluation of the N.T. dollar at that time might have generated a larger anti-inflationary effect through the demand side.

NOTES

1.   It was the highest inflation rate since the Korean War.

2.   With the United Kingdom and Ireland as exceptions.

3.   Council for International Economic Cooperation and Development, Executive Yuan.

4.   Import Price Elasticity of Taiwan
                        (1951—1971)

Origin of Imports	Import Price Elasticity
Total Imports	−0.01
Japan	−0.03
United States	−0.02
Germany, West	−0.02
United Kingdom	−0.06
Canada	0.06
France	0.01
Other Countries	−0.02

Source: Je-Ho Hsu, "The Income Elasticity and Price Elasti-
    city of Exports and Imports of Taiwan," National Taiwan
    University, The Graduate Institute of Economics, April
    1973.

5. The contents of each category are as follows:

(1) Agriculture, Forestry and Fishing: 01 Paddy Rice, 02 Other
Common Crops, 03 Sugarcane, 04 Crops for Processing, 05 Horticul-
tural Crops, 06 Hogs, 07 Other Livestock, 08 Forestry, 09 Fisheries
and 15 Rice.

(2) Processed Foods: 16 Sugar, 17 Canned Foods, 20 Monosodium
Glutamate, 24 Tea and 25 Misc. Food Products.

(3) Tobacco, Wine and Other Beverages: 19 Tobacco & Alcoholic
Beverages and 23 Non-Alcoholic Beverages.

(4) Mining and Energy: 10 Coal & Products, 11 Metallic Minerals,
12 Crude Petroleum & Natural Gas, 13 Salt and 14 Non-Metallic
Minerals.

(5) Construction Materials: 45 Cement, 46 Cement Products and 48
Misc. Non-Metallic Mineral Products (90.12%).

(6A) Intermediate Products I: 22 Edible Vegetable Oil & By-Products,
31 Lumber, 32 Plywood, 36 Leather & Products (31.64%), 38 Chemi-
cal Fertilizer, 39 Medicines, 40 Plastics & Products, 41 Petroleum
Products, 42 Non-Edible Vegetable & Animal Oils, 43 Industrial
Chemicals, 44 Misc. Chemical Manufactures, 47 Glass, 48 Misc.
Non-Metallic Mineral Products (9.88%), 49 Steel & Iron and 53 Misc.
Metals & Products (52.69%).

(6B) Intermediate Products II: 26 Artificial Fibres, 27 Artificial Fab-
rics, 28 Cotton Fabrics, 29 Woolen & Worsted Fabrics, 30 Misc.
Fabrics & Apparel, Accessories (8.34%), 33 Products of Wood,
Bamboo & Rattan, 34 Pulp, Paper & Paper Products, 36 Leather &

Products (14.72%), 37 Rubber & Products 50 Steel & Iron Products, 52 Aluminum Products and 53 Misc. Metals & Products (47.31%).
(7) Non-Durable Consumer Goods: 30 Misc. Fabrics & Apparel, Accessories (91.66%), 36 Leather & Products (53.64%) and 61 Misc. Manufactures.
(8) Durable Consumer Goods: 56 Communication Equipment, 59 Motor Vehicles and 60 Other Transport Equipment (7.83%).
(9) Machinery: 54 Machinery, 55 Household Electrical Appliances and 57 Other Electrical Apparatus & Equipment.
(10) Transportation Equipment: 58 Shipbuilding and 60 Other Transport Equipment (92.17%).

10

Growth, Inflation, and Policies in the Wake of the Oil Crises

The quadrupling of oil prices in November 1973 had significant effects on the world economy, as oil was not only used as a prime energy source but also as a primary material input for countless products. The shock manifested itself in worldwide stagflation, in balance of payments deficits for most non-OPEC countries, and in deterioration in the terms of trade of the oil importing countries. The second oil crisis in 1979 hampered the recovering world economy, causing the growth rate to decline and the inflation rate to rise again.

This chapter is aimed at analyzing the growth and inflation of the Taiwan economy in the wake of the two oil crises. Government measures taken in response to the oil shocks will also be discussed.

I. Growth and Inflation in the 1970s

1. The First Oil Crisis

The performance of the Taiwan economy in the 1960s was characterized by rapid growth and stable prices. During 1961-71, the real GNP grew at an annual average rate of 10.2%. Prices were stable, increasing at an annual average of 1.6% measured by the wholesale price index, 2.9% by the consumer price index, and 3.6% by the GNP deflator. This good performance was interrupted by the 1973 oil crisis.

The abrupt price rise of 22.9% in 1973 was a severe shock, although the growth rate still remained high that year. In 1974 the inflation rate jumped to 40.6%, and the growth rate dropped to 1.1%. This was quite a new experience for the Taiwan economy. Various, drastic government measures were taken. In 1975 inflation was controlled and dropped to a negative 5.1%, and the economy recovered to register a 4.2% growth. Thereafter, the Taiwan economy enjoyed renewed rapid growth with stable prices. For the three post-oil crisis years, 1976—78, the average growth rate was a high 12.4%, and the inflation was a low 3.0%. Taiwan enjoyed a prosperous and stable period before the second oil crisis.

2. The Second Oil Crisis

The rise of oil prices in 1979 and 1980 again shocked the Taiwan economy. Prices rose at annual rates of 13.8% in 1979 and 21.5% in 1980. On the other hand, the growth rate declined to 8.1% in 1979 and 6.6% in 1980. Thus, the inflation rate during the second oil shock was about half that of the first shock, and the reduction in the growth rate was also smaller. No widespread and drastic government measures were taken at this time; only mild monetary steps were taken. The economy adjusted itself gradually in the environment of tighter money. In 1981 the inflation rate was brought down to 7.6%, but the growth rate was not very high, 5.5%. Although the recorded growth rate for the first half of 1982 was only 3.5%, the inflation rate became negative in June 1982.

II. Causes of Inflation

1. Cost-Push and Demand-Pull

The two inflationary periods of 1973—74 and 1979—80 can be explained as having been induced by both cost-push and demand-pull. The cost-push side will be explained first. Among four components of cost—wages, profits, cost of inter-

Table 10.1   Fluctuations of Growth and Inflation Rates

(%)

Year	GNP Growth	Rate of Inflation		
		Wholesale Prices	Consumer Prices	GNP Deflator
1961–71 (annual average)	10.2	1.6	2.9	3.6
1971	12.9	0.02	2.8	3.1
1972	13.3	4.5	3.0	5.8
1973	12.8	22.9	8.2	14.9
1974	1.1	40.6	47.5	32.3
1975	4.2	−5.1	5.2	2.3
1976	13.5	2.8	2.5	5.6
1977	9.9	2.8	7.0	6.2
1978	13.9	3.5	5.8	4.7
1979	8.1	13.8	9.8	11.3
1980	6.6	21.5	19.0	16.1
1981	5.5	7.6	16.3	12.1
1982/II*	3.5	−0.3	3.7	4.5

Source: Directorate-General of Budget, Accounting and Statistics, Executive Yuan, *National Income of the Republic of China*, 1981; Directorate-General of Budget, Accounting and Statistics, Executive Yuan, *Commodity-Price Statistics Monthly, Taiwan Area, the Republic of China*, July 1982; Directorate-General of Budget, Accounting and Statistics, Executive Yuan, *Quarterly National Economic Trends, Taiwan Area, the Republic of China*, May 1982.

Note: * The second quarter of 1982.

mediate inputs, and indirect taxes—wages were not a factor of cost-push in Taiwan, because the island's labor market was quite competitive and able to generate a market-determined wage rate.   Cost-push due to profit maximization was not significant either, because monopoly power in Taiwan was not generally strong.   The cost of intermediate goods depended heavily on import prices, as intermediate inputs comprised about 70% of manufactures and some 40% of these intermediates were imported.   According to the cost-price model constructed

Table 10.2   Inflation Rates and Changes in Import Prices
and Money Supply

(percent per annum)

Year	Change in Wholesale Price Index $\left(\begin{matrix}\text{Year Average}\\\text{Comparison}\end{matrix}\right)$	Change in Import Price Index $\left(\begin{matrix}\text{Year Average}\\\text{Comparison}\end{matrix}\right)$	Growth Rate of Money Supply, M_1 $\left(\begin{matrix}\text{End of Year}\\\text{Comparison}\end{matrix}\right)$
1961–71 (annual average)	1.6	1.7	17.9
1970	2.7	3.6	11.3
1971	0.02	5.1	24.8
1972	4.5	8.0	37.9
1973	22.9	22.1	49.3
1974	40.6	47.0	7.0
1975	−5.1	−5.0	26.9
1976	2.8	2.1	23.1
1977	2.8	7.7	29.1
1978	3.5	9.2	34.1
1979	13.8	16.6	7.0
1980	21.5	20.2	19.9
1981	7.6	8.6	11.1
1982/June	−0.4	−1.5*	7.8

Source: Directorate-General of Budget, Accounting and Statistics, Executive Yuan, *National Income of the Republic of China,* 1981; Directorate-General of Budget, Accounting and Statistics, Executive Yuan, *Commodity-Price Statistics Monthly, Taiwan Area, the Republic of China,* July 1982; Directorate-General of Budget, Accounting and Statistics, Executive Yuan, *Quarterly National Economic Trends, Taiwan Area, the Republic of China,* May 1982; Economic Research Department, The Central Bank of China, *Financial Statistics Monthly, Taiwan District, the Republic of China,* May 1982 and July 1982.
Note: * The second quarter of 1982.

in Chapter 9, the quadrupling of oil prices alone will incur about a 40% cost-price increase. However, since a large part of the rise in oil prices in 1973 and 1974 was absorbed by the government-owned China Petroleum and Taiwan Power Companies, the 40.6% inflation rate that occurred in 1974 was not all due to the increase in the oil price. Various econometric models, based on observations for the past two decades or so, show that import price changes accounted for about 50% of all past price changes.[1]

Second, the presence of demand-pull can be seen from the high growth rates in the money supply, which were mostly generated one year prior to the rise in prices. That is, a 37.9% growth rate in the money supply in 1972 preceeded a 22.9% price rise in 1973; and a 49.3% growth in the money supply preceeded a 40.6% price rise in 1974. Likewise, the 34.1% growth in the money supply in 1978 apparently led to price increases in 1979. The only exception was the inflation in 1980 which was not preceeded by a large monetary growth in the previous year.   Generally speaking, the close relationship between the money supply (M_1) and the rate of inflation can be observed from Fig. 10.1, where the two variables are depicted in terms of money per unit of output and rate of inflation. This relationship seems to show that "money matters" in the Taiwan case for the period 1971–81.[2]

2.   Sources of Change in the Money Supply

Given the above observation, we would like to study how this large money supply was created. Sources of change in the money supply can be decomposed into three categories: changes in net foreign assets, changes in net claims upon the government, and changes in the banks' excess loans (see Table 10.3).   These three sources are determined respectively by changes in the balance of payments, changes in government deposits and withdrawals, and changes in banks' loans and investment minus changes in deposits and banks' net worth.

For the four critical years, 1972, 1973, 1977 and 1978, when the money supply increased by more than or close to 30%, we note three things from the decomposition in Table 10.4: first, that the increase in net foreign assets was the dominant source; second, that the performance of the government sector was a stabilizing force rather than an expansionary factor, especially since the portion of the money supply absorbed

Fig. 10.1   Relationship Between Money Per Unit of Output
and Rate of Inflation (1971~1981 = 100)

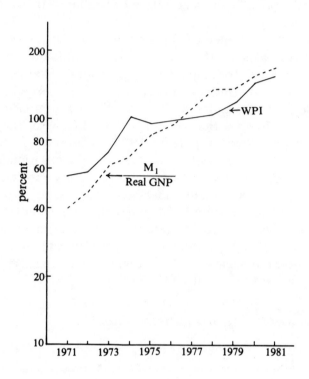

by government deposits was high in 1973 and 1978; and third,
that excess bank loans were not the major source of a higher
growth rate of the money supply except in 1973. In 1973,
a high rate of excess bank loans together with a large increase
in net foreign assets forced an almost 50% increase in the
money supply.   However, the contribution made by banks'
excess loans to the increase in money supply in 1978 was about
one third of that due to the net increase in foreign assets.

3. Trade Surplus and Balance of Payments

In the previous section, we observed that the net increase

Table 10.3   Sources of Change in the Money Supply

(NT$ million)

End of Year	Changes in the Money = Supply ΔM_1	Due to Changes in Net Foreign Assets	Due to Changes in + Net Claims + upon the Government	Due to Changes in Banks' + Excess Loans	Due to Others
1971	7,945	10,067	−648	93	−1,567
1972	15,146	24,227	−5,885	−2,461	−735
1973	27,184	20,619	−18,110	25,762	−1,087
1974	5,769	−24,444	1,292	41,977	−13,056
1975	23,701	−7,910	−8,603	32,839	7,375
1976	25,780	37,201	−2,706	−7,940	−775
1977	40,015	40,414	14	−601	188
1978	60,504	61,823	−24,543	17,591	5,633
1979	16,624	−6,353	−30,196	68,703	−15,530
1980	50,741	−13,046	6,191	71,397	−13,801
1981	34,020	32,754	31,900	5,945	−36,579

Source: Economic Research Department, The Central Bank of China, *Financial Statistics Monthly, Taiwan District, the Republic of China,* May 1982.
Notes:
  1. The term changes in banks' excess loans is defined as: Changes in banks' loans and investment − Changes in (deposits + CD's + net worth of deposit banks).
  2. The figures in this table are adjusted figures. About the adjustment, please see Note 3.

in foreign assets was the decisive factor in generating a high growth rate of the money supply. In this section, we would like to examine this change by breaking the net increase in foreign assets down into trade balance and basic balance.[4]   As can be seen from Table 10.5, the Taiwan economy had favorable trade balances and favorable basic balances throughout the period 1970–81, except for 1974 and 1975. One characteristic was that in the four critical years of rapid monetary growth, the trade surpluses were particularly large in terms of their percentages of the GNP: 8.2% in 1972, 6.8% in 1973, 5.5% in 1977, and 8.3% in 1978. Such large trade surpluses not only created a vast pool of additional money, but also caused a large

Table 10.4　Sources of Change in the Money Supply
(Percentage Distribution)

(%)

End of Year	Changes in the Money Supply ΔM_1	=	Due to Changes in Net Foreign Assets	+	Due to Changes in Net Claims upon the Government	+	Due to Changes in Banks' Excess Loans
1971	100		127		−8		1
1972	100		160		−39		−16
1973	100		76		−67		95
1974	100		−424		22		728
1975	100		−33		−36		138
1976	100		144		−10		−31
1977	100		101		0		−2
1978	100		102		−40		29
1979	100		−38		−182		413
1980	100		−26		12		141
1981	100		96		94		18

Source: Same as Table 10.3.

portion of domestic savings to flow out to foreign countries.

Trade surpluses can be attributed to a superiority in export competitiveness. The competitiveness of exports is affected by two factors: relative prices and foreign exchange rates. Table 10.6 reviews these two factors in terms of purchasing power parity (PPP) and effective exchange rate (EER).

The purchasing power parity measures the weighted average of the ratio of foreign prices to domestic prices. The year 1980 is used as the base because that year's trade balance and basic balance were both close to zero, i.e., equilibrium. When PPP is greater than 100, it means that foreign prices rise at a rate higher than domestic prices; when PPP is less than 100, it means that domestic prices rise at a higher rate. As can be seen from Table 10.6, all figures for PPP were greater than 100 in the

+ Due to Others	Annual Growth Rate of the Money Supply M_1	End of Year
−20	24.8	1971
−5	37.9	1972
−4	49.3	1973
−226	7.0	1974
31	26.9	1975
−3	23.1	1976
1	29.1	1977
9	34.1	1978
−93	7.0	1979
−27	19.9	1980
−108	11.1	1981

1970s, except in 1974, indicating that throughout the 1970s, the inflation rate in Taiwan was lower than the aggregated inflation rates of Taiwan's trading partners. In particular, the relative price stability in 1970, 1971, 1972 and 1978 was noticeable. Another factor, the effective exchange rate (EER), is a weighted average of foreign exchange rates. For the same reason, 1980 is again used as the base year. An effective exchange rate greater than 100 means over-valuation of the domestic currency, while one less than 100 means under-valuation.

The change in the competitiveness of exports can be measured by EER/PPP, which is the real effective exchange rate. When the real effective exchange rate is greater than 100, competitiveness in that year is lower than in the base year; when the real effective exchange rate is less than 100, competi-

Table 10.5   Major Items in Balance of Payments

(U.S. $ million)

Year	Current Account Balance =	Trade Balance +	Balance on Services etc.	Net Direct Investment	Net Long-Term Capital
1970	1	106	−105	61	62
1971	173	292	−119	52	37
1972	513	647	−134	24	45
1973	566	734	−168	61	137
1974	−1,113	−830	−283	83	304
1975	−589	−255	−334	34	497
1976	292	688	−396	68	531
1977	920	1,177	−257	44	305
1978	1,669	2,234	−565	110	243
1979	241	1,408	−1,167	122	361
1980	−965	147	−1,112	119	1,087
1981	497	1,970	−1,473	101	738

Source: Economic Research Department, The Central Bank of China, *Financial Statistics Monthly, Taiwan District, the Republic of China,* January 1977, May 1981 and July 1982.

Notes: 1.   Basic balance = current account balance + net direct investment + net long-term capital

tiveness in that year is superior to that of the base year. From Table 10.6 we know that whether we use exports or two-way trade as weights, the real effective exchange rates in the 1970s were all less than 100—except in 1974, when prices skyrocketed. This shows that during the 1970s except for 1974, export competitiveness, in terms of relative price and foreign exchange rates combined, was favorable to exports when 1980 is used as the base year for comparison. We should also note that the real effective exchange rates in 1972 and 1978 were especially low, and generated large trade surpluses which in turn resulted in a vast expansion of the money supply.

From the above observations, we know that Taiwan's economic environment immediately before the two oil shocks

Basic[1] Balance	Overall[2] Balance of Payments	Year
124	135	1970
262	254	1971
582	607	1972
764	610	1973
−726	−597	1974
−58	−149	1975
891	981	1976
1,269	1,132	1977
2,022	1,951	1978
724	96	1979
241	−127	1980
1,336	1,299	1981

2. Overall balance of payments
= changes in net foreign assets
of the banking system

was such that prices had been particularly stable for some time, and that speedy export growth was creating a large physical demand on the one hand and inducing money supply growth on the other.   Both oil crises occurred in the midst of this environment.   Strong demand plus the available money supply easily absorbed the higher intermediate costs.   The two inflations in the 1970s were thus caused by both demand-pull and cost-push.

III. Government Policies

The government measures for the first oil crisis were mostly taken in 1974.   In order to cope with the skyrocketing inflation

Table 10.6   Purchasing Power Parity, Effective Exchange Rate and Real Effective Exchange Rate

(%)

Year	Purchasing Power Parity (PPP)		Effective Exchange Rate (EER)	
	Export Weighted	Trade Weighted	Export Weighted	Trade Weighted
1970	114.0	116.1	109.2	117.0
1971	116.1	118.1	103.9	113.2
1972	115.9	116.9	100.0	104.8
1973	107.3	108.1	101.0	103.1
1974	90.2	93.4	101.7	106.3
1975	103.3	105.1	102.9	106.5
1976	106.2	107.8	103.9	107.5
1977	108.5	109.6	101.3	103.2
1978	110.2	110.1	97.3	96.1
1979	106.8	106.2	99.6	99.1
1980	100.0	100.0	100.0	100.0
1981	100.4	99.4	100.1	99.3

Source: International Monetary Fund, *International Financial Statistics*, 1981; Directorate-General of Budget, Accounting and Statistics, Executive Yuan, *Commodity-Price Statistics Monthly, Taiwan Area, the Republic of China*, December 1981; Department of Statistics, Ministry of Finance, *Monthly Statistics of Exports and Imports, the Republic of China*, December 1981.

rate, they were rather active and drastic. The measures for the second oil crisis, which were taken after 1979, were comparatively mild and gradual. These measures will be discussed below.

1.   Government Measures in the Wake of the First Oil Crisis

Government measures taken in the wake of the first oil crisis can be categorized as a high interest rate policy, a one-shot adjustment of oil prices, significant tax reductions, and heavy public spending.

Real Effective Exchange Rate (EER/PPP)		Year
Export Weighted	Trade Weighted	
95.8	100.8	1970
89.5	95.9	1971
86.3	89.6	1972
94.1	95.4	1973
112.7	113.8	1974
99.6	101.3	1975
97.8	99.7	1976
93.4	94.2	1977
88.3	87.3	1978
93.3	93.3	1979
100.0	100.0	1980
99.7	99.9	1981

Notes:
1. Export weights are based on the export value of the 9 largest exporting countries in that year.
2. Trade weights are based on trade value of the 9 largest trading countries in that year.

(1) High Interest Rate Policy

As prices started to rise in 1973, interest rates were upped in April and July of that year. As a result of these two increases, the secured loan rate rose by two percentage points to 13.25%, and the discount rate by one and three quarters points to 11.75%. However, the price index continued to rise at a monthly rate of about 4% per month in the second half of 1973. Inflationary expectations became widespread over the entire island. Time and savings deposits started to decrease in October 1973. Finally, in January 1974, inflation soared at a monthly rate of 12.9%. At this juncture "Stabilization Measures" were promulgated, on January 27, 1974. The high interest rate policy was implemented as one of the two essential components of the "Stabilization Measures."

The characteristics of this interest rate policy can be noted as follows: first, a significant one-shock rise in interest rates: on January 27, 1974 deposit rates were raised by 33.4% on average, and loan rates by 25.8% (Table 10.7); second, a greater rise in shorter-term interest rates than in longer-term interest rates; third, a greater rise in deposit rates than in loan rates; and fourth, an allowance of the new deposit rates and bond rates to be applicable to all previous deposits and previously issued public bonds. The effectiveness of this interest rate policy can be seen by the prompt upturn of and the continuous

Table 10.7   Changes in Interest Rates on January 27, 1974

(percent per annum)

	Date of Change		Rate of Change
	Oct. 24, 1973	Jan. 27, 1974	(%)
Deposit rate			
1 month	7.00	10.00	42.9
3 months	8.00	11.50	43.8
6 months	9.00	12.50	38.9
9 months	9.50	13.00	36.8
1 year	11.00	15.00	36.4
2 years	11.50	15.00	30.4
3 years	12.00	15.00	25.0
Weighted average rise in deposit rate			33.4
Loan rate			
Unsecured	13.75	17.50	27.3
Secured	13.25	16.50	24.5
Weighted average rise in loan rate			25.8

Source: Economic Research Department, The Central Bank of China, *Financial Statistics Monthly, Taiwan District, The Republic of China*, December 1981.

increase in time and savings deposits after February 1974 (see Table 10.8).

Table 10.8   Monthly Changes in Time Deposits and Wholesale Prices

(monthly rate)

Year and Month	Time Deposits and Savings Deposits	Changes in Time Deposits and Savings Deposits	Growth Rate of Time Deposits and Savings Deposits	Growth Rate of Wholesale Prices
	(end of month)	(comparison with the previous month)		
	(NT$ million)	(NT$ million)	(%)	(%)
1973 May	105,776	3,238	3.2	0.9
Jun.	108,217	2,441	2.3	2.0
Jul.	110,501	2,284	2.1	3.1
Aug.	113,790	3,289	3.0	4.5
Sep.	114,744	954	0.8	4.6
Oct.	114,322	−422	−0.4	4.3
Nov.	114,114	−208	−0.2	2.8
Dec.	114,543	429	0.4	4.6
1974 Jan.	112,706	−1,837	−1.6	12.9
Feb.	114,524	1,818	1.6	12.9
Mar.	118,140	3,616	3.2	−1.8
Apr.	121,958	3,818	3.2	−3.0
May	125,849	3,891	3.2	−1.8
Jun.	130,775	4,926	3.9	−1.1
Jul.	135,543	4,768	3.6	−0.9
Aug.	140,933	5,390	4.0	−0.1
Sep.	145,430	4,497	3.2	−0.9
Oct.	149,728	4,298	3.0	−1.4
Nov.	152,375	2,647	1.8	−1.5
Dec.	157,638	5,263	3.5	−0.1

Source: Economic Research Department, The Central Bank of China, *Financial Statistics Monthly, Taiwan District, the Republic of China*, January 1974, January 1975.

(2) A One-Shot Adjustment of Oil Prices

As a government monopoly enterprise, the China Petroleum Corp. had   enjoyed a considerable rate of profit up until the oil crisis broke, which allowed it to absorb a part of the cost increase. However, the increase in the oil price was much more than the Chinese Petroleum Corp. alone could absorb. On January 27, 1974, the domestic prices of oil and its related products were raised to meet the higher costs of oil products. This was the other essential part of the "Stabilization Measures."   In order to eliminate the psychology of inflation, which had prevailed for several months, a one-shot adjustment rather than a gradual change was adopted. Prices were raised by 88.4% on the average for various kinds of oil products, and the price rise for electricity was 78.7%. The price level rose by 12.9% in February. However, the one-shot oil price adjustment together with the high interest rates started to bring the price level down in March 1974, and it declined continuously in each month thereafter. Thus, the inflation after the first oil crisis was controlled by 1975, as the inflation rate in that year became a negative 5.1%.

(3) Tax Reductions

Tax reductions in 1974 were mainly designed to reduce the cost of products and to promote a faster recovery of the economy. Major reductions were directed at income taxes, customs duties, commodity taxes and harbor dues.

The amendment of the income tax law in October 1974 raised the exemption levels of individual and business income taxes. The income brackets of the business income tax were also amended.

It has been estimated that this change reduced individual income taxes by NT$460 million but increased the business income tax by NT$100 million. Thus, the net reduction in income taxes in 1974 was estimated at NT$360 million.

The tariff rate adjustment in 1974 lowered the tariff on 200 import items and raised the tariff on only 7 items. At

Table 10.9   Changes in Domestic Prices of
Fuel Oil and Electricity

(%)

Year	Changes in the Price of Fuel Oil	Changes in the Price of Electricity
1971	2.6	0.5
1972	2.0	−0.6
1973	0	2.1
1974	88.4	78.7
1975	2.8	3.9
1976	0	−1.2
1977	0	20.9
1978	0.5	−0.3
1979	44.7	11.5
1980	71.3	45.3
1981	23.1	35.4

Source: Council for Economic Planning and Development, Executive
Yuan, *Economic Situation,* 1979 and 1981.

the same time, the Executive Yuan utilized its authority to
greatly reduce the tariff rates on many imports. These reductions were estimated to amount to NT$6,740 million, or 25%
of the total tariff revenue in 1974.

According to tax regulations, commodity tax amounts
should be based on the "taxing price," which is determined by
the wholesale price of the taxed commodity. In order to reduce
the commodity tax, the "taxing prices" of sugar, cement, and
oil products, which accounted for about one half of total
commodity taxes paid, were frozen in July 1973. The reduction in 1974 taxes caused by this freeze was estimated to
amount to 28% of the total commodity tax revenue collected
that year.

Table 10.11 gives a general picture of the tax reduction
in 1974. The total tax reduction in 1974 was estimated to be
NT$11.11 billion, which was equivalent to 12.9% of total tax

Table 10.10   Inflation Rates in 1974

(%)

Month in 1974	Changes in WPI (Comparison with the Same Month of Previous Year) (Percent Per Annum)
Jan.	52.0
Feb.	67.4
Mar.	62.8
Apr.	58.2
May	54.1
Jun.	49.3
Jul.	43.5
Aug.	37.1
Sep.	29.9
Oct.	22.8
Nov.	17.6
Dec.	12.3

Source: Directorate-General of Budget, Accounting and Statistics,
Executive Yuan, *Commodity-Price Statistics Monthly, Taiwan
Area, the Republic of China,* No. 139, July 1982.

revenue and 2.1% of the GNP in 1974. Thus, the tax reduction in 1974 was quite significant.

(4) Public Spending — The Ten Major Projects

The ten major construction projects started in 1973 and ended in 1978.   They included six transportation projects, three heavy industry projects and one nuclear power generation project.   Investment in the ten major projects comprised 4.5% of total investment in the years 1973 and 1974, and about 20% in 1975 and 1976.   Actually, the ten major projects were not designed to counter the business cycle or other such phenomenon, but rather to develop the infrastructure and heavy industry.   It was a nice coincidence that this

Table 10.11   An Estimation of Tax Reductions in 1974

Taxes	Tax Revenues (NT$ billion)	Estimated Tax Reductions (NT$ billion)	Percentage of Tax Reductions (%)
Income taxes	15.77	0.36	2.3
Customs duties	26.66	6.74	25.3
Commodity taxes	13.90	3.94	28.3
Harbor dues	5.88	0.07	1.2
Total	86.45	11.11	12.9

Source: Economic Planning Council, Executive Yuan, "An Estimation of Tax Reductions in 1974" (mimeo.).

Table 10.12   Investment in the Ten Major Projects and GNP Growth Rate

(%)

Year	Percentage of Investment in the Ten Major Projects in Total Investment	Growth Rate of GNP
1973	4.5	12.8
1974	4.5	1.1
1975	19.3	4.2
1976	19.6	13.5
1977	13.1	9.9
1978	8.1	13.9

Source: Council for Economic Planning and Development, Executive Yuan, *An Evaluation of Ten Major Projects,* 1979; Directorate-General of Budget, Accounting & Statistics, Executive Yuan, *National Income of the Republic of China,* 1981.

public spending was well-timed. Thus, the implementation of the ten major projects contributed greatly to the fast recovery in 1975 and to prosperous growth thereafter.

2. Policies in the Wake of the Second Oil Crisis

The impact of the second oil crisis was comparatively mild in terms of the rise in inflation and the decline in the growth rate.   However, the process of adjustment took more time than in the previous crisis.   No radical government measures were taken this time; the mild and gradual measures that were adopted were directed to the more rational pricing of oil and its products, a foreign exchange rate determined more by market forces, and a more liberalized interest rate. These points will be elaborated on below.

(1) Pricing of Oil and Its Products

After the one-shot increase in oil and electricity prices in 1974, their domestic prices were kept relatively low in order to prevent serious price fluctuations, lessen the economic burden of low-income people, and maintain the competitiveness of manufactured exports. As a result of the low energy pricing policy, manufacturing firms were slow to adjust and improve their equipment and production processes.   Consequently, the entire manufacturing structure adjusted rather slowly to the oil-induced changes in the 1970s.

Greater reliance has been placed on the price mechanism following the second oil crisis. Domestic oil prices have been allowed to change in a manner more reflective of import costs. During 1979–81, prices of both oil and electricity were raised every year (see Table 10.9). However, there is still much room for improvement in the use of the price mechanism to promote more efficient energy use and to encourage further energy conservation.

(2) Foreign Exchange

In order for the foreign exchange rate to reflect the market rate more closely, the foreign exchange system was converted to a floating rate system from the previous fixed rate system in February 1979. Since then, the value of the New Taiwan dollar has changed more frequently: six times in 1979; 17 times in 1980; 39 times in 1981; and 32 times in the first eight months of 1982. However, the fluctuations were very mild.

The exchange rate was set by the Foreign Exchange Center, which based its decisions on the cumulative excess demand or excess supply of foreign exchange, counting from the day when the foreign exchange banks cleared their balance with the Central Bank of China. Since August 12, 1981, when the New Taiwan dollar was devalued by 4.6% against the U.S. dollar in one day, the real effective exchange rate has also been taken into consideration in the determination of the exchange rate. This was done in order to prevent over-valuation or under-valuation of the New Taiwan dollar.

(3) Interest Rates

According to the present banking law, the maximum rates for different types of deposits are prescribed by the Central Bank of China, and the range of interest rates for different loan categories are proposed by the Bankers' Association and submitted to the Central Bank of China for endorsement and enforcement. In order to move towards interest rate liberalization, the Central Bank of China promulgated the "Essentials of Interest Rate Adjustment" in November 1980. This regulation allows for a larger spread between maximum and minimum interest rates, and flexible interest rates on CD's. With the intention of moving closer to market-determined interest rates, interest rates were adjusted ten times from November 1980 to September 1982. As can be seen in Fig. 10.2, the movement of interest rates during this period was rather close to the movement of money market rates and call rates, which were not strictly subject to ceiling regulations. Actually, the permissible range of the call rate has been expanded gradually, which has made it possible for the rate to reflect the excess reserves in the banking system. As interest liberalization was emphasized, the movement of the interest

Fig. 10.2   Changes in Interest Rates on Commercial Paper, Interbank Call Loans, Bank Loans, and Net Excess Reserves of Domestic Banks [5/] (August 1980 – October 1982)

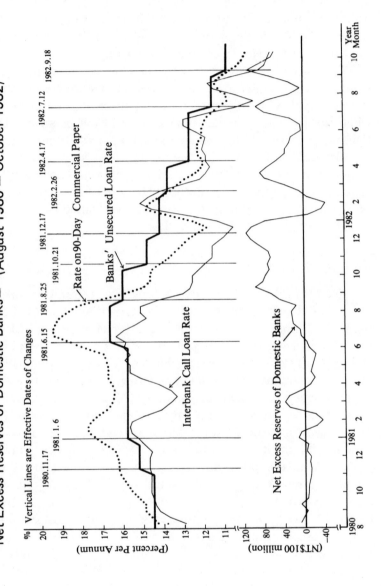

rate became even closer to the money market rate and the call rate after January, 1982.

(4) Fiscal Policies

No particularly active fiscal policies were implemented during this period. This was partly due to the desire to prevent a crowding out of money by heavy public investment, and partly due to the fact that the government budget, which had been in surplus every year for more than a decade, started to show a deficit after 1980.

Although the impact of the second oil shock was large, prolonged, and widespread, it seems to be approaching its end. Inflation, as of August, 1982, had been brought down significantly and the Taiwan economy seemed to be bottoming out. It is our hope that the past experience will be of some use in solving future problems.

NOTES

1. e.g., Sung Y. Kwack, Jane-yu Li, and Fenwick W. Yu, "A Model of the Taiwan, R.O.C. Economy for Analysis of Policy Effects and External Influences," SRI/WEFA World Economic Program Discussion Papers, No. 7 (Virginia 1980); Directorate-General of Budget, Accounting and Statistics, Executive Yuan, *Econometrics Model of Taiwan* (Taipei: DGBAS 1978).

2. Fig. 10.1 is comparable to figures used by Professor Milton Friedman, in Milton Friedman, "Money and Inflation" (Taipei: Academia Sinica, The Institute of Economics, 1981).

3. The increment of net worth of deposit banks is the additional self-owned capital of those banks, which naturally can be used for loans and investment. Therefore, in the calculation of excess loans, this item should also be taken into account. The present *Financial Statistics Monthly* places the change in the net worth of deposit banks and of the Central Bank in the "others" category. In order to be able to see the sources of change in the money supply, therefore, we need to take these two kinds of net worth out from the "others"

category, and put them in the right place. Namely, first, in the calculation of changes in excess loans, the change of net worth of deposit banks should be included in the subtraction; second, in the calculation of changes in net foreign assets as a source of changes in money supply, the change in net worth of the Central Bank is subtracted from the amount of changes in net foreign assets. This is based on the evidence that the change in net foreign assets exceeds the change in net worth of the Central Bank which does not constitute a source of money supply.

4. By basic balance we mean the balance of the current account plus the net long-term capital inflow plus net direct investment.

5. (1) Rates on 90-day commercial paper are the moving average of three end-of-10-day-period figures.
    (2) Banks' unsecured loan rates are the average of maximum and minimum rates.
    (3) Interbank call loan rates and net excess reserves of domestic banks are the moving average of means of three 10-day periods.

PART IV

11

Technical Change and Factor Utilization

The rate of technical progress measures the rate of increase in output that is not caused by an increase in input but by an advancement in the efficiency of production. This concept has many other names: "change in total factor productivity," "change in productive efficiency," "change in output per unit of input," "residual," etc. are the typical ones.

The purpose of this chapter is to analyze the rates of technical change of the nonagricultural sectors in Taiwan for the period 1952–80. During these three decades the Taiwan economy grew very rapidly. But how did technical change contribute to this rapid growth? Did the contribution of technical progress play the same role in the different periods? How did the economy's leading industries behave during this period? What role did the domestically produced and imported intermediate inputs play in the course of development? These are the main questions we will focus on in this chapter.

Two types of measures will be used. They are the value added production function developed by Professor R.M. Solow,[1] and the gross production function inclusive of intermediates based on an input-output method.[2] The value added production function is in the form of Equation (1) and the gross production function is in the form of Equation (2):

(1) Y = $h(t) \, f(L, K)$

(2) X = $H(t) \, F(L, K, x^d, x^m)$

where Y =   value added

L =   labor

K =   capital stock

X =   gross output

x^d =   domestically produced intermediate inputs

x^m =   imported intermediate inputs

t =   time

$h(t)$ and $H(t)$ = technical change

Although two types of production function are used, the same theoretical framework will be applied on them. Namely,

(1) the production functions are assumed to exhibit constant returns to scale;

(2) the necessary conditions for a producer equilibrium hold, so that factors are paid the value of their marginal products; and

(3) quantities of output and input entering the production functions are identified with real products and real factor inputs.

Data used in the two measurements are different. For the value added production function, national income data are used. The manufacturing sector is examined only at the aggregate level, and observations are yearly series for the period 1952–80.   For the gross production function, the input-output data deflated into consistent domestic constant prices are used.[3]   The measurements are done for 46 disaggregated nonagricultural sectors, and observations are for the four years 1961, 1966, 1971 and 1976. Accordingly, the period of observation by this approach is 1961–76.

I. Technical Change Assessed by Value Added Production Function, 1952–1980

In this section, technical changes in the nonagricultural, manufacturing, and service sectors of the Taiwan economy for the period 1952–80   will be measured by a Solow type of production function.   The production function in a Cobb-Douglas form can be written as

$$(3) \quad Y \; = \; A_o \, e^{gt} \, K^{\alpha} \, L^{1-\alpha}$$

where

Y = value added (net of indirect taxes)

e = base of natural logarithm

g = rate of technical change

t = year

K = capital

L = labor

α = capital share

The period of observation is divided into two sub-periods, 1952–61 and 1961–80.[4]   The results show that the rates of technical progress in the nonagricultural, manufacturing, and service sectors are all much higher in the first period than in the second.   Their contributions to the growth of the respective sectors were accordingly much higher in the first period than in the second.   Technical progress explained approximately 50% of the growth in the first period, but only 12% of non-agricultural, 17% of service, and 7% of manufacturing growth in the second period.   The rates of technical progress in the 1960s were not smaller than those in the 1950s: 6.4% vs. 6.5% for the manufacturing sector; 4.6% vs. 4.0% for the service sector; and 5.1% vs. 5.0% for the nonagricultural sector.   However, due to higher growth rates of value added realized in the 1960s than in the 1950s, the percentage of contribution to the growth rate made by technical progress was smaller in the

1960s than in the 1950s, ranging from 20% to 34%. Technical progress deteriorated significantly in the 1970s; e.g., technical change in manufacturing registered a very meager rate of 1.1% for the period 1971—80.

Table 11.1   Technical Change Rates and Their Contributions to Growth Rates in the Nonagricultural, Manufacturing, and Service Sectors (1952—1980)

(%)

Sector and Period	Rate of Technical Change	Value Added Growth Rate	Contributions of Technical Change to Growth Rate
Nonagricultural sector			
1952—61	5.0	8.3	53
1961—80	3.1	11.1	12
1961—71	5.1	12.2	30
1971—80	1.3	9.9	9
Manufacturing sector			
1952—61	6.5	12.1	42
1961—80	3.4	14.4	7
1961—71	6.4	18.1	20
1971—80	1.1	10.5	7
Service sector			
1952—61	4.0	6.9	51
1961—80	3.1	9.4	17
1961—71	4.6	10.3	34
1971—80	1.6	8.3	15

Source: Directorate-General of Budget, Accounting and Statistics, Executive Yuan, *National Income of the Republic of China* (1980); Shirley W.Y. Kuo, "Labor Absorption in Taiwan, 1954—1971," *Economic Essays*, Vol. 7 (Taipei: National Taiwan University, Graduate Institute of Economics, November 1977); Directorate-General of Budget, Accounting and Statistics, Executive Yuan, *Yearbook of Labor Statistics, Republic of China* (1980).

The slowdown in the rate of technical progress in the manufacturing sector deserves attention. This slowdown was caused by the fact that during 1971—80 capital stock grew at a much higher rate than value added, 14.0% vs. 10.5%. At the same time, labor grew at 6.2%, bringing the weighted average of the growth rates of capital and labor very close to the growth rate of value added in manufacturing.

Table 11.2   Growth Rates of Capital Stock, Labor
and Value Added in Manufacturing
(1952—1980)

(%)

Period	Value Added Growth Rate	Labor Growth Rate	Capital Stock Growth Rate
1952—61	i2.1	2.7	8.7
1961—80	14.4	6.6	14.8
1961—71	18.1	7.0	15.5
1971—80	10.5	6.2	14.0

Source: Same as Table 11.1.
Note: Capital stock refers to capital in use.

In short, assessment by a Cobb-Douglas production function shows that economic growth in the 1950s was largely attributable to technical progress.   The contribution of technical change decreased in the 1960s.   In 1971—80, the high rate of manufacturing growth was largely attributable to the large amount of investment and rapid labor absorption, namely, more to factor utilization than to technical change.

To give a clearer look at manufacturing, we shall use another approach in terms of gross production function to assess the technical changes of manufacturing and manufacturing sub-industries for this later period.

II. Technical Change Assessed by Gross Production Function, 1961–1976

1. The Model

In this section, the rates of technical change of the non-agricultural, manufacturing, and service sectors of the Taiwan economy over the period 1961–76 are measured by a gross production function.

For the model, the following notations will be used:

n   = number of sectors in the input-output table

X   = domestic production

x_{ij}^{d} = amount of domestically produced input i that is used in the production of output j

x_{ij}^{m} = amount of imported input i that is used in the production of output j

L_j = amount of labor used in the production of output j

K_j = amount of capital used in the production of output j

a_{ij}^{d} = value share of domestically produced input i in output j

a_{ij}^{m} = value share of imported input i in output j

ℓ_j = labor income share in output j

k_j = capital income share in output j

T_j = amount of indirect taxes paid on output j

A_o = constant

g   = rate of technical change

t   = year

p_j^{d} = domestic price index of output j

p_j^{m} = import price index of output j

A gross production function in a Cobb-Douglas form can be written as follows.

$$X_j = A_{oj} e^{g_j t} \prod_{i=1}^{n} x_{ij}^{d}{}^{a_{ij}^d} \prod_{i=1}^{n} x_{ij}^{m}{}^{a_{ij}^m} L_j^{\ell_j} K_j^{k_j}$$

(4)   and

$$\sum_{i=1}^{n} a_{ij}^d + \sum_{i=1}^{n} a_{ij}^m + \ell_j + k_j = 1$$

$$(j = 1, 2, \cdots, n)$$

or in the logarithm form,

$$(5) \quad \ell n\, X_j = \ell n\, A_{oj} + g_j t + \sum_{i=1}^{n} a_{ij}^d \, \ell n\, x_{ij}^d + \sum_{i=1}^{n} a_{ij}^m \, \ell n\, x_{ij}^m$$

$$+ \ell_j \, \ell n\, L_j + k_j \, \ell n\, K_j \qquad (j = 1, 2, \cdots, n)$$

where the term $\ell n\, A_{oj} + g_j t$ measures the status of technology. Writing this technology term as a dependent variable $\ell n\, G_j$, we have Equation (6) to express the status of technology of industry j in a particular year:

$$(6) \quad \ell n\, G_j = \ell n\, A_{oj} + g_j t = \ell n\, X_j - \sum_{i=1}^{n} a_{ij}^d \, \ell n\, x_{ij}^d$$

$$- \sum_{i=1}^{n} a_{ij}^m \, \ell n\, x_{ij}^m - \ell_j \, \ell n\, L_j - k_j \, \ell n\, K_j$$

$$(j = 1, 2, \cdots, n)$$

Since no yearly time series of I-O data are available, we can only calculate the rate of technical change by a discrete comparison. The growth rate of any variable Q can be expressed as $\Delta Q / Q$, which is equal to $\Delta \ell n\, Q$. Using g to denote the rate of technical change, we therefore have

$$g_j \;=\; \Delta \ln G_j$$

$$(7) \qquad =\; \Delta \ln X_j \;-\; \sum_{i=1}^{n} a_{ij}^{d} \,\Delta \ln x_{ij}^{d} \;-\; \sum_{i=1}^{n} a_{ij}^{m} \,\Delta \ln x_{ij}^{m}$$

$$-\; \ell_j \,\Delta \ln L_j \;-\; k_j \,\Delta \ln K_j \qquad (j = 1, 2, \cdots, n)$$

Equation (7) is the one used to calculate the rate of technical change in this study.[5]   The results of observations for j = (12 − 57) nonagricultural sectors, as combined into 20 sectors, are shown in Table 11.3.

As can be seen in Table 11.3 rates of technical change estimated by the gross production function show the same tendency as that estimated by the value added production function: slower rates of technical change in 1971−76 than in 1961−71. Of the twenty nonagricultural industries, only three had higher rates of technical change in 1971−76: food-beverage−tobacco, petroleum-coal products, and wholesale-retail trade.   Chemical industry had a negative rate of technological change, possibly due to heavy investment in the petrochemical industry both in the public and private sectors for the production of high-valued new petrochemical products, but with a time lag before the beginning of production. The deterioration   in   technical   progress   during   1971−76   in machinery, electrical machinery, and transport equipment is noteworthy, for those industries have been the leading manufacturing industries.

In Table 11.4 the rates of technical change are aggregated to the nonagricultural, manufacturing, and service sectors. In this aggregation, domestic productions X_j are used as weights.   These aggregated magnitudes show the following characteristics:

1) The rates of technical progress in all sectors were higher in 1961−71 than in 1971−76.

2) The service sector had a higher rate of technical progress than manufacturing in 1961−71, but the order was reversed in 1971−76.

3) Heavy manufacturing had a higher rate of technical

Table 11.3   Rate of Technical Change in Nonagricultural Industries

(%)

(Number of Industry by I-O Classification)	Industry	Rate of Technical Change	
		1961 ~71	1971 ~76
1. (12+13+14+15+16 +17+18+19+20)	Food, beverage, tobacco	0.9	2.3
2. (21+22+23+24+25)	Textiles and footwear	2.6	1.7
3. (26+27+28)	Wood, furniture	2.8	2.1
4. (29)	Paper, printing, publishing	2.9	0.6
5. (30)	Leather	1.6	1.1
6. (31)	Rubber	3.4	−1.0
7. (32+33+34+36+37)	Chemicals	4.3	−0.2
8. (35)	Petroleum and coal products	0.4	1.7
9. (38+39)	Non-metallic mineral products	3.4	2.2
10. (40)	Basic metal	2.2	0.9
11. (41+42+43)	Metal products	2.5	1.5
12. (44)	Machinery	4.7	1.4
13. (45+46+47)	Electrical machinery	6.0	5.0
14. (48)	Transportation equipment	3.6	1.4
15. (49)	Miscellaneous manufactures	8.1	3.6
16. (50)	Construction	2.4	0.3
17. (51+52+53)	Electricity, gas and city water	2.6	1.1
18. (56)	Wholesale and retail trade	1.1	2.9
19. (54+55)	Transportation, warehousing and communications	3.9	2.6
20. (57)	Services	4.1	0.6

Source: Based on recompiled and deflated Input-Output Tables for 1961, 1966, 1971 and 1976. As to the sector names, see Appendix IV.

progress than light manufacturing in both sub-periods. The difference, however, was much greater in 1961—71. This was similar to Japan's case in the period 1955—63. The United States also had a higher rate of technical progress in heavy industry than in light industry in 1946—57, although the difference between heavy and light industries was smaller than in the cases of Japan in 1955—63 and Taiwan in 1961—71 (See Tables 11.4 and 11.5).

Regarding the deterioration of technical progress in 1971—76, a few points should be noted. First, during this period, capital increased at a very high annual rate of 16.2%. It is our general understanding that rapid capital investment will increase productivity. However, the situation in this period was just the opposite. One possible reason is that much capital was invested in heavy industries during this period—the typical

Table 11.4   Rate of Technical Change in Nonagricultural Sector (Based on I-O measurement)

(%)

Sector	Rate of Technical Change	
	1961—71	1971—76
Nonagricultural sector	2.9	1.9
Industrial sector	2.8	1.9
Service sector	3.1	1.6
Manufacturing sector	2.9	2.1
Light manufacturing	2.1	2.0
Heavy manufacturing	4.1	2.3

Source: Same as Table 11.3.
Note: Light manufacturing includes food, beverages and tobacco, textiles and footwear, wood and furniture, leather, basic metal, metal products, and miscellaneous manufactures. Heavy manufacturing includes paper, printing and publishing, rubber, chemicals, petroleum and coal products, non-metallic mineral products, machinery, electrical machinery, and transportation equipment.

Table 11.5   Rates of Technical Change, Japan and
the U.S. (Based on I-O measurement)

(%)

Sector	Japan (1955—63)	U.S. (1946—57)
	Gross Output	Value Added
Manufacturing sector	1.72	1.93
Light manufacturing	0.95	1.71
Heavy manufacturing	2.20	2.04
Service sector	4.07	—

Source: Mitsuo Saito, *General Equilibrium and Price* (Tokyo: Sobunshia, 1975) p. 88.
Note: The estimations are based on the Input-Output Model.

ones were electricity (particularly nuclear power), a steel mill, a shipyard, and petrochemical plants. It is probable that while investment had already been made, the added output had not yet been fully produced. In other words, during this period, production in heavy industries might have greatly lagged behind investment.

Second, in 1974 and 1975 the Taiwan economy experienced a serious recession due to the oil crisis and the worldwide recession. The growth rates of the value added in these two years were respectively 1.1% and 4.2%, dropping from 12.8% in 1973. However, the number of employed did not decrease very much because adjustments for the decline in demand were made mostly through hours of work and wage changes rather than through the number of workers. Thus, the growth rate of labor shown in the statistics was not so much affected by the recession.

Third, there was a significant deterioration in the speed of development of leading industries in 1971—76. By leading industries we mean the top six manufacturing industries as ranked by the growth rates of gross output, exports and employment during the 1960s. They were electrical machinery,

machinery, transportation equipment, textiles, leather, and miscellaneous manufacturing. The rates of technical change in these six industries all decreased in 1971—76.

Among the six leading industries, the product share of leather was trivial, and the contents of miscellaneous manufacturing too sundry. Thus only four industries—electrical machinery, machinery, transportation equipment, and textiles—will be taken up for further observation.

The growth rates of gross output, value added, and exports of these four leading industries were all smaller in 1971—76 with no single exception (Table 11.6). We also notice the tremendously rapid expansion of the electrical machinery industry in 1961—71 and the slowdown of its expansion in 1971—76.

Table 11.6   Growth Rates of Gross Output, Value Added and Exports of the Four Leading Industries

(%)

Industry	Growth Rates of Gross Output		Growth Rates of Value Added	
	1961—71	1971—76	1961—71	1971—76
Textiles and footwear	28.9	17.0	19.7	7.2
Machinery	29.5	10.4	18.6	13.8
Electrical machinery	49.6	26.2	36.1	12.9
Transportation equipment	28.4	16.5	23.3	12.1
Manufacturing average	19.6	15.0	15.7	11.4

Source: Gross output and Exports: based on the recompiled Input-Output data in 1971 constant prices.
Value added: Directorate-General of Budget, Accounting and Statistics, Executive Yuan, *National Income of the Republic of China*, 1961, 1971 and 1976.

The relative rapidity of growth of these four leading industries can be measured by the ratio of the growth rate of each industry to the average manufacturing growth rate. A significant decline in these relative growth rates in 1971—76 shows a weakened leading force of the four leading industries during those years.

The faster relative growth of these four industries in the 1960s significantly increased their shares of gross output and value added in manufacturing during 1961—71, from 22.7% to 37.1% in the case of gross output and from 22.9% to 41.3% in the case of value added. However, the relative deterioration in the growth of the four industries in the 1970s reduced their shares in manufacturing to even smaller levels

Growth Rates of Exports		Industry
1961—71	1971—76	
33.3	22.9	Textiles and footwear
38.0	20.8	Machinery
71.9	30.2	Electrical machinery
50.5	28.6	Transportation equipment
24.4	21.4	Manufacturing average

than 1971. The past success of manufacturing development in Taiwan was characterized by product cycles: first food processing, then textiles, and then electrical machinery and transportation equipment took the lead. In the early period before 1971, the textile industry successfully took the place of declining food processing. However, the evidence shown in Table 11.7 seems to indicate that the three leading industries which emerged in the 1960s—electrical machinery, machinery, and transportation equipment—were not able to satisfactorily replace the outgoing old industries (including textiles) in the 1970s. Since technical progress and rapid growth of output influence each other, the slowdown of the growth rates in the leading manufacturing industries acted unfavorably on the advancement of technology in the 1970s.

Table 11.7   Changes in the Shares of Leading Industries in Manufacturing

(%)

Industry	Shares of Gross Output				
	1952	1961	1971	1976	1980
Textiles and footwear	17.0	16.9	21.5	18.3	14.9
Machinery	1.5	1.9	2.8	2.9	2.6
Electrical machinery	0.7	1.8	9.4	10.3	11.5
Transportation equipment	0.7	2.1	3.4	4.0	6.2
Sum of the above four industries	19.9	22.7	37.1	35.5	35.2

Source: Directorate-General of Budget, Accounting and Statistics, Executive Yuan, *National Income of the Republic of China,* various years.

The inclusion of intermediate inputs in the assessment of

technical change enables us to decompose the sources of output growth into the following five categories: technical change, domestically produced intermediate inputs, imported intermediate inputs, labor inputs, and capital inputs. Contributions by each of these categories can be identified through each term which appears on Equation (7) (on page 230). These contributions are summarized in Table 11.8.

The main conclusions drawn from Table 11.8 are as follows:

1) Contributions made by technical change to output growth in the nonagricultural sector decreased from 18.5% in 1961–71 to 15.0% in 1971–76. Contributions made by technical change to output growth in the manufacturing sector did not change much in the two periods, accounting for about 15%. However, for the service sector, contributions to output growth made by technical change decreased from 30% in 1961–71 to 22% in 1971–76.

2) Intermediate inputs comprised the dominant source of output growth, accounting for about 60% in the nonagricultural sector and 70% in the manufacturing sector. The growth in domestically produced intermediate inputs for manufacturing use contributed about 45% of manufacturing growth, while that of imported intermediate inputs contributed 25%, in both periods.

3) Light manufacturing showed a different pattern compared with heavy manufacturing, in that light manufacturing had a much larger contribution by domestically produced intermediate inputs than by imported intermediate inputs, 52.7% vs. 21.5% in 1961–71 and 51.1% vs. 18.2% in 1971–76. On the other hand, the contributions of domestic and imported intermediate inputs in heavy manufacturing were much closer, 38.8% vs. 29.7% in 1961–71 and 36.3% vs. 29.8% in 1971–76.

4) The contribution made by growth in capital input to output growth in 1971–76 was much larger than that made in 1961–71, accounting for 16.5% vs. 12.1% for the nonagricultural sector, 11.3% vs. 9.7% for the manufacturing sector, and 36.5% vs. 17.3% for the service sector. The larger contribution of capital growth in the service sector was attributable to implementation of "the ten major projects," through which

Table 11.8   Sources of Output Growth
(Percentage Distribution,
1961—1976)

(%)

Sector	Due to Technical Progress	Due to Growth in Labor Input	Due to Growth in Capital Input
1961—1971			
Nonagricultural sector	18.5	9.5	12.1
Manufacturing sector	14.8	6.1	9.7
Light manufacturing	12.9	5.5	7.4
Heavy manufacturing	14.8	5.8	10.9
Service sector	29.8	23.1	17.3
1971—1976			
Nonagricultural sector	15.0	11.0	16.5
Manufacturing sector	14.0	6.7	11.3
Light manufacturing	14.6	6.6	9.5
Heavy manufacturing	13.7	7.1	13.1
Service sector	21.6	31.1	36.5

Source: Same as Table 11.3.
Note: In aggregation, the shares of gross output of sub-industries in the I-O classification are used as weights.

a large amount of investment was made in transportation in
1974—77.

From the above observations, we may conclude that the
rates of technical change in Taiwan's nonagricultural sectors
were not the same for different periods. During the 1950s,
technical progress explained about one half of economic
growth. However, this contribution declined to about 20%

Due to Growth in Domestic Intermediates	Due to Growth in Inported Intermediates	Sector
		1961–1971
39.5	20.4	Nonagricultural sector
44.4	25.0	Manufacturing sector
52.7	21.5	Light manufacturing
38.8	29.7	Heavy manufacturing
23.1	6.7	Service sector
		1971–1976
38.6	18.9	Nonagricultural sector
43.3	24.7	Manufacturing sector
51.1	18.2	Light manufacturing
36.3	29.8	Heavy manufacturing
8.1	2.7	Service sector

in the 1960s and to around 15% in the 1970s. The high rate of economic growth in the 1970s was mostly attributable to the high rates of growth in capital and in manufactured intermediate inputs. The implementation of the ten major projects, through which a large amount of investment was made in infrastructure and heavy industry, contributed greatly to this capital growth.

NOTES

1. Robert M. Solow, "Technical Change and the Aggregate Production Function," *The Review of Economics and Statistics*, Vol. 39 (Aug. 1957).

2. Evsey D. Domar, "On the Measurement of Technological Change," *Economic Journal*, Vol. 71 (1961); Mieko Nishimizu and Charles R. Hulten, "The Sources of Japanese Economic Growth: 1955–71," *The Review of Economics and Statistics*, Vol. 60 (Aug. 1978); Mitsuo Saito, *General Equilibrium and Price* (Tokyo: Sobunshia, 1975); Tsunehiko Watanabe, "A Note on Measuring Sector Input Productivity," *Review of Income and Wealth*, Vol. 17 (Dec. 1971).

3. Among the four tables used in this study, 1966 and 1971 are original tables and 1961 and 1976 are extension tables. The quality of the 1971 table is superior to that of 1966, as the census in 1966 is considered to be biased. All four tables are consistently deflated in 1971 domestic constant prices. The original I-O table valued products for exports at world prices and products for domestic use at domestic prices. Consistency means the valuation of products for exports and domestic use both at domestic prices. $p_i^d x_{ij}^d$ are deflated first by nominal rates of protection at commodity level for each of the 58 sectors with some service sectors as exceptions. After this is done, domestic price indices at industry level are applied to deflate $p_i^d x_{ij}^d$ and $p_i^m x_{ij}^m$. Some service sectors and value added terms are deflated by the GDP deflator. In the deflation of price changes 1971 is used as the base year; however, the 1971 table is also deflated by nominal rates of protection for consistency.

4. The reasons for using 1961 as the demarcation year are:

    1) The second monetary reform was successfully achieved by 1961, as the average annual rate of price inflation came down from 10.5% in 1952–60 to 2.0% in 1961–65 and 2.9% in 1966–70.

    2) In 1961 the multiple exchange rate was abandoned, and the simple exchange rate became effective.

    3) The real wage rate, having remained nearly fixed, began to rise rapidly after 1961.

    4) The rate of labor absorption into the nonagricultural sector, having kept pace with the increase in total population, started to exceed population growth rapidly after 1962.

    5) The rate of investment in the manufacturing sector accelerated after 1961.

6) The average propensity to save increased from 4.5% of Net National Product in 1951–59 to 8.0% in 1963 and 12.0% thereafter. It can be inferred that a fundamental change in saving capability occurred between 1960 and 1963.

5. The double deflation technique for an I-O table is still an undeveloped area. The approach applied in the double deflation of the four tables of the Taiwan case follows the design of Dr. Larry Westphal and the late professor T. Watanabe. Although four years' x_{ij}'s in real terms were thus made and were used for decomposition of sources study elsewhere (Shirley W. Y. Kuo, "Economic Growth and Structural Change in the Republic of China" (Mimeo, prepared under the auspices of the World Bank, 1979), an intensive analysis of their "residuals" may not be very appropriate. Since a study of technology change is a study solely focusing on the change of residuals, any errors due to deflation may produce too great a weighting in the change and thereby obscure the true picture. Therefore, in this study, the x_{ij}'s other than those of 1971 are estimated via equilibrium conditions of profit maximizations as shown in Equations (A1) and (A2).

$$(A1) \quad x_{ij}^d = \frac{a_{ij}^d \, p_j^d \, (1 - t_j) \, X_j}{p_i^d}$$

$$(A2) \quad x_{ij}^m = \frac{a_{ij}^m \, p_j^d \, (1 - t_j) \, X_j}{p_i^m}$$

where

$$t_j = \frac{T_j}{\sum_{i=1}^{n} p_i^d x_{ij}^d + \sum_{i=1}^{n} p_i^m x_{ij}^m + W_j + R_j + T_j}$$

T_j = indirect taxes paid by industry j

W_j = compensation for labor used in industry j

R_j = compensation for capital used in industry j

In the calculation, 1971 data of a_{ij}^d, a_{ij}^m, ℓ_j, k_j and t_j are used. In the calculation of these output elasticities, indirect taxes are excluded. Other variables, X_j, L_j, K_j, p_j^d, p_i^d, and p_i^m are the respective figures for the calculation year. Measures of changes in 1961–71 are based on the observations for 1961–66 and 1966–71.

12

Structural Change and Technology of Tertiary Industry

The economic development of Taiwan in the past three decades was quite satisfactory, as rapid growth was accompanied by stable prices, achievement of full employment, and speedy industrialization. Studies on economic development in Taiwan are rather numerous. However, very few studies have been done on tertiary industry, which comprises about a half of the GNP. In order to shed some light on this under-explained area, this chapter attempts to analyze the structural change and technology of tertiary industry in Taiwan for the period 1952–81.

From the point of view of service rendered, tertiary industry can be divided into two parts: transportation and communications, and service industries. Transportation and communications in this study will be abbreviated to transportation. Service industries will be divided into commerce (consisting of wholesale and retail trade), finance (consisting of banking, insurance and real estate), all other services (consisting of dwelling services, government services, and miscellaneous services). One essential characteristic of tertiary industry is its dual character. That is, tertiary industry exists not only for itself, but also for others. Therefore, its positive external contributions to other industries deserve serious attention.

The first section of this chapter will examine growth, price change and employment in tertiary industries. The second section will analyze productivity and investment in tertiary industries. The third section will study the linkages of tertiary industries in the framework of input-output analysis. Finally, section four provides conclusions.

I. Growth, Price Change and Employment in Tertiary Industries

1. Growth of Tertiary Industries

The Taiwan economy has enjoyed very rapid growth over the past three decades. From 1952 to 1981, the real national product grew twelve times, increasing at an annual rate of 8.9%. Per capita income grew six times, increasing at an annual rate of 6.1%. Overall growth was accompanied by important changes in the structure of the economy. The share of primary industry in net domestic product dropped from 35.6% to 7.3%, and that of secondary industry rose from 17.8% to 44.1%. During this course of change, however, the share of tertiary industry remained around 49%. During the last 28 years, tertiary industry in Taiwan has grown at about the same rate as the NDP. The growth of secondary industry was much higher, while that of primary industry was much lower.

Breaking tertiary industry into the transportation and service industries, we find that the share of value added of transportation in tertiary industry increased from 8.2% in 1952 to 17.8% in 1981, with the growth rate increasing after 1961. Commerce, one of the service industries, decreased its share from 40.1% to 31.7%, while finance increased its share from 1.7% to 8.1%; other services, which include government services, decreased from 50% to 42.4%.

2. Price Change in Tertiary Industries

Price change in tertiary industry as a whole was slightly slower than that of the NDP during 1952–61, mainly due to the fact that the availability of abundant surplus labor during that period made the price change in service industries much

Table 12.1   Structure of the Net Domestic Product
(% of NDP, 1952–1981)

(in 1971 constant prices; %)

Year	NDP	Primary Industry	Secondary Industry	Tertiary Industry
1952	100.0	35.6 (32)	17.8 (22)	46.6
1961	100.0	27.7	23.9	48.4
1971	100.0	14.5	36.1	49.4
1981	100.0	7.3 (7)	44.1 (51)	48.6

Source: Directorate-General of Budget, Accounting & Statistics, Executive Yuan, *National Income of the Republic of China*, 1982.
Note: Figures in parentheses are shares in current prices.

Table 12.2   Growth Rate of Value Added of
the Three Industries (1952–1981)

(%)

Period	NDP	Primary Industry	Secondary Industry	Tertiary Industry
1952–56	7.4	3.8	13.2	7.6
1956–61	6.3	3.9	8.0	6.9
1961–66	9.8	5.6	12.9	10.4
1966–71	10.6	1.1	16.8	10.5
1971–81	9.0	1.8	11.3	8.9

Source: Same as Table 12.1.

slower than average. The situation started to change in 1961, as the economy moved closer to a state of full employment.

During the period 1966–71, service industries had an annual price increase of 6.7%, much higher than that of the primary and secondary sectors, as the economy reached its turning point in 1968 and achieved full employment in 1971. The high price change observed in 1971–76 was due to the influence of the first oil crisis, which caused the wholesale price

Table 12.3   Structure and Growth of Tertiary Industries
(Value Added, 1952—1981)

(in 1971 constant prices; %)

Year and Period	Tertiary Industry	Transportation	Service Industries	Commerce	Finance Finance	Finance Banking
Share of value Added						
1952	100.0	8.2	91.8	40.1	1.7	1.6
1961	100.0	8.0	92.0	29.5	3.5	2.8
1971	100.0	12.0	88.0	32.5	5.1	3.6
1981	100.0	17.8	82.2	31.7	8.1	6.1
Annual Growth Rate						
1952—56	7.6	7.9	7.6	4.6	25.4	24.8
1956—61	6.9	6.2	7.0	3.0	8.8	5.7
1961—66	10.4	13.8	10.1	12.1	16.5	14.2
1966—71	10.5	16.3	9.8	11.0	12.7	11.9
1971—81	8.9	13.3	8.1	8.6	14.0	14.8

Source: Same as Table 12.1.

index to jump 40% in 1974.

3. Employment and Labor Absorption by Tertiary Industries

The rapid growth of the economy was accompanied by substantial growth and structural change in employment. Employment in primary industry decreased dramatically over the last

In-surance and Real Estate	Other Services				Year and Period
	Other Services, Total	Dwelling Services	Govern-ment Services	Misc. Services	
				Share of value Added	
0.1	50.0	15.2	23.0	11.8	1952
0.7	59.0	12.2	36.2	10.6	1961
1.5	50.4	12.5	27.4	10.5	1971
2.0	42.4	11.9	18.6	11.9	1981
				Annual Growth Rate	
36.8	9.1	6.9	11.3	7.3	1952–56
33.9	9.4	2.9	13.9	5.0	1956–61
24.3	8.7	9.5	6.7	13.6	1961–66
14.6	8.8	12.0	8.1	7.3	1966–71
11.9	7.0	8.4	4.7	10.2	1971–81

thirty years, while that in nonagricultural industry increased: for secondary industry from 20.4% to 42.2%, and for tertiary industry from 28.2% to 39.0%.

One of the most important features of the economic development of Taiwan was the achievement of full employment by 1971. In the period 1961–81 employment in Taiwan increased by 3 million persons, equivalent to 99% of the number

Table 12.4   Price Change in the Three Industries
(1952–1981)

(%)

Period	NDP	Primary Industry	Secondary Industry	Tertiary Industry	Transpor- tation	Service Industries
1952–56	9.6	9.6	9.6	9.6	9.6	9.6
1956–61	8.6	11.0	9.2	6.8	12.9	6.2
1961–66	2.2	2.5	2.1	2.3	0.8	2.4
1966–71	4.5	2.0	4.0	6.2	1.9	6.7
1971–76	11.4	15.8	11.5	10.3	3.5	11.5
1976–81	9.9	8.8	9.5	10.8	8.6	11.2
1952–61	9.1	10.4	9.4	8.0	11.4	7.7
1961–71	3.4	2.2	3.0	4.2	1.4	4.5
1971–81	10.7	12.3	10.5	10.5	6.0	11.3

Source: Same as Table 12.1.

Table 12.5   Percentage Distribution of Employment in
the Overall Economy (1952–1981)

(%)

Year	Grand Total	Primary Industry	Secondary Industry	Tertiary Total	Transpor- tation
1952	100.0	51.4	20.4	28.2 100.0	11.2
1961	100.0	46.2	22.4	31.4 100.0	14.5
1971	100.0	35.1	30.3	34.6 100.0	15.3
1981	100.0	18.8	42.2	39.0 100.0	14.9

Source: Shirley W.Y. Kuo,"Labor Absorption in Taiwan, 1952–1971," *Economic Essays*,Vol. VII, National Taiwan University, Graduate Institute of Economics, November 1977; Directorate-General of Budget, Accounting & Statistics, Executive Yuan, *Year Book of Labor Statistics, Republic of China,* 1982.

employed in 1961. Appling the decomposition equations (4) and (4)' of Chapter 7, we can trace out sources of job opportunities.

In Table 12.7 causes of employment expansion are listed by sectoral origin. We note that productivity in manufacturing advanced most rapidly, so the employment release due to productivity advancement in this sector was largest throughout the period 1961—76.   But manufacturing also created the greatest number of job opportunities through export expansion. Particularly   during the second and third periods, the employment increase due to export expansion in manufacturing was large enough to account for more than 50% of its employment increase.

Labor absorption by tertiary industry was 193 thousand persons in 1961—66, 481 thousand persons in 1966—71, and 418 thousand persons in 1971—76, accounting for 51%, 47%, and 45%, respectively, of the increment of employment of the whole economy in each period.   Export expansion created a substantial amount of employment in tertiary industry

Industry

Commerce and Finance	Other Services	Year
37.7	51.1	1952
36.5	49.0	1961
41.8	42.9	1971
48.4	36.7	1981

Table 12.6   Relative Labor Absorption in the Eight Industries of the Economy

(%)

Industry	Increment of Employment of that Particular Industry in Total Increment of the Whole Economy				
	1954 ~61	1961 ~66	1966 ~71	1971 ~76	1976 ~81
The Whole Economy (thousand persons)	100.0 (420)	100.0 (377)	100.0 (1,015)	100.0 (925)	100.0 (1,009)
1. Agriculture	14.0	18.4	4.7	−1.7	−38.8
2. Mining	2.4	2.2	3.5	−2.0	−3.4
3. Manufacturing	25.2	23.8	37.5	63.1	54.6
4. Construction	5.5	5.1	14.0	7.8	23.2
5. Electricity, gas and water supply	1.2	1.1	0.6	−1.0	0.0
6. Transportation	7.6	7.1	6.9	9.1	5.3
7. Commerce and Finance	18.6	17.9	23.5	15.6	39.6
8. Others	25.5	24.4	9.3	9.1	19.5

Source: Same as Table 12.5.
Note: Figures in parenthesis are numbers of increase in employment during the period.

throughout the three periods. The contribution by export expansion to employment in tertiary industry reached as high as 28%, 28%, and 42% in the three respective periods.[1] In economic theory, particularly in pure theory, services are often treated as nontradables. In reality, however, services are also exported greatly, as seen in the Taiwan case.

II. Productivity and Investment in Tertiary Industries

The simultaneous achievement of stability and rapid growth

Table 12.7   Causes of Employment Expansion by Industrial Origin (1961–1976)

(%)

Period and Industry	In % of Employment Expansion Due to Output Expansion			
	Employ-ment Expan-sion Due to Output Expan-sion	Employ-ment Expan-sion Due to Domestic Expan-sion	Employ-ment Expan-sion Due to Export Expan-sion	Employ-ment Expan-sion Due to Import Substitution and I-O Changes
1961–66				
Agriculture	100	68	30	2
Manufacturing	100	44	43	13
Tertiary	100	87	28	−15
Whole economy	100	66	33	1
1966–71				
Agriculture	100	109	39	−48
Manufacturing	100	29	60	11
Tertiary	100	81	28	−9
Whole economy	100	65	45	−10
1971–76				
Agriculture	100	67	33	0
Manufacturing	100	20	81	−1
Tertiary	100	71	42	−13
Whole economy	100	45	59	−4

Source: Same as Table 7.6 on page 149. Calculation is based on the decomposition equations (4) and (4)' of Chapter 7 on page 147.

in the past three decades in Taiwan was possible only because of a significant rise in labor productivity. The industrial sector had a substantial increase in labor productivity, which in 1979 grew to 5.2 times that of 1952. Labor productivity in the tertiary and primary industries increased to 3.4 times and 2.5 times, respectively, over the 1952 levels. This substantial increase can be attributed to such factors as the use of high-efficiency machinery, the introduction of new equipment, improvements in management, and the advancement of workers' knowledge.

Table 12.8   Annual Labor Productivity Growth Rate of Tertiary Industries

(%)

Period	Tertiary Industry Total	Transpor-tation	Commerce and Finance	Other Services
1952–61	4.1	0.9	1.8	6.6
1961–71	5.7	9.6	5.6	5.4
1971–81	3.9	8.4	3.6	3.1

Source: Same as Tables 12.1 and 12.5.

Within tertiary industry, transportation, commerce and finance, and other services had different patterns of growth in their labor productivities. The labor productivity of transportation grew very slowly at an 1% annual rate in the period 1952–61, but then grew rapidly at 9.6% and 8.4%, respectively, in 1961–71 and 1971–81. Other services grew faster in the earlier period, and slowed down later. The relative contribution to the advancement in labor productivity of tertiary industry by each sub-industry can be seen in Table 12.9. We see that during the period 1952–61, the growth of labor productivity of other services accounted for as much as 80% of the total, while the contribution of transportation was almost nothing. The situation changed in later periods. The contribution of transportation increased to account for 24% and 31%,

Table 12.9   Relative Contributions to the Growth of
Labor Productivity of Tertiary Industry
by Each Sub-industry

(%)

Period	Labor Productivity Growth Rate of Total Tertiary Industry	Contribution by Transportation	Contribution by Commerce and Finance	Contribution by Other Services
1952–61	4.1	2.9	16.3	80.8
1961–71	5.7	23.5	36.4	40.1
1971–81	3.9	30.6	38.7	30.7

Source: Calculated as

$$\frac{w_i G_i}{\sum\limits_{i=1}^{3} w_i G_i}$$

where w_i = share of employment
G_i = growth rate of labor productivity
i = each sub-industry

and the contributions of commerce and finance each shared more than one third.   Some of the features which are closely related to this change and to productivity are explored below.

1. Investment and Capital Intensity

The growth rate of capital stock in tertiary industries showed a quite similar pattern to the growth of their labor productivity.   Investment was very low in all sub-industries during the early period of 1952–61, but tended to increase in 1961–71.   A rapid growth in capital was seen in transportation and other services during 1971–79.   This was brought about by the completion of the "ten major projects" that started in 1974 and were finished in 1979.[2]   Among these ten major

Table 12.10   Annual Growth Rate of Capital Stock
of Tertiary Industries

(%)

Period	Tertiary Industry Total	Transportation	Commerce and Finance	Other Services
1952–61	1.6	0.9	1.4	3.1
1961–71	5.9	4.7	4.0	8.4
1971–79	10.9	10.1	5.6	13.2

Source: Same as Tables 12.1 and 12.5.

projects, six were in transportation: North-South Expressway, Railway Electrification, North-link Railway, Chiang Kai-Shek International Airport, Taichung Harbor, and Suao Harbor Expansion. Government investment was also heavy during this period because some of the expenditures in the ten major projects were classified as government investment. Thus, investment in transportation was a decisive factor in the advancement of labor productivity of tertiary industry in the 1970s.

2.   Labor Productivity and Capital Intensity

The relationship between labor productivity and capital intensity in tertiary industries in Taiwan underwent a very interesting pattern as can be seen in Fig. 12.1. First, the capital intensity of tertiary industries in total did not increase at all before 1971, but labor productivity increased. Secondly, the capital intensity of the transportation sector significantly decreased every year before 1965. Thirdly, in the commerce and finance sector, a significant negative correlation is observed between labor productivity and capital intensity. Fourthly, other services, which include government services, experienced productivity advancement without any increase in capital

Fig. 12.1 Labor Productivity and Capital Intensity of Tertiary Industries (1952—1979)

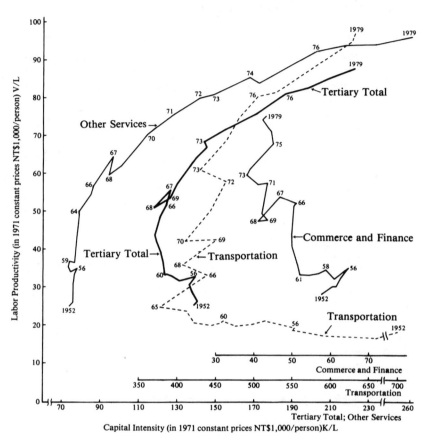

intensity before 1964.

One reason for the decrease in capital intensity of transportation as measured by capital/labor ratio in the early period may be that transportation was in relatively excess capacity at that early time, so that it could absorb a relatively larger portion of labor force. However, after it reached the point of full utilization, capital had to increase vis—a—vis the increase in labor force. Another conceivable reason is that at the same time, transportation had relatively capital-intensive technology change over the period.

Correlation between labor productivity (V/L) and capital intensity (K/L) shows the following results:

Total Tertiary Industry
(1952–79)   Significance level

$$\frac{V}{L} = -24 + 0.529 \frac{K}{L} \qquad R = 0.76 \qquad 1\%$$
$$(t = 6.02)$$

Transportation
(1952–65)   Significance level

$$\frac{V}{L} = 30 - 0.019 \frac{K}{L} \qquad R = -0.81 \qquad 1\%$$
$$(t = -4.82)$$

Transportation
(1965–79)   Significance level

$$\frac{V}{L} = -75 + 0.283 \frac{K}{L} \qquad R = 0.90 \qquad 1\%$$
$$(t = 7.46)$$

Commerce and Finance
(1952–79)   Significance level

$$\frac{V}{L} = 125 - 1.534 \frac{K}{L} \qquad R = -0.81 \qquad 1\%$$
$$(t = -7.03)$$

Other Services
(1952–79)   Significance level

$$\frac{V}{L} = 14 + 0.381 \frac{K}{L} \qquad R = 0.91 \qquad 1\%$$
$$(t = 10.90)$$

These results indicate that (1) in the total tertiary industry, labor productivity is highly correlated with capital intensity throughout the whole period; (2) transportation first had a negative correlation with a very small slope (1952–65), which then turned to a positive correlation (1965–79); (3) commerce and finance had a negative correlation, and other services had a positive correlation throughout the period. These observations seem to show that in the transportation sector, an increase in labor productivity cannot be achieved without an enhancement in capital intensity, while this may not be the case for the commerce and finance sector.

3. Investment in Transportation Compared with Direct Investment

Hirschman's theory of unbalanced growth is famous. It is also known as zigzag development due to the fact that during the course of development, the speed of direct and indirect investment will alternate. The relative speed of direct investment, which is defined here as the residual of total investment minus investment in transportation and electricity, and transportation investment in Taiwan for the period 1952–79, can be seen in Fig. 12.2. Each point on the figure designates both the growth rate of direct investment and the growth rate of transportation investment in that particular year. All those points which lie on the left hand side of the 45° line show a growth rate of direct investment higher than that of transportation investment. Conversely, all those points which lie on the right hand side of the 45° line show the growth rate of transportation investment exceeding that of direct investment.

From this figure we know that higher growth rate in investment in the directly producing industries (direct investment) alternated with investment in transportation every two or three years in past development in Taiwan.[3] We also note that investment in transportation grew at a particularly more rapid rate in 1975, 1976 and 1977, the period of implementation of the ten major projects, compared with direct investment. The much higher growth in labor productivity in transportation in the later period was mostly attributable to this rapid increase in capital intensity.

Fig. 12.2   The Relative Speed of Direct and Transportation Investment   (1952—1979)

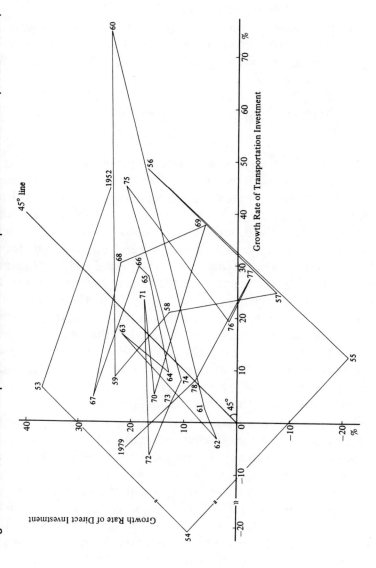

4. Scale of Operation in Commerce

In the very early stage of development, the commerce sector had a relatively higher labor productivity to start with. However, labor productivity in the commerce sector started to lag behind beginning in the late 1960s so as to make per-worker income of commerce only 85% of the per-worker income of the total tertiary industry in 1979. One possible important reason for this low productivity is that during the course of economic development, the commerce sector had very little expansion in its operation scale. In 1976, operation units with nine or fewer employees still comprised 96.3% of the total units, 254,977 out of 264,680, although this figure was down from 99.2% in 1961. Operation units with 10-19 employees comprised 2.6%; 20-99 employees, 1.0%; and 100-499 employees, 0.1%. Operation units employing

Table 12.11   Operation Scale Seen in the Distribution of Operating Units

(%)

Number of Employees	Percentage Share of the Number of Operating Units			
	1961	1966	1971	1976
1 – 9	99.2	98.4	97.8	96.3
10 – 19	0.6	1.2	1.7	2.6
20 – 99	0.2	0.4	0.5	1.0
100 – 499	0.02[1]	0.03	0.04	0.1
More than 500	0.001[2]	0.002	0.003	0.01

Source: The Committee on Industrial and Commercial Censuses of Taiwan-Fukien District of the Republic of China, Executive Yuan, *Industrial and Commercial Censuses of Taiwan-Fukien District of the Republic of China,* 1961, 1966, 1971 and 1976.

Notes:
1   for 100-399
2   for more than 400

more than 500 persons comprised only 0.01% of the total units in 1976, although the number of such units increased from one unit in 1961 to two units in 1966, 5 units in 1971, and 17 units in 1976.

The scale of operation in commerce can also be seen by its distributions of employment and wage income. As Table 12.12 shows, the distributions of employment and wage income are not as concentrated in the 1-9 employee category as are operation units. For example, employment in 1-9 employee category comprised only 70.2% of total employment in 1976, and wage income, 65.3% of the total.

Comparing the relative shares of employment and wage income of each category in each year, we note that only in the 1-9 employee category was the employment share bigger than the wage income share; for the rest, the wage income share was greater. This obviously shows that operations with 10 or more employees have higher labor productivity than those with less than 10. With more than 250 thousand small shops of less than 10 employees constituting more than 96% of the total commerce sector, and with only 17 units operating with more than 500 employees, it is apparent that one way to increase labor productivity in commerce is to rely heavily upon an expansion in operation scale.

III. Linkages of Tertiary Industries

Through the delivery of services to other sectors, tertiary industry has important impacts on the development of the whole economy. These impacts are called linkages of the service sector. Linkages have two dimensions, positive and negative. Better transportation facilities that provide efficient transportation of commodities are positive linkages; they can increase efficiency and reduce costs in the manufacturing sector. However, the reverse is also true for inefficient transportation facilities. Those services—communications, financial intermediaries, wholesale and retail trade, etc.—all have a very close relationship with other industries in this regard.

Since the problems of linkages are so broad and com-

Table 12.12   Relative Shares of Employment and Wage Income for Different Operating Scales

(%)

Number of Employees	Percentage Share of Employment				Percentage Share of* Wage Income		
	1961	1966	1971	1976	1966	1971	1976
1 – 9	90.8	86.4	81.2	70.2	81.3	74.1	65.3
10 – 19	3.6	6.3	8.2	11.1	8.0	10.4	12.7
20 – 99	3.8	4.6	6.9	11.7	7.1	9.9	13.5
100 – 499	1.6^1	2.1	2.8	4.9	2.3	4.7	5.7
More than 500	0.2^2	0.6	0.9	2.1	1.3	0.9	2.8

Source: Same as Table 12.11.
Notes:
     * No data available for 1961.
     1 for 100-399
     2 for more than 400

plicated, we will confine ourselves in this chapter to an examination of the linkage effects of tertiary industries in the framework of input-output analysis. The points upon which we will focus are the power of dispersion and the sensitivity of dispersion.

1.   Definitions of Power of Dispersion and Sensitivity of Dispersion

The concept of power of dispersion and sensitivity of dispersion will be used to examine the linkages of tertiary industries. The index of power of dispersion of industry j as raised by Rasmussen is composed of two parts, a numerator and a denominator.[4] The numerator R_j is the sum of direct and indirect increments in all industries induced by a unit increment of final demand in industry j . This is,

$$R_j = \sum_{i=1}^{n} r_{ij}$$

where r_{ij} is an element of Leontief's inverse matrix. From the interpretation of r_{ij} it follows readily that this sum of column elements can be interpreted as the total increase in output from the whole system of industries needed to cope with an increase in final demand for the products of industry j by one unit. The other part, the denominator, is an average of all r_{ij}, i.e. $\dfrac{1}{n} \sum_{j=1}^{n} \sum_{i=1}^{n} r_{ij}$. This denominator is used for normalization in order to be able to make inter-industry comparisons.

In this study, in order to identify the effects on other sectors but not on its own sector, power of dispersion is defined along the same line drawn by Professor Saito[5] by excluding the own effect, the diagonal element of the inverse matrix, r_{ii}. Thus, power of dispersion P_j is defined as:

$$P_j = \frac{\sum_{i=1, i \neq j}^{n} r_{ij}}{\dfrac{1}{n} \sum_{j=1}^{n} \sum_{i=1, i \neq j}^{n} r_{ij}} \qquad \ldots \ldots \ldots (1)$$

What does it mean when P_j for a given j is found to be larger than unity? According to the definition just given, it means that the industry j will need a comparatively large production increase in other industries to cope with a unit increase in final demand for the products of industry j. In other words, P_j would in this case express that industry j draws heavily on the system of industries, and *vice versa* when $P_j < 1$. It is for this reason that the index P_j is called the power of dispersion. The meaning of P_j may also be explained by saying that it expresses the extent of the expansion that industry j will cause in the system of industries.

The index of the sensitivity of dispersion of industry i as raised by Rasmussen is also composed of two parts. The numerator R_i is the sum of direct and indirect increments induced in industry i when all industries increase one unit each in final demand. This is,

$$R_i = \sum_{j=1}^{n} r_{ij}$$

Similarly, this sum of the row elements is taken to be the increase in output in industry i needed in order to cope with a unit increase in final demand for the product of each industry. The other part, the denominator, is $\dfrac{1}{n} \sum\limits_{i=1}^{n} \sum\limits_{j=1}^{n} r_{ij}$.

In order to identify effects by other sectors but not by its own, the sensitivity of dispersion is again defined along the same line drawn by Professor Saito by excluding the own effect, the diagonal element of the inverse matrix, r_{ii} . Thus, the sensitivity of dispersion S_i is defined as:

$$S_i = \frac{\sum\limits_{j=1, j \neq i}^{n} r_{ij}}{\dfrac{1}{n} \sum\limits_{i=1}^{n} \sum\limits_{j=1, j \neq i}^{n} r_{ij}} \quad \ldots \ldots \ldots \ldots (2)$$

It follows that when S_i is greater than unity, it means that industry i will have to increase its output more than other industries for a given increase in demand, and *vice versa* for $S_i < 1$. This is why S_i is termed the sensitivity of dispersion for the industry considered. Obviously, this index expresses the extent to which the system of industries draws upon industry i or, in other words, the extent to which industry i is affected by an expansion in the system of industries.

2. The Power of Dispersion and Sensitivity of Dispersion in 1966 and 1976

The power and sensitivity of dispersions for 1966 and 1976 are plotted respectively in Fig. 12.3 and Fig. 12.4. The vertical axis measures the power of dispersion; the horizontal axis measures the sensitivity of dispersion. The dotted lines indicate the average of all industries, which is normalized to be unity. Therefore, those points that lie in quadrant I have larger power and sensitivity than the average. In other words, their degree of dispersion is above average, while those that lie in quadrant III have a lesser degree of dispersion in terms of both power and sensitivity. Needless to say, those points that lie in quadrant II have larger power but smaller sensitivity, while those that lie in quadrant IV have smaller power but stronger sensitivity.

As we can see from these figures, land transportation, finance and insurance, and wholesale and retail trade (commerce) all lie in quadrant IV, indicating strong sensitivity of those tertiary industries. However, the points for air transportation, water transportation, warehousing, communications, and miscellaneous services lie in quadrant III, showing their little influence on and by other industries. Incidentally, we also note that the residential building industry had a very big power of dispersion.

It is studied and pointed out by Professor Saito in his excellent book, *General Equilibrium and Price*,[6] that when consumption is taken as an endogenous variable in the input-output system, the sensitivity of dispersion of the tertiary industries will be larger than that based on the Leontief system, due to the fact that the increase in consumption will generate stronger effects on the service sector, which will generate an additional need for services for final use. If this point is taken into consideration, the sensitivity of dispersion of commerce could be much bigger than we have observed based on the Leontief system.

3. Change in the Sensitivity of Dispersion of Tertiary Industries

By the above observation, we know that commerce and finance had a large sensitivity of dispersion in 1966 and 1976. In order to observe the transportation sector as a whole, land transportation, air transportation, water transportation, communications, and warehousing are further taken together as

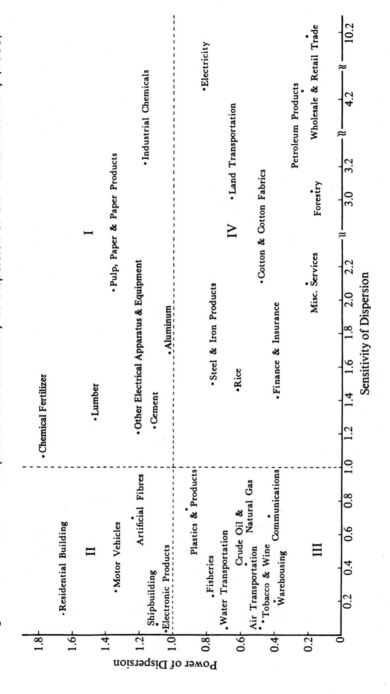

Fig. 12.3 The Power of Dispersion and Sensitivity of Dispersion of the Taiwan Economy (1966)

Fig. 12.4 The Power of Dispersion and Sensitivity of Dispersion of the Taiwan Economy (1976)

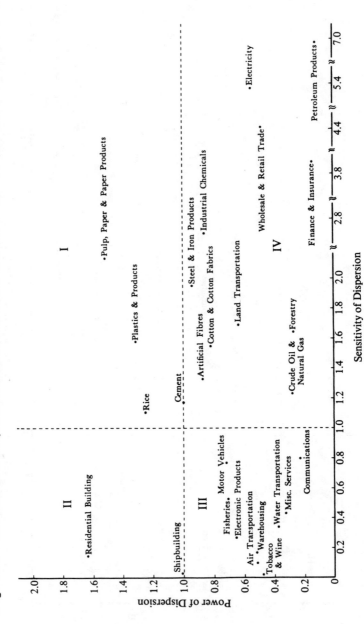

one sector to calculate the sensitivity of dispersion (their relative share of domestic production is used as the weight). We note that when this is done, the transportation sector shows a larger than one sensitivity of dispersion due to the large sensitivity in transportation.

It may be interesting to observe changes in sensitivity of dispersion of tertiary industries over time. The changes in sensitivity of dispersion of commerce, finance, and transportation for the period of 1956–76 can be seen in Fig. 12.5. The different pattern of movement is very impressive. First, the sensitivity of dispersion of commerce decreased over time, from 7.85 in 1956 to 4.41 in 1976. Second, transportation also had a decreasing tendency, falling from 4.60 in 1956 to 1.16 in 1976. Land transportation, which has the dominant share of about 65% in transportation, also had a decreasing sensitivity.   Third, the sensitivity of finance increased rapidly, from 1.42 in 1966 to 3.88 in 1976. These observations need further explanation.

Some details will be studied in the following:

(1) Transportation

We know that indices of sensitivity of dispersion of transportation in Japan for 1965, 1970, and 1975, and in Korea for 1975, were 2.92, 2.37, 2.43 and 2.27, respectively—similiar to Taiwan's case in 1966 and 1971. Their compositions of sensitivity are also very similar.   Judging from these data, one thing we are not very sure of is whether sensitivity of dispersion of transportation in 1976 was too small (it was very small compared with that of the past, and that of other countries), since the sensitivity calculated was a realized figure which does not tell us whether transportation service was enough to cope with the needs of intended growth at that time.

Breaking down the transportation sector into five subsectors: land transportation, water transportation, air transportation, communications, and warehousing, we find that it was land transportation that made the sensitivity of transportation greater than unity. The decrease in sensitivity of dispersion

Fig. 12.5   The Change in Sensitivity of Dispersion of Tertiary Industries in Taiwan (1956—1976)

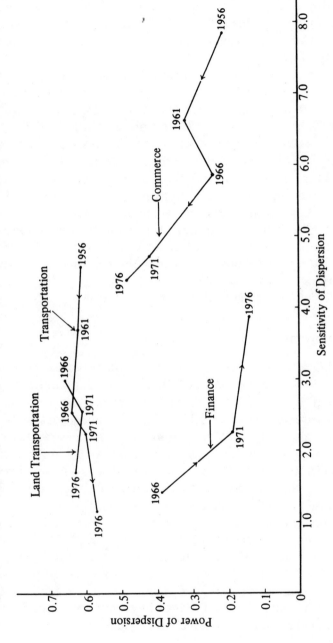

Table 12.13   Power of Dispersion and Sensitivity of Dispersion
of Tertiary Industries (1956—1976)

Year	Transportation		Commerce		Finance	
	Sensitivity of Dispersion	Power of Dispersion	Sensitivity of Dispersion	Power of Dispersion	Sensitivity of Dispersion	Power of Dispersion
1956	4.60	0.61	7.85	0.21	–	–
1961	3.70	0.62	6.61	0.32	–	–
1966	2.53	0.64	5.86	0.24	1.42	0.39
1971	2.25	0.60	4.73	0.42	2.26	0.19
1976	1.16	0.57	4.41	0.48	3.88	0.14

Source:
1. 1956—71 figures for transportation and commerce sectors are calculated from Input-Output Tables, recompiled by Shirley W.Y. Kuo, which are consistently deflated into 1971 domestic constant prices (for the deflation, see Note 8 of Chapter 7 on pages 172-173).
2. 1976 figures for all sectors and figures of the finance sector for all years are calculated from the Taiwan Input-Output Table, which is in current prices, compiled by the Council for Economic Planning and Development.

of the transportation sector was due solely to a rapid decrease in the sensitivity of land transportation, from 3.01 in 1966 to 1.69 in 1976. Water transportation and air transportation both had an increasing sensitivity of dispersion; however, their shares in transportation are still very small, comprising only 18.5% and 15.8% of all transportation in 1976. The sensitivity of communications is relatively high among the sub-sectors, although it is less than unity.

As to the causes of the larger sensitivity of dispersion in transportation, a decomposition in Table 12.15 shows us that the main factor was manufacturing. Manufacturing accounted for about 70% of the sensitivity of transportation in 1971 and 63% of the sensitivity of land transportation in 1976.

Since manufacturing was the dominant cause of the large

Table 12.14   Power of Dispersion and Sensitivity of
Dispersion of Transportation Sub-sectors
(1966—1976)

Industry	1966		1971	
	Sensitivity of Dispersion	Power of Dispersion	Sensitivity of Dispersion	Power of Dispersion
Land transportation	3.01	0.66	2.55	0.61
Water transportation	0.04	0.68	0.11	0.44
Air transportation	0.04	0.48	0.06	0.31
Communications	0.71	0.44	0.75	0.36
Warehousing	0.20	0.40	0.13	0.62

Source: Calculated from Input-Output Table, which is in current prices, compiled
by the Council for Economic Planning and Development.

sensitivity of dispersion of transportation, we would like to
decompose this effect further to observe the influence of
manufacturing sub-sectors.   The sub-sectors which have relatively large influence on the sensitivity of dispersion of transportation are: food processing, chemicals, lumber and wood
products, and non-metallic mineral products. A rapid decrease
in the share of final demand of food processing, from 36% of
total manufacturing in 1971 to 28% in 1976, and the reduction
of the shares of non-metallic mineral products and lumber and
wood products by 3% and 16% respectively, thus contributed
greatly to the reduction of the burden on transportation.

(2) Commerce

The sensitivity of dispersion of commerce in Taiwan had a

1976		
Sensitivity of Dispersion	Power of Dispersion	Industry
1.69	0.63	Land transportation
0.34	0.38	Water transportation
0.10	0.52	Air transportation
0.80	0.23	Communications
0.17	0.52	Warehousing

decreasing tendency, falling from 7.85 in 1956 to 4.41 in 1976. Manufacturing accounted for more than 80% of the total influence in the early period, and fell slightly to 73% in 1976. Taking its place was miscellaneous services, which accounted for 4% of commerce in 1976. Agriculture accounted for about 10% of commerce.

The sensitivity of dispersion of commerce in Japan, on the contrary, had a slightly increasing tendency, raising from 4.10 in 1965 to 4.93 in 1975. Manufacturing accounted for close to 60%, and miscellaneous services induced about 20% of commercial services. The Korean case shows a 6.77 sensitivity of dispersion in 1975. Manufacturing accounted for 70% of the total influence, while miscellaneous made up 10%.

With these results, it is too early for us to draw any conclusions about the changes in sensitivity of dispersion of commerce

Table 12.15   Influence by Each Sector on Sensitivity of Dispersion of Transportation and Land Transportation (1956–1976)

Sensitivity of Dispersion Caused by	On Transportation			
	1956	1961	1966	1971
Agriculture	0.17	0.13	0.14	0.17
Mining	0.56	0.46	0.13	0.15
Manufacturing	3.25	2.56	1.88	1.57
Construction	0.15	0.12	0.08	0.12
Electricity, gas, water supply	0.29	0.23	0.13	0.07
Transportation other than land transportation	—	—	—	—
Communications	0.11	0.09	0.08	0.06
Commerce	0.04	0.03	0.04	0.04
Finance	—	—	—	—
Misc. services	0.03	0.02	0.02	0.02
Undistributed	—	0.06	0.03	0.05
Total	4.60	3.70	2.53	2.25

Source:
  1. 1956–71 figures for the transportation sector are calculated from Input-Output Tables, recompiled by Shirley W.Y. Kuo, which are consistently deflated into 1971 domestic constant prices (for the deflation, see Note 8 of Chapter 7 on Pages 172-173).

in Taiwan. We can only say that 1) the linkage of commerce is pretty large; 2) manufacturing was the dominant sector which caused commerce to grow, or we may say that commerce should grow in order to cope with manufacturing expansion; 3) commerce provides heterogeneous services. The very small scale of commercial services in Taiwan may be somewhat different from that of Japan, although we can also see many

On Land Transportation			Sensitivity of Dispersion Caused by
1966	1971	1971	
0.18	0.19	0.16	Agriculture
0.13	0.11	0.06	Mining
2.01	1.74	1.07	Manufacturing
0.22	0.30	0.20	Construction
0.11	0.06	0.02	Electricity, gas, water supply
0.24	0.07	0.10	Transportation other than land transportation
			Communications
0.02	0.02	0.01	Commerce
0.04	0.01	0.003	Finance
0.02	0.01	0.06	Misc. services
0.04	0.04	0.01	Undistributed
3.01	2.55	1.69	Total

2. 1966–76 figures for the land transportation sector are calculated from the Taiwan Input-Output Table, which is in current prices, compiled by the Council for Economic Planning and Development.

small shops in Japan.

(3) Finance

It is interesting to note that sensitivity of dispersion of finance in Taiwan increased rapidly during 1966–76, jumping from 1.42 to 3.88. The major cause of expansion arose from

Table 12.16 Sensitivity of Dispersion of Transportation Caused by Manufacturing Sub-sectors (1971)

Food (processed), including tobacco and drinks	0.1870
Textiles	0.0655
Lumber and wood products	0.1234
Papers and pulp products, printing and publications	0.0294
Leather products	0.0176
Rubber products	0.0173
Chemicals	0.1310
Petroleum and coal products	0.0034
Non-metallic mineral products	0.0914
Basic metals	0.0835
Machinery	0.0628
Transportation equipment	0.0121
Misc. manufacturing products	0.0146
Manufacturing	0.8390

Source: Calculated from Input-Output Tables, recompiled by Shirley W.Y. Kuo, which are consistently deflated into 1971 domestic constant prices(for the deflation, see Note 8 of Chapter 7 on Pages 172-173).

manufacturing, which increased from 0.70 to 2.69. The influence from miscellaneous services also increased rapidly, from 0.01 to 0.14.

Japan's sensitivity of dispersion increased slightly, from the previously high index of 2.83, to 3.51 from 1965 to 1975. Again, manufacturing accounted for the largest share. Also noticeable in Japan's case is a relatively important influence

Table 12.17 Influence of Each Sector on Sensitivity of Dispersion of Transportation in Japan and Korea

Sensitivity of Dispersion of Transportation Caused by	Japan			Korea
	1965	1970	1975	1975
Agriculture	0.19	0.19	0.19	0.12
Mining	0.18	0.16	0.18	0.07
Manufacturing	1.77	1.37	1.40	1.40
Construction	0.14	0.12	0.11	0.17
Electricity, gas, water supply	0.08	0.07	0.07	0.08
Transportation	—	—	—	—
Communications	0.04	0.03	0.03	0.03
Commerce	0.05	0.03	0.03	0.04
Finance	0.02	0.01	0.01	0.03
Misc. services	0.39	0.34	0.32	0.27
Undistributed	0.06	0.05	0.09	0.06
Sensitivity of Dispersion of Transportation	2.92	2.37	2.43	2.27

Source: Input-Output Table of Japan and Input-Output Table of Korea.

by miscellaneous services on finance. In other words, it is obvious that the financial sector provided more service to the miscellaneous services sector in Japan than in Taiwan or Korea. The sensitivity of dispersion in Korea was still small in 1975.

The expansion in externalities of the financial sector can also be seen from the indicators in Table 12.20.

During the period 1962 to 1979, the ratio of assets of all financial institutions in the GNP increased from 40.8% to 109.9%; their ratio of loans to GNP, from 31.0% to 69.2%; and their ratio of portfolio investments to GNP, 2.2% to 9.2%.

Table 12.18   Influence of Each Sector on Sensitivity of Dispersion of Commerce in Taiwan (ROC), Japan and Korea   (% Allocation)

Sensitivity of Dispersion of Commerce Caused by	Taiwan (ROC)				
	1956	1961	1966	1971	1976
Agriculture	8.8	7.9	8.0	10.6	11.3
Mining	3.2	3.6	2.9	4.2	2.2
Manufacturing	81.0	80.9	81.4	77.6	73.5
Construction	1.2	1.0	2.2	2.8	5.9
Electricity, gas, water supply	4.3	4.1	2.4	1.7	0.7
Transportation	0.6	0.6	0.7	0.4	1.6
Communications	0.8	0.6	0.5	0.4	
Commerce	—	—	—	—	—
Finance	—	—	—	—	0.1
Misc. services	0.1	0.2	0.4	0.4	3.6
Undistributed	—	1.1	1.5	1.9	1.1
Total (%)	100.0	100.0	100.0	100.0	100.0
Sensitivity of Dispersion of Commerce	7.85	6.61	5.86	4.73	4.41

Source:
1. 1956−71 figures are calculated from Input-Output Tables, recompiled by Shirley W.Y. Kuo, which are consistently deflated into 1971 domestic constant prices (for the deflation, see Note 8 of Chapter 7 on Pages 172-173).

During the same period, the ratio of total market value of listed stocks to GNP increased from 8.9% to 15.4%, and the ratio of the amount of bank clearings to GNP increased from 233% in 1964 to 568% in 1979. The relative expansion of financial activities is obvious.

Japan			Korea	Sensitivity of Dispersion
1965	1970	1975	1975	of Commerce Caused by
4.6	5.3	5.3	4.0	Agriculture
4.4	4.3	5.3	3.1	Mining
58.8	56.1	57.8	68.4	Manufacturing
4.9	4.5	4.5	4.4	Construction
1.5	1.7	2.0	3.5	Electricity, gas, water supply
0.7	0.6	0.8	1.5	Transportation
0.3	0.4	0.6	0.7	Communications
—	—	—	—	Commerce
0.2	0.4	0.6	0.6	Finance
23.4	23.0	18.9	11.4	Misc. services
1.2	3.7	4.2	2.4	Undistributed
100.0	100.0	100.0	100.0	Total (%)
4.10	4.87	4.93	6.77	Sensitivity of Dispersion of Commerce

2. 1976 figures are calculated from ROC Input-Output Table, which is in current prices, compiled by the Council for Economic Planning and Development.
3. Input-Output Table of Japan and Input-Output Table of Korea.

From the above analyses we may try to conclude that tertiary industries in Taiwan possess great linkages induced by other sectors' production activities. Manufacturing in particular induced a lot of services; on the other hand, a lot of service development is needed to cope with manufacturing develop-

Table 12.19   Influence of Each Sector on the Sensitivity of Dispersion of Finance in Taiwan (ROC), Japan and Korea

Sensitivity of Dispersion of Finance Caused by	Taiwan (ROC)		
	1966	1971	1976
Agriculture	0.14	0.24	0.24
Mining	0.11	0.15	0.19
Manufacturing	0.70	1.47	2.69
Construction	0.06	0.06	0.14
Electricity, gas, water supply	0.03	0.07	0.18
Transportation	0.16	0.23	0.19
Communications	—	—	—
Commerce	0.02	0.02	0.08
Finance	—	—	—
Misc. services	0.01	0.01	0.14
Undistributed	0.19	0.01	0.03
Sensitivity of Dispersion of Finance	1.42	2.26	3.88

Source:
   1. Calculated from Input-Output Table, which is in current prices, compiled by the Council for Economic Planning and Development.

ment.   The linkages of transportation and commerce have decreased over the past two decades, while the linkages of finance have increased rapidly over the past decade.   The decrease in the linkages of transportation may be due partly to an inadequacy of land transportation capacity to cope with the added demand, though this point needs further analysis.

4. *The Intensity of Serving as Intermediate Demand of Tertiary Industries*

Japan			Korea	Sensitivity of Dispersion
1965	1970	1975	1975	of Finance Caused by
0.16	0.18	0.21	0.11	Agriculture
0.25	0.25	0.33	0.11	Mining
1.50	1.51	2.03	1.29	Manufacturing
0.09	0.09	0.10	0.07	Construction
0.08	0.07	0.16	0.09	Electricity, gas, water supply
0.03	0.05	0.08	0.03	Transportation
0.02	0.02	0.02	0.01	Communications
0.07	0.07	0.07	0.02	Commerce
−	−	−	−	Finance
0.42	0.41	0.43	0.12	Misc. services
0.21	0.13	0.08	0.02	Undistributed
2.83	2.78	3.51	1.87	Sensitivity of Dispersion of Finance

2. Input-Output Table of Japan and Input-Output Table of Korea.

In the above sections, we examined the linkages of tertiary industries through observation of their direct and indirect use. In this section, we will observe their direct use. Tertiary industries are identified as having the characteristic of serving a greater portion as final demand than as intermediate demand. The case in Taiwan was not an exception. Table 12.21 shows the ratio of tertiary industries being used as intermediate demand.

Table 12.20   Percentages of Assets, Loans, Portfolio Invest-
ments, Total Market Value of Listed Stocks and
Amount of Bank Clearings of All Financial
Institutions in GNP

(%)

Year	Assets GNP	Loans GNP	Portfolio Invest- ments GNP	Total Market Value of Listed Stocks GNP	Amount of Bank Clearings GNP
1961	40.8	31.0	2.2	8.9	223*
1971	65.4	44.0	3.5	8.0	338
1979	109.9	69.2	9.2	15.4	568

Source: Directorate-General of Budget, Accounting & Statistics, Executive Yuan,
National Income of the Republic of China, 1980; Economic Research Department, the Central Bank of China, *Financial Statistics Monthly, Taiwan District,
the Republic of China,* November 1981.
Note: * 1964 figure.

Table 12.21   Ratio of Tertiary Industry Services Used as
Intermediate Demand (1956—1976)

(%)

Year	Transpor- tation	Commerce	Other Services
1956	0.54	0.23	0.12
1961	0.47	0.24	0.13
1966	0.37	0.32	0.13
1971	0.39	0.32	0.16
1976	0.41	0.44	0.20

Source: Same as Table 12.13.

The ratio of intermediate use of transportation decreased
from a relatively high 0.54 in 1956 to 0.37 in 1966, and then

increased again to 0.41 in 1976. The commerce sector's ratio of intermediate use increased from 0.23 in 1956 to 0.44 in 1976; other services also had an increasing tendency, from 0.12 to 0.20. However, by their very nature, commerce and other services have a big portion served as final demand, the contributions of which to economic growth and employment were studied in section one.

IV. Conclusions

The tertiary sector, products of which are services and not visible commodities, comprised about 48% of the GNP every year during the past three decades. It is a very important sector, yet analyses of it are very few.

Breaking tertiary industry into transportation, commerce, finance and other services (including government service), we find that over the period 1952–81, the shares of value added of transportation in tertiary industry changed from 8% to 18%, commerce from 40% to 32%, finance from 2% to 8%, and other services from 50% to 42%.

Labor productivity of transportation grew hardly at all in the 1950s, but it grew rapidly, at 9.6% and 8.4%, respectively, during the following two decades. The much higher growth in labor productivity of transportation in the later period was mostly attributable to the deepening of capital intensity. The implementation of the ten major projects made the greatest contribution.

Tertiary industry absorbed a huge amount of employment. During the three periods, 1961–66, 1966–71, and 1971–76, tertiary industry absorbed 193,000 persons, 481,000 persons, and 418,000 persons respectively, accounting for 51%, 47%, and 45% of the increment of employment of the whole economy in each period. The contribution of export expansion to employment in tertiary industry reached as high as 28%, 28%, and 42% of total employment expansion which was caused by export expansion in the three respective periods. Thus, services were also exported in large quantity.

The income per worker in the commerce sector was

lowest, reaching only 85% that of total tertiary industry in 1979. The operation scale in commerce has been very small, with 96.3% of operating units still belonging to the 1-9 employee category in 1979, and only 0.001% of operating units being in the more than 500 employee category. It is apparent that one way to increase labor productivity in commerce is to expand its operation scale.

Tertiary industries in Taiwan possess great linkages induced by the production activities of other sectors. Particularly, services induced by manufacturing comprised about 60–70% of the total. This also means that a lot of service development is needed to cope with manufacturing development.

The linkages of transportation and commerce have been decreasing over the past two decades, while the linkages of finance have been rapidly increasing over the last decade. The decrease in the linkages of transportation may be partly due to an inadequate land transportation capacity; however, this point needs further study. The increase in the linkages of the finance sector was made possible by faster growth of financial activities. Financial intermediaries offered more credit to individuals and businesses. However, statistics cannot adequately reflect qualitative changes within the banking world. Whether a relatively conservative and disciplined attitude toward lending, liquidity and leveraging made any improvement is not yet known.

Comprising about 48% of the GNP, the tertiary sector has been a very large part of the Taiwan economy. In this study, only a few important aspects of the tertiary sector are analyzed. It is beyond this study's scope to deal with details such as the tourist industry, restaurants, barber shops, coeffee shops and the like, although a study of these businesses may also be of some interest. Government service is also an unexplained area, as is the determination of prices of services. These subjects will be left for future studies.

NOTES

1. Shirley W.Y. Kuo, "Effects of Trade on Growth, Employment, and Income Distribution in Taiwan, Republic of China, 1952–1979," (paper read at Conference on United States-Asia Economic Relations, April 1981, Rutgers University).

2. Council for Economic Planning and Development, *Evaluations on the Ten Major Projects* (Taipei: Council for Economic Planning and Development, 1979).

3. Professor Kowie Chang also did a study on direct and indirect investment for the period 1952–69 as reported in Kowie Chang, "Economic Growth and Investment–Social Overhead Capital versus Directly Productive Activities, *"Economic Essays,* Vol. II (Taipei: National Taiwan University, The Graduate Institute of Economics, November, 1971).

4. P. N. Rasmussen, *Studies in Inter-Sectoral Relations* (Amsterdam: North-Holland Publishing Company, 1957).

5. Mitsuo Saito, *General Equilibrium and Price* (Tokyo: Sobunshia, 1975).

6. Mitsuo Saito, ibid.

PART V

13

Stabilization Policies of the Early 1950s

Toward the end of World War II, Taiwan was subject to intense bombing by the allies and was isolated from the outside world. Production decreased, external trade was at a standstill, there was a serious shortage of commodities, and inflation had reached serious proportions. Soon after the restoration in 1945, it was found that Taiwan needed a tremendous amount of capital for rehabilitation and reconstruction. Also due to its peculiar political situation on the island, an independent financial system from mainland China was set up.

During the period from December 15, 1945 through the end of 1951, a special temporary budget was used by the government to administer the public revenues and expenditures in Taiwan. Because of the limited tax revenues, the government expenditures in 1947 and 1948 were dependent heavily on the issuance of paper currency. Compared with the volume of paper money issuance at the end of 1946, the volume of issuance rose by 3.2 times by the end of 1947, 26.5 times by the end of 1948, and soared to 99 times by the eve of the reform of the monetary system which came into force on June 15, 1949.[1]

Prices in Taiwan rose at an annual five-fold rate in 1946—48 and then accelerated to about 30-fold in the first half of 1949. The inflation in Taiwan during this period was mainly due to the following reasons: (1) extension of big loans for rehabilitation and reconstruction, (2) colossal government expenditures, and (3) the vicious inflation on the mainland. Although the purpose of automatic adjustment of the exchange rate of the old Taiwan dollar against the Chinese National Currency was to ward off the impact of the rapid depreciation of the Chinese National Currency, for many reasons the extent of the adjustment was not adequate to be really effective. Furthermore, there was no way to stop the influx of capital from the mainland; consequently, it failed to achieve the expected result of suppressing the inflationary trend in Taiwan.

At this stage, the most urgently needed action, more vital than any other, was thus price stabilization. Stabilization policies were implemented by various measures, among which monetary reform, preferential interest rate deposits, and a balanced government budget were essential. Those three measures will be discussed below.

I.   Monetary Reform and Other Measures

1.   The Reform

The New Taiwan Dollar Reform was put into effect on June 15, 1949, when the economy was suffering from hyper-inflation. The old Taiwan currency was devalued at a rate of forty thousand to one, and the value of the New Taiwan dollar was linked up with that of the U.S. dollar at the rate of NT$5 to US$1. The new currency was backed by a hundred percent reserve in gold, silver, and foreign exchange, and the ceiling on the issuance of currency was set at NT$200 million.

These stipulations, if strictly enforced, would unquestionably have inspired confidence of the people in the currency and prevented the resurgence of inflation. However, due to a big government deficit, advances from the Bank of Taiwan, which was functioning as the central bank at that time,[2] continued to accumulate. By the end of December 1949, the currency issue was close to the ceiling of NT$200 million, causing a rapid depreciation of the new currency and a steady rise in the price of the U.S. dollar in the black market. In

July 1950, the maximum issuance limit was abolished.   By December 1950, the issue of the N.T. dollar had reached NT$267 million, and the black market price of the U.S. dollar had risen to NT$16.

2. Gold Savings Deposits

During this early period, from May 1949 to December 1950, a noteworthy financial measure taken by the government to check inflation was the redemption of gold. The redemption of gold was done in the form of "gold savings deposits," the deposits redeemable in gold in one month at the official price which was set lower than the market price of gold. Due to the continuous rise of prices, however, a large discrepancy soon developed between the official and market prices of gold. From June 1, 1950, Patriotic Savings Coupons were allotted against gold savings deposits, and the number of coupons thus allotted varied daily in accordance with the discrepancy between the official and market prices of gold. These Patriotic Saving Coupons were substituted by Patriotic Bonds after July 16, 1950.   The liquidity of the Coupons and Bonds was very low.   Their maturity being two years for the Coupons and seventeen years for the Bonds, allotment of these securities was actually an increase of the price of gold in disguise. The gold savings deposits, which were aimed to absorb currency and to dump gold for price stabilization, were finally suspended on December 27, 1950.[3]

3. Other Measures

After that, new financial measures were incorporated in two decrees: (1) "Measures Governing Control of Gold and Foreign Currencies" and (2) "Prohibition of Importation of Luxury Goods."   The former, while permitting the possession of gold and foreign currencies, prohibited free buying and selling of these items.   The purpose was to outlaw black market dealings and strengthen foreign exchange and foreign trade control.   The latter was designed to check the outflow of gold and foreign currencies through rigid suppression of smuggling and prohibition of illicit remittances and the trading of imported luxury goods. The authorities believed that prevention of smuggling and prohibition of imported luxury goods would help eradicate the black market dealings in gold and foreign currencies.

In addition to these, the following measures are noteworthy. As of December 19, 1950, an importer, when applying for import exchange allocation, was required to put up a marginal deposit equivalent to 50% of the amount of foreign exchange he was applying for. On March 23, 1955, the requirement was raised to 100%. This requirement, which was not abolished until June 29, 1964, was originally designed as a foreign exchange control measure, but because of its usefulness in calling in a sizable amount of money supply in circulation, it became one of the important monetary tools of the government. Frequently, the amount of foreign exchange that an importer applied for would be several times the amount that was eventually approved, and it would usually take several weeks for an application to be processed and approved. Thus, the requirement for a marginal deposit could freeze a large amount of currency for a considerable period of time.

According to the Chinese Banking Law, the guarantee reserve is banks' deposits with the Central Bank which represent a fixed percentage of the total deposits banks have received from their clients. In July 1948, the Bank of Taiwan was designated by the Central Bank to accept guarantee reserves from other banks. At that time, it was agreed that the reserve requirement for "industrial banks" should be applicable to the Land Bank of Taiwan, the Cooperative Bank of Taiwan, and the Central Trust of China and that the reserve requirement for "commercial banks", to all other banks.

Before 1956, banks never fully complied with the payment of reserves requirement and failed to deposit a sufficient amount with the Bank of Taiwan. In early 1956 the Bank of Taiwan considered that bank credit was being over-expanded, and began to enforce this requirement rigidly. At the same time the

Bank of Taiwan demanded that all banks should, in principle, transfer all payment reserves deposited with other banks to the Bank of Taiwan. But since the reactivation of the Central Bank of China in July 1961, the deposits of banks' guarantee reserves and payment reserves have been transferred to the Central Bank.

II. Interest Rate Policy

Another very important measure promoting stabilization was the introduction of "preferential interest rate savings deposits" in March 1950. Due to the then prevailing hyper-inflation, the duration of the deposits was set very short, starting from one month at the outset. Deposits received by the banks had to be transferred to the Bank of Taiwan. Loans could be given to the depositors based on their deposit certificates, but the amount of a loan could not exceed 70% of the amount of the deposit.

The principal characteristic of the preferential interest rate savings deposits was their high interest rate. At that time, the yearly interest rate on one-year time deposits was 20%. The interest rate on these new deposits was 7% per month, which, if compounded, would amount to 125% per year. Although the interest rate was actually still below the inflation rate in 1950, the setting of such a high interest rate required intelligence and determination on the part of the government.

The preferential interest rate savings deposits were very effective. At the beginning of 1950, time deposits in all banks amounted to only NT$2 million. After the inauguration of the preferential interest rate deposits, the amount increased to NT$35 million in eight months, comprising about 7% of the money supply. The interest rate was later lowered from 7% per month to 3.5% and then to 3% in 1950. A decrease in deposits resulted, however, and the interest rate was again raised to 4.2%. The interest rate was then gradually reduced, dropping to 2% by November 1952. At that time, preferential interest rate savings deposits accounted for 44% of the money supply.

After 1953 the government gradually implemented longer-term preferential interest rate savings deposits, and these longer-term deposits increased gradually. On March 5, 1956, the authorities established a new kind of time deposit that matured in either six months or one year, could not be mortgaged, and bore monthly interest rates of 1.5% and 1.8%, respectively. These rates were higher than those for deposits that could be accepted as security for loans, interest on which had   been

Table 13.1   Rates of Preferential Interest Deposits

(percent per month)

Effective on	Usable as a Mortage					
	Half Month	One Month	Two Months	Three Months	Six Months	One Year
Mar. 25, 1950	—	7.00	—	—	—	—
Apr. 17, "	6.0	7.00	8.0	9.00	—	—
Jul. 1, "	3.0	3.50	4.0	4.50	—	—
Oct. 1, "	—	3.00	3.3	3.30	—	—
Mar. 26, 1951	—	4.20	4.5	4.50	—	—
Apr. 28, 1952	—	3.80	4.0	4.00	4.2	—
Jun. 2, "	—	3.30	—	3.60	3.9	—
Jul. 7, "	—	3.00	—	3.20	3.4	—
Sep. 8, "	—	2.40	—	2.60	2.8	—
Nov. 30, "	—	2.00	—	2.15	2.3	—
Apr. 10, 1953	—	2.00	—	2.15	2.3	3.0
Jul. 16, "	—	1.50	—	1.70	2.0	2.5
Oct. 10, "	—	1.20	—	1.30	1.5	2.0
Jul. 1, 1954	—	1.00	—	1.10	1.3	1.6
Mar. 5, 1956	—	0.85	—	1.00	1.3	1.6
Jun. 18, "	—	0.85	—	1.00	—	—
Jul. 16, 1957	—	—	—	0.85	—	—

Source: Chih-chi Pan, Jen-ming Chang, and Yin-sheng Yuan, "Monetary Situation and Price Movements," in Kowie Chang ed., *Economic Development in Taiwan* (Taipei: Cheng Chung Book Company, 1968).

reduced to 0.85% and 1%, respectively, for deposits in one-month and three-month accounts. Because of the reduction in interest rates on shorter-term deposits, deposits of longer maturity increased significantly. At the end of 1956, deposits in one-year accounts comprised 27% of the total deposits.

On July 16, 1957, the Bank of Taiwan began to accept time deposits maturing in two years, and also abolished the

Not Usable as a Mortgage			Effective on
Six Months	One Year	Two Years	
—	—	—	Mar. 25, 1950
—	—	—	Apr. 17, "
—	—	—	Jul. 1, "
—	—	—	Oct. 1, "
—	—	—	Mar. 26, 1951
—	—	—	Apr. 28, 1952
—	—	—	Jun. 2, "
—	—	—	Jul. 7, "
—	—	—	Sep. 8, "
—	—	—	Nov. 30, "
—	—	—	Apr. 10, 1953
—	—	—	Jul. 16, "
—	—	—	Oct. 10, "
—	—	—	Jul. 1, 1954
1.50	1.80	—	Mar. 5, 1956
1.50	1.80	—	Jun. 18, "
1.35	1.65	1.80	Jul. 16, 1957

one-month deposits.   The interest rate on deposits of three-month duration was further lowered to 0.85%, and the rate on deposits of two-year duration was fixed at 1.8%. During 1958, the total amount of one-year deposits more than doubled, and from the middle of 1957 to the end of 1958, the amount of six-month deposits almost doubled.[4]

At the end of 1958, the authorities suspended preferential interest rate savings deposits. Total outstanding deposits at that time amounted to NT$1,500 million, or 29% of the money supply. In a period of about nine years, from March 1950 to the end of 1958, the financial authorities had relied on these savings deposits to call in a tremendous amount of idle capital from the market, thus contributing greatly to the stability of the island's economy during these years.

The inflation rate slowed right after monetary reform, with prices increasing only three-fold in 1950. Compared with the 30-fold increase experienced in the first half of 1949, this was a great success. Inflation was controlled further after 1951; the annual increase in prices was 8.8% from 1952 to 1960, dropped to 2% in 1961, and then only 3% after 1961. Although it took twelve years to accomplish this, the contribution of monetary reform and other measures to price stabilization and to general economic development was great.

During the period of high interest rates and the period of lowering interest rates, there were heated arguments from many quarters. Those who favored a low interest rate policy were of the opinion that it would stimulate economic growth; that it would lower the cost of production, and hence, the prices of the finished products; that regulation of interest rates would serve to secure the supply of financial capital for equity investment; and that the prerogative of the government enterprises to obtain low interest rate loans from government banks was only a way of subsidizing their products and services which were frequently sold at low prices.

Discrediting entirely the points mentioned above, those who favored high interest rates claimed that the functions of interest rates should be to provide inducement for savings and to channel them to banking institutions for capital investment, and to allocate the capital to different, competitive use. With the short supply of capital in Taiwan, a high interest rate, determined by the market demand for capital, would tend to direct capital investment to more efficient enterprises, so that the less efficient enterprises might not have the same chance to expand. Conversely, if the interest rates were arbitrary fixed, the result would be indiscriminate allocation of the limited supply of capital, permitting the diversion of a part of the funds into less productive uses.

Amidst these different opinions, the government gradually decreased interest rates. The market interest rates also gradually declined. This was mainly attributable to the increase in national income and in the savings of the people, and to the relative stability of prices. At the same time, after the period of runaway inflation was over, many enterprises were bankrupted due to poor management and to the excessive burden of interest payments. Private money lenders learned a lesson from these changes and would rather deposit their money with banks than earn interest from private borrowers. Bank deposits increased greatly under these circumstances, making it possible for the authorities to lower interest rates further.

III. The Balanced Government Budget

During this period, the authorities concerned concentrated on eliminating factors that could cause economic instability. On the fiscal side, a great effort was made to achieve a balanced budget (see Chapter 2). A part of U.S. aid was efficiently utilized to supplement the government deficits up until 1961. The government budget, inclusive of transfer receipts, actually was in surplus every year even before 1961, which provided an important financial source of investment in infrastructure.

In conclusion, the experience of Taiwan showed an anti-inflation policy that was implemented through three dimensions: first, an elimination of inflationary psychology by implementation of monetary reform: second, an absorption of money supply by manipulation of interest rate and other measures; and third, the maintenance of a balanced government

Table 13.2   Foreign Transfers and Government
Current Surplus

Period	Foreign Transfers to the Government Sector in Percent of Government Expenditure	Government Current Surplus Net of Foreign Transfers in Percent of Government Expenditure	Government Current Surplus Inclusive of Foreign Transfers in Percent of Government Expenditure	Government Expenditure in Percent of GNP
1951–56	29.2	−4.6	24.6	18.1
1956–61	22.7	−4.7	18.0	19.8
1961–66	7.2	4.2	11.4	18.1
1966–71	0.1	19.8	19.9	17.9
1971–76	−0.1	46.6	46.5	15.3
1976–81	−0.1	52.6	52.5	15.5

Source: Directorate-General of Budget, Accounting and Statisitcs, Executive Yuan, *National Income of the Republic of China* (1981).

budget. The policies in these three dimensions were effectively implemented over the period 1949–58. The hyper-inflation of the early 1950s was thus effectively cured. Although it took a decade to accomplish, the success of this anti-inflation policy laid down a sound foundation for continuing rapid growth in the following decades.

NOTES

1. Kowie Chang, Ming-jen Lu, Teh-an Hsu, "Fiscal Operations," in Kowie Change ed., *Economic Development in Taiwan* (Taipei: Cheng Chung Book Company, 1968).

2. Before the reactivation of the Central Bank of China on July 1, 1961,

the Bank of Taiwan was, in fact, the central bank in Taiwan.

3. Chih-chi Pan, Jen-ming Chang, and Yin-sheng Yuan, "Monetary Situation and Price Movements," in Kowie Chang ed., *Economic Development in Taiwan* (Taipei: Cheng Chung Book Company, 1968).

4. Chih-chi Pan, Jen-ming Chang, and Yin-sheng Yuan, ibid.

14

From Import Substitution to Export Promotion Policies in the 1960s

At the beginning of the 1950s, the government was faced with a difficult choice between inward-looking and outward-looking policies. Both policy choices were problematic. From the inward-looking point of view, the size of the domestic market was clearly too small to be depended upon as a source of sustained growth, and from the outward-looking viewpoint, the ready markets of Japan and mainland China were no longer available. At the same time, surpluses of rice and other agricultural products were substantially reduced by increased domestic demand caused by the abrupt population increase resulting from the influx of people from the mainland.

Notwithstanding the obstacles to inward-looking measures, import controls had to be implemented for two reasons. By 1951 Taiwan was confronted with a sizable trade deficit, which was to continue throughout the 1950s. Numerous small enterprises had started up business immediately after the war, partly by acquiring old Japanese facilities and producing simple manufactures of poor quality but at high cost. Many of these enterprises not only encountered difficulties in marketing abroad, but also had to compete with the superior Japanese products that re-entered Taiwan. Under these conditions, import substitution policies were adopted.

297

I. Import Substitution Policies

Import substitution policies were reflected in the adoption of a foreign exchange policy and in the implementation of a pricing policy to encourage domestic production of substitutes for imported goods. These two dimensions will be discussed below.

1. The 1950s Foreign Exchange Policy

In 1949 when monetary reform was put into effect, a functionally simple exchange rate was adopted. The operation was such that the receipt of domestic currency in exchange for foreign money was given partly in cash, at a rate of NT$5 to US$1, and partly in exchange settlement certificates (ESCs). These ESCs were freely negotiable on the market and could be sold to the Bank of Taiwan at the official rate. For importers, foreign exchange was approved rather liberally, and the ESCs were sold for importation of permissible items at the official rate. However, because of the large trade deficit and continued inflation, applications for foreign exchange soon outgrew the available supply. The official supply price of ESCs was repeatedly devalued.

In 1951, along with substantial currency devaluation, a multiple exchange rate was introduced. Goods imported by the public sector, and plant and important raw materials and intermediate inputs imported by the private sector, were given a lower official rate; imports of other goods were given a higher ESC rate. Export earnings of the major exports, sugar, rice, and salt, were given a lower ESC rate than private export earnings. After 1951 the New Taiwan dollar became overvalued due to continuous inflation, which hampered exports and encouraged imports and import substitution.

The revision of the foreign exchange system in November, 1958, was decisive and paved the way for a move to a simple exchange system. The essence of this revision was to allow exchange settlement cretificates to be applied to all kinds of exports and imports. In addition, the price of exchange settlement certificates was fixed at a level close to the market price. The Taiwan Sugar Corporation, which earned more than a half of the island's total foreign exchange, was permitted to sell its ESCs at a price very close to the market price. Furthermore, the ESCs of the Taiwan Sugar Corporation were fixed at a price lower than market price after July 1, 1960; and then, from August, 1960, the price of an ESC incorporated the official basic foreign exchange rate. After this, the market exchange rate was gradually stabilized at the rate of US$1 to NT$40. The Taiwan Sugar Corporation earned a large amount of foreign exchange in 1963 due to the high international sugar price that year. Making use of this abundance of foreign exchange, the government abolished the ESC system. Thus, the direct exchange settlement system came into being, and the over-valuation of the New Taiwan dollar was ended.

2. Higher Prices of Import Goods vs. Export Goods

Due to various reasons, mostly import restrictions and high tariffs, the price ratio of import substituting goods to export goods went up appreciably in the beginning of the 1950s. This was manifested in the dramatic rise of the relative price of cotton textiles to rice, which increased from 2:1 during 1949–50 to 4~5:1 in 1951–52.[1] This change was of particular significance, because rice was Taiwan's main agricultural product and an export commodity, while textiles were important imports. By the rise of the domestic price, therefore, import substitution of textile goods received significant support.[2]

Import substitution was not only encouraged through foreign exchange measures and pricing, but also through allocation of raw materials and financial funds. Mr. K.Y. Yin, then vice chairman of the Taiwan Production Board, an organization in charge of U.S. aid, emphasized the long-run comparative advantage for development. He organized a joint textile group to give full support to the expansion of cotton yarn fabrics production by providing necessary raw materials to manufacturing firms through U.S. aid and allocation of financial funds. Thus, the textile industry grew rapidly.

Some export promotion measures were in fact started in the early 1950s. For example, a system of tax rebates for reimbursing import duties on raw materials was introduced in 1954. A system offering certain proportions of foreign exchange earnings for the import of raw materials was initiated in 1956. Basically, however, the overvaluation of currency and the multiple exchange rate structure tilted policy in favor of import substitution.

Easy import substitution soon came to an end due to the limited domestic market and urgently needed foreign exchange earnings. By 1958 the investment climate was gloomy and more fundamental policy changes were called for. The strategy of development was then turned toward export promotion.

II. Export Promotion Policies in the 1960s

The change of policy was made in 1956—60. An ambitious annual growth target of 8% was set for the Third Four-Year Plan, running from 1961 to 1964, and an important 19-point Economic Financial Reform was introduced.

1. Nineteen-Point Economic and Financial Reform

The essential elements of the 19-point Economic and Financial Reform were as follows:

1) To make a thorough review of various control measures taken in the past, for the purpose of liberalizing those measures.

2) To give private business preferential treatment in the areas of tax, foreign exchange and financing.

3) To reform the tax system and tax administration to enhance capital formation.

4) To reform the foreign exchange and trade systems in order to establish a unitary exchange rate, and to liberalize trade control.

5) To broaden measures encouraging exports, to improve procedures governing settlement of foreign exchange earned by exporters, and to increase contacts with foreign business organizations.

2. Investment Incentives

The Statute for Encouragement of Investment was enacted pursuant to the above 19-point supporting measure. The main purposes of this Statute were to facilitate the acquisition of plant sites and to provide tax exemptions and deductions. The salient points of the Statute for Encouragement of Investment may be given as follows:

1) Income tax holiday: The strongest incentive was the "five-year tax holiday" set forth in Article 5, whereby a productive enterprise conforming to the Statute's criteria was exempted from income tax for a period of five consecutive years.

2) Business income tax: The maximum rate of income tax, including all forms of surtax payable by a productive enterprise, would not exceed 18% of its total annual income, which was comparable to 32.5% for ordinary profit-seeking enterprises.

3) Tax exemption for undistributed profit: The amount reinvested for productive purposes was deductible from taxable income.

4) Tax deduction of exports: Within certain limits a deduction from taxable income of 2% of annual export proceeds was permissible.

5) Exemption or reduction of stamp tax: This tax was either waived or reduced in a large number of cases.

6) Productive enterprises were allowed to set aside 7%, to be regarded as profits before taxation, of the unpaid balance of foreign currency debt calculated in local currency as a reserve against possible loss caused by exchange rate revision.

The response of industry toward export expansion in the early 1960s was still slow. In 1965, the Statute was revised and its scope was expanded. The Kaohsiung Export Processing Zone was set up, within which no duties were imposed on imports. Development strategy at the time became entirely export-oriented.

3. Tax Reduction and Rebates

The reduction of taxes as a result of the Statute for Encouragement of Investment, and the tax and duty rebates for exportation, amounted to a large proportion of the levied taxes, as seen in Table 14.1.

Table 14.1 Tax Rebates
(as Percentage of the Corresponding Tax)

(%)

Fiscal Year	Income Tax	Stamp Tax	Customs Duties	Commodity Tax	Total Rebates of the Four Taxes
1955	—	—	2.3	0.2	1.5
1961	2.4	25.3	14.5	12.5	11.9
1966	21.4	51.1	32.6	20.1	28.1
1971	13.5	73.5	77.3	34.3	47.5
1972	14.9	60.0	86.1	37.3	52.4
1973	15.9	57.0	72.3	37.6	48.0
1974	22.0	50.9	46.2	31.7	36.9
1975	12.2	51.8	54.6	37.7	38.2
1976	15.3	48.7	42.2	37.3	34.3
1977	12.7	50.5	57.2	40.6	40.0
1978	14.9	34.2	40.5	36.0	31.8
1979	13.2	12.8	40.3	35.2	29.9
1980	11.7	23.3	41.5	20.2	25.8
1981	9.7	17.8	39.2	5.7	18.7

Source: Department of Statistics, Ministry of Finance, *Yearbook of Financial Statistics of the Republic of China, 1981* (1982, p.p. 130-131, 134).
Note: Fiscal year 1958 runs July 1958-June 1959, and fiscal year 1960 runs July 1959-June 1960, due to a change in the fiscal year system.

The largest income tax reductions in percentage terms, 25.2% and 23.4%, were enacted in 1963 and 1967, respectively. The income tax reduction remained around 15% in the 1970s, although it accounted for 22% of income tax in 1974 due to the higher earnings in the boom year 1973.

ERRATA

THE TAIWAN ECONOMY IN TRANSITION

Shirley W. Y. Kuo

p. 303

The third and fourth line from the bottom of the page
should read as follows:

"by domestic sales, dropped from 0.535 in 1961
to 0.395 in 1966 and then to 0.300 in 1971."

The customs duties exempted and refunded increased rapidly from 1971 to 1973 due to the rapid expansion of exports relative to imports. Conversely, the sudden reduction of the percentage in the rebate of customs duties in 1974 was due to the relatively rapid increase in the denominator — the tariff revenue — that resulted from the abrupt increase in oil prices and other imports. The commodity tax rebate showed the same tendency as customs duties. The total rebates of all four taxes in the boom period, 1971 to 1973, accounted for as much as a half of the total revenue of the four taxes.

The basic policy in the most recent years has been to reduce the tariff rate on imports of necessary raw materials and inter-mediate inputs, so as not to rebate levied tariffs. Successive measures have been taken along this line since 1976 and will be intensified in the future.

4. Favorable Interest Rate

A special export loan program was initiated in 1957, and favorable interest rates for export financing have been available since then. However, the proportion of loans granted under this favorable interest rate has been relatively small. After 1974, outstanding loans extended under favorable rates in Taiwan declined to less than 3% of the total outstanding amount, as can be seen in Table 14.2.

III. Nominal Rate of Protection

Although the most important features of the tariff structure remained unchanged between 1961 and 1971, the nominal rate of protection changed appreciably during this period. As can be seen in Table 14.3, the nominal rate of protection for manufacturing (which is measured by a comparison of domestic prices with international prices at commodity level[3]), weighted by domestic sales, dropped from 0.535% in 1961 to 0.395% in 1966 and then to 0.300% in 1971.

The decrease from 1961 to 1966 was larger than that from 1966 to 1971. The nominal rates of protection weighted by

Table 14.2   Favorable Interest Rate Export Loans

End of Year	Favorable Rate Export Loans (in millions of NT dollars)	Total Loans (in millions of NT dollars)	Percentage of Favorable Rate Export Loans to Total Loans
1972	6,544	104,599	6.3
1973	8,742	151,514	5.8
1974	7,470	214,759	3.5
1975	8,000	284,507	2.8
1976	8,857	317,704	2.8
1977	11,108	375,892	3.0
1978	12,947	470,186	2.8
1979	12,398	544,650	2.3
1980	13,367	693,599	1.9
1981	15,927	760,369	2.1

Source: Economic Research Department, The Central Bank of China, *Financial Statistics Monthly, Taiwan District, The Republic of China*, various years.

exports were about the same by size and by decreasing tendency. The nominal rates of protection weighted by imports were not only comparatively lower than those weighted by domestic sales or exports, but also evidenced a different tendency, decreasing faster in the period 1966 to 1971 than in the period 1961 to 1966. The high rate of protection in 1961 was due to the high rate of protection given to food processing at that time. If food processing is excluded, the rate or protection is reduced considerably.

When manufactured products are classified into four categories — export competing, export-import competing, import competing and non-import competing,[4] it is very interesting to observe that the highest rate of protection was extended to export competing industries. Export-import competing industries ranked second and non-import competing industries third. The difference among the rates of protection for these four categories was large in 1961, but decreased considerably by 1971. The rate for export competing industries was high in

Table 14.3   Nominal Rate of Protection of Manufacturing
(Ratio of Domestic Prices to International
Prices — 1)

Item	1961	1966	1971
Nominal rate of protection weighted by domestic sales			
Manufacturing (including food processing)	0.535	0.395	0.300
Manufacturing (excluding food processing)	0.384	0.309	0.285
Nominal rate of protection weighted by exports			
Manufacturing (including food processing)	0.563	0.391	0.360
Manufacturing (excluding food processing)	0.330	0.331	0.373
Nominal rate of protection weighted by imports			
Manufacturing (including food processing)	0.411	0.361	0.283
Manufacturing (excluding food processing)	0.416	0.368	0.288

Source: Shirley W.Y. Kuo, "Economic Growth and Structural Change in the Republic of China," Appendix II A (Mimeo, prepared under the auspices of the World Bank, 1979).

1961 due to the high rates for monosodium glutamate and sugar, non-alcoholic beverages and miscellaneous fabrics. Monosodium glutamate and sugar retained high rates throughout the period, although their shares in manufacturing decreased tremendously. The rates of protection for non-alcoholic beverages and miscellaneous fabrics had decreased appreciably by 1971, causing a decrease in the average rate for this category.

In the category of export-import competing industries, the rate of protection for artificial fabrics was the highest, particularly in 1961. Also benefiting from high rates in 1961 were woolen fabrics and household electric appliances.

IV. Real Effective Exchange Rate

The change in the competitiveness of exports can be measured by the real effective exchange rate. When the real effective exchange rate is greater than 100, competitiveness in that year is lower than in the base year; when the real effective exchange rate is less than 100, competitiveness in that year is superior to that of the base year (for the definitions and the details, see Chapter 10, Pages 206-208). Export weighted, import weighted and trade weighted effective exchange rates are shown in Table 14.4. During the last two decades the effective exchange rate, as adjusted by purchasing power parity using exports as weight, remained higher than 100 up until 1968. However, it dropped to under 100 during 1969–73, indicating that the rate of foreign exchange in real terms increased the competitiveness of Taiwan's export commodities. The basic reason for this change was the price stability experienced during this period. As a result, exports grew at a 44% annual rate, yielding huge trade surpluses every year which in turn fostered a rapid growth in the money supply. The 1973 oil crisis caused the inflation rate to shoot up to 40% in 1974, which pushed the real effective exchange rate above 100 again in that year. However, due to a negative price change of 5% in 1975 and a relatively low inflation rate thereafter, the real effective exchange rate dipped below 100 after 1975.

The foreign exchange system was converted from a fixed system to a floating system in February 1979. Since then, the value of the New Taiwan dollar has fluctuated. The fluctuation, however, has been very mild.

The real effective exchange rate was under 100 (with 1980 as the base year) for the entire 1976–81 period, indicating that in terms of the weighted foreign exchange rate, with the relative price change (domestic price against foreign prices) taken into account, the value of the New Taiwan dollar was favorable for foreign trade during these six years.

We also note that the Taiwan economic environment immediately before the two oil shocks was such that prices had

Table 14.4   Real Effective Exchange Rate
of the New Taiwan Dollar
(Index 1980 = 100)

Year	Export Weighted	Import Weighted	Trade Weighted
1960	103.7	98.8	100.3
1961	102.2	98.9	100.1
1962	104.9	102.9	103.7
1963	112.8	107.0	109.5
1964	114.8	112.0	113.3
1965	107.9	105.5	106.5
1966	105.0	105.4	105.3
1967	103.5	106.1	105.0
1968	101.6	108.4	105.4
1969	97.6	106.3	102.8
1970	95.8	104.8	100.8
1971	89.5	101.9	95.9
1972	86.3	93.5	89.6
1973	94.1	96.6	95.4
1974	112.7	114.7	113.8
1975	99.6	102.6	101.3
1976	97.8	101.8	99.7
1977	93.4	95.0	94.2
1978	88.3	86.2	87.3
1979	93.3	93.4	93.3
1980	100.0	100.0	100.0
1981	99.7	100.0	99.9

Source: International Monetary Fund, *International Financial Statistics*, 1981; Directorate-General of Budget, Accounting and Statistics, Executive Yuan, Republic of China, *Commodity-Price Statistics Monthly*, December 1981; Department of Statistics, Ministry of Finance, *Monthly Statistics of Exports and Imports*, December 1981.

Notes:
1. The index of the real effective exchange rate is the index of the effective exchange rate adjusted for inflation differentials which are measured by wholesale prices of nonfood manufactures.
2. Weighted by data of nine major trading countries.

been particularly stable for some time, and that speedy export growth was creating a large physical demand on the one hand and inducing money supply growth on the other. Both oil crises occurred in the midst of this environment. Strong demand plus the available money supply easily absorbed the higher intermediate costs. The government measures in the wake of these oil crises have been discussed intensively in Chapter 10.

In concluding this chapter, we may note the following: Export was the true essential factor contributing to the past rapid growth and successful labor absorption. In particular, export expansion was the dominant source of manufacturing growth after the 1960s.

Appropriate government policies are considered to have been essential to the rapid export expansion. In the early 1950s, policies stimulated import substitution. An adoption of a multiple exchange rate system, an over-valuation of the New Taiwan dollar, and the maintenance of higher prices of import goods vs. export goods during this period were all in favor of import substitution.

However, from the late 1950s, export expansion was emphasized. Various export promotion schemes were implemented. Through the 19-point Economic and Financial Reform and the Statute for Encouragement of Investment, outward-looking trade policies were emphasized and carefully designed. Nominal rates of protection, exchange rates, investment policy, tax rebates, and trade loans all provided a favorable direction for export promotion. Thus, the outward-looking government economic policies and measures contributed greatly to the successful transition growth in Taiwan.

NOTES

1. T.H. Lee, *Intersectoral Capital Flows in the Economic Development of Taiwan, 1895–1960* (Ithaca, N.Y.: Cornell University Press, 1971).

2. C.Y. Lin, *Industrialization in Taiwan, 1946–72* (New York: Praeger Publishers, 1973).

3. Shirley W.Y. Kuo, "Economic Growth and Structural Change in the Republic of China" (Mimeo, prepared under the auspices of the World Bank, 1979).

4. For the definition of these categories, see Chapter 7, Table 7.7.

15

Problems and Policies of the 1980s

The Taiwan economy experienced successful transition growth in the last three decades, which was manifested in rapid growth, speedy export expansion, and achievement of full employment. Although this success was in no small way attributable to the concerted efforts of both the people and the government, several factors that were particularly important during the 1950s and 1960s greatly helped this growth: availability of cheap energy, the rapidly expanding world economy, a sound international finance system, abundant reserves of low-cost labor, and speedy technological progress. In the 1970s, however, the climate changed significantly in the areas of energy, trade, finance, manpower, and technology.

The quadrupling of oil prices in 1973 brought on the world recession of 1973–75, which was followed by worldwide stagflation. The impact of the second oil shock, which occurred in 1978, hampered the recovery of the world economy. World trade in the 1970s grew at a much slower pace than in the prosperous 1960s, and the outlook for the 1980s is gloomy. Foreign exchange and interest rates entered a new era in the 1970s. The Breton Woods System that had supported smooth trade expansion in the postwar period collapsed after the Nixon shock in 1971. Inflationary anticipations rose along with actual inflation and thus became incorporated into high interest rates. This not only created innovations in the financial markets, but also instigated novel difficulties in the financial area.

In its domestic economy, Taiwan is facing a new manpower problem in the 1980s. Unskilled labor has been virtually fully employed. Wages have been rising, and the abundant numbers of high school and college graduates need more training. Also, the speed of technical progress, which accounted for about half of the economic growth in the 1950s, started to slow down in the 1960s and decelerated further in the 1970s.

In order to pursue the national goals of a suitable rate of growth, stable prices, full employment, and improved welfare, it is important to address the nation's response to these new problems of the 1980s. Government and business must respond promptly to these new changes, and effective economic policies must be designed and implemented to meet the new circumstances. Following are some basic directions for major economic policies that should be followed in the 1980s.

I. Energy Policies

An important concept in energy policy is "to achieve a certain economic growth rate with a minimum consumption of energy." Energy policies, therefore, should not be designed only for energy conservation, but also for economic growth. Accordingly, to lower energy elasticity becomes a most important task for the entire nation. Energy elasticity refers to the percentage of increase in energy input required to raise the gross domestic product by one percent.

The crux of the energy problem lies in the high price of petroleum, which not only increases costs of production but also results in a huge loss of real national income through adverse changes in the terms of trade. The loss due to unfavorable terms of trade in 1974 was 4.2% of the GNP (in 1971 prices); and the losses in 1979 and 1980 were equivalent to 2.4% and 5.2% of the real GNP for each respective year in 1976 prices. The large outflow in the real GNP due to unfavorable terms of trade reduces demand for domestic commodities and imports. Thus, even if petroleum prices remain relatively stable in the near future and rise only moderately over the long term, an efficient use of petroleum is still urgently required for the continuous growth of the economy. Three major approaches are important in reducing oil consumption without affecting economic growth:

(1) Develop a sophisticated energy saving program: promote energy conservation through the use of energy-efficient machinery and equipment rather than simply limit total electricity usage

One of the current energy saving policies merely discourages or limits electricity usage by large unit users. We should bear in mind, however, that energy policy should be designed for both energy conservation and economic growth. Energy elasticity, not energy usage, should be the indicator used to measure efficiency. Limiting electricity usage by large users is inappropriate for increasing energy efficiency. For example, in 1978 steel production by the China Steel Corporation comprised 30% of the Taiwan's total steel production, while its electricity consumption comprised only 13% of total electricity consumption by the entire steel industry. Some two hundred other small steel firms consumed the remaining 87% of electricity to produce 70% of the steel. This shows that a large unit user can be a more efficient user of electricity, and proves the necessity of sophisticated energy saving programs designed to reduce energy elasticity.

(2) Improve the industrial structure by expanding the output shares of energy efficient, skill-intensive and high-value-added industries

For example, in order to produce one dollar of output, the average amount of electricity consumed by the three industries of machinery, electrical machinery, and transportation equipment is only one third of the average usage in the manufacturing sector, and their average usage of oil is only one eleventh of the sector's average usage. Therefore, if the shares of these industries can be expanded, the economy can generate the same amount of value added with less energy.

(3) Save oil by diversification of energy utilization, particularly in power generation

The current ten-year plan (1980–89) calls for diversifying energy sources by using coal and nuclear energy in place of oil. The plan anticipates a rise in installed nuclear power-generating capacity from 17% of the total installed capacity of the Taiwan Power Company in 1979 to 29% in 1989. Over the same period, the proportion of the company's coal burning power plants is expected to rise from 12% to 31%. Aside from the Taiwan Power Company, some private industries should also shift from oil to coal as a source of energy. The move to coal will result in a rapid increase in coal consumption, which is expected to exceed 30 million tons in 1989. In order for this plan to be realized, however, the construction of port handling and storage facilities, and of new coal-burning power plants, is a matter of utmost urgency.

In order to encourage a factory to convert to energy-efficient machinery and equipment, and to direct the economy to adjust to an energy-saving structure, appropriate fiscal and monetary measures are important. For example, tax credits and low interest rate loans for investment in energy saving machinery and equipment will accelerate the move. In the revised Statute for Encouragement of Investment, the scope of tax credits for investment in energy-efficient machinery and equipment was expanded. For the development of energy-saving and high-technology industries, such as machinery, electronics, information, electrical machinery, and electrical appliances, low interest loans were designed to be offered through the Bank of Communications. However, these fiscal and monetary measures are inadequate in terms of both scope and degree. For example, low interest loans are designed to be offered to technology-intensive industries for purchases of machinery, but it is equally important—if not more so—to have loans designed for the purchase of their products. That is, while loans for their production are important, loans for their sales are no less important.   Provision for installment buying, for both domestic and foreign customers, should be intensified and facilitated, particularly in the field of machinery.   In general, much stronger incentives should be provided for the adjustment towards an energy-efficient structure.

At the same time, energy pricing policies are no less important than fiscal and monetary measures for energy conservation and should not be overlooked.   After the oil crisis in 1973, government enterprises were initially directed to absorb the increases in world oil prices.   Domestic prices and fees were raised in stages in order to prevent price fluctuations, lessen the economic burden of low-income people, and maintain the competitiveness of manufactured exports. Nevertheless, the low energy pricing policy caused manufacturing firms to be sluggish in adjusting and improving their equipment and production processes.   The manufacturing structure adjusted at a rather slow pace in the 1970s.

A greater reliance has been placed on the price mechanism in recent years.   Domestic oil prices have been allowed to change in a manner more reflective of import costs.   However, for greater efficiency in energy use and for the encouragement of further energy conservation, there is still much room left for improvement in the pricing strategy.

II. Trade and Structural Change

Export expansion has been an important factor contributing to economic growth in Taiwan.   The shares of exports and imports in the GNP were, respectively, 49% and 46% in 1981. Exports will continue to play an important role in the growth process of Taiwan due to the island's small economic scale and the need for increasing imports.

Exports grew at a 22% annual rate in real terms during 1961-71, and at 19.2% during 1971-81.   Such a high rate of export expansion was attributable to both worldwide prosperity in the 1960s and to Taiwan's rapid transition growth from an agriculture-oriented to an industry-oriented economy.   In view of the current slowdown in world trade, a further export expansion in the future should rely more heavily on the enhanced competitiveness of Taiwan's products in the international market. Important directions toward this goal are as follows:

1. Upgrade the Industrial Structure

Export expansion and improvement of the industrial structure interact with each other. Rapid export expansion was the result of rapid improvement in the production structure, and the growth of manufacturing was in turn fostered by rapid export expansion. Manufacturing exports accounted for about one half of total manufacturing production in 1981.

The past success of manufacturing development in Taiwan was characterized by product cycles of food processing, textiles, and then electrical machinery as leading industries. By the middle of the 1960s, the textile industry successfully took the place of the then declining food processing industry which was the leader in the 1950s. However, there was a significant deterioration in the speed of the development of leading industries in the 1970s. Evidence shows that electrical machinery, which developed most rapidly in the 1960s, was not able to satisfactorily take the place of the outgoing old industries in the 1970s, when textiles began deteriorating. For example, the share of textiles in manufacturing production decreased from 21.5% in 1971 to 14.9% in 1981, and the share of textile exports in total exports dropped from 35.4% to 24.2% over the same period. While the share of electrical machinery production increased from 1.8% in 1961 to 9.4% in 1971, it still remained no higher than 11.5% in 1981.

The era of low wages has passed due to the achievement of full employment. At the same time, newcomers in the international market are accelerating their exports of cheap-labor products. The only way to increase the competitiveness of ROC products is through advancement in technology and the industrial structure, so as to produce and export higher value added and more sophisticated products which utilize more skilled labor and less unskilled labor. Export expansion will be continuously generated by profitability. A prompt move from labor-intensive, light industries to skill-intensive, heavier industries is the most important change in enabling the economy to be continuously profitable in the international market.

Structural change must be pursued in two directions: increasing the share of heavier industries from the macro point of view, and upgrading the quality of products and managerial techniques within an industry from the micro point of view. For example, China Steel's participation in production upgraded the steel industry, for CSC produces products of higher quality at lower cost than do the small steel firms. An introduction of new machinery and equipment into the textile industry for improvement in the quality of products and production efficiency is most urgently needed, because the textile industry comprises a big share in manufacturing and faces keen competition from newcomers in the world market.

2. Promote Big Trading Companies

Big trading companies become more important as the scale of the economy expands and the importance of marketing increases. Big trading companies are important not only for the expansion of export markets, but also for facilitating imports of raw materials and intermediate goods at lower cost. They even provide information on new materials and intermediate goods and new methods of production. However, in the mind of the general public, the importance of commerce, marketing, and coordination has been neglected. Big trading companies have not been treated as production units until very recent days. Promotion of big trading companies is urgently needed not only for trade development, but also for advancing the industrial structure and reducing production costs.

3. Intensify Import Liberalization

In upgrading the industrial structure, the use of high tariffs and/or restriction of imports should be avoided. Due to the fact that products of the heavier industries are mostly used as intermediate inputs, levying high tariffs on or restricting imports of these products will raise their domestic prices and so increase the cost of their downstream products. Thus, the imposition of high tariffs and restriction of imports will reduce international competitive power and will generate adverse effects on exports.

Moreover, the industries receiving protection will often reap easily obtainable profits as a consequence, and have less pressure to improve quality and reduce cost. Thus, protection may make them remain in the status of infant industries for a long time.

Tariff rates in Taiwan have been reduced in recent years. However, the rates remained high as tariffs still comprised 19% of government tax revenues in 1981. Tariff reduction is particularly beneficial to an open, small, resource-poor economy, for it permits acqusition of cheaper external resources in terms of raw materials, machinery, and inter-mediate inputs. Import restriction is more objectionable than heavy tariffs, for it not only raises prices and costs but also blocks the availability of better quality and more suitable machinery and intermediate inputs. Its adverse effects on the export expansion of downstream industries are much bigger.

Taiwan's tariff structure should be rationalized. According to the present system, tariffs levied on many parts and components are higher than those on the final products. Also, substantial differences exist among items at the same level of fabrication and entering the same production process. The tariff structure should be rationalized to benefit economic development. One important consideration in tariff rationaliza-tion is that a timetable for the change in tariff structure covering several years should be worked out and made public in advance. It is very important to let entrepreneurs know in advance about changes in tariffs, so that they can adjust their plan of production accordingly.

Tax rebates, including rebates on the income tax, tariffs, commodity tax and stamp tax, contributed to the past expansion of exports. However, as the economy expands its scope horizontally and vertically to the production of more sophisticated products with more complicated procedures, tax rebates become technically unmanageable. It is beyond the government's ability and duty to calculate detailed import contents and tax burdens for close to a million export cases. The era of tax rebates has passed as the economy has upgraded to a more intensive and complex production system. It is wiser to invigorate export expansion by charting a development course that calls for low tariffs and no tax rebates.

Import liberalization has another advantage for export expansion through its effects on foreign exchange reserves and the foreign exchange rate. The Taiwan economy had a continuous positive basic balance over the past six years, 1976-81. The surpluses amounted to US$2 billion in 1978 and US$1.3 billion in 1981, piling up a big amount of foreign exchange reserves. Too much foreign exchange reserves is considered to constitute an inefficient use of financial resources, a cause of too much money supply, and a factor inducing revaluation of the New Taiwan dollar. Import liberalization will cure these adverse effects on export expansion. On the positive side, a decrease in the trade surplus will make it easier to accept foreign capital inflow and direct foreign investment, which are important, among other factors, for technical progress, structural change and further export expansion.

III. Fiscal Policies

The characteristics of the fiscal situation of the last ten-odd years were: a favorable budgetary balance, and accordingly a very small amount of public bonds issuance; a low percentage of government consumption in the GNP; and a large ratio of government savings, which was a source of funds for national construction. The situation in the 1980s may be somewhat different. The following are some points for consideration.

1. Government Budget

In the 1980s, the maintenance of a large amount of government savings may become more difficult due to the fact that the growth of government revenue may slow down along with the growth of the economy, while the requirements for government spending may increase with the need of more social welfare and infrastructural construction. Reliance on more public bonds seems unavoidable. The issuance of public bonds requires careful planning in terms of quantity, timing, conditions and technique.

Almost no fiscal policies have been designed and adopted in Taiwan for counter-cyclical purposes. In the issuance of public bonds, short-run business cycles should be taken into consideration. Also, the establishment of a sound and active secondary market for bonds transaction is very important.

2. Taxation and Government Expenditures

The impact of taxation on economic development is enormous. Its indirect effects, particularly, need careful study. Government consumption should be strictly regulated. Government investment should be encouraged in the area of infrastructure, such as transportation and communications, harbors, and land development, to create a good environment.

IV. Monetary Policies

1. Develop Capital and Secondary Markets

In the past the financial sector contributed greatly to the economic development in Taiwan, with a significant financial deepening in terms of money supply and banking loans. Over the period 1962–81, the percentage of M_1 in the GNP increased from 10.5% to 26.5%, M_2, from 24.8% to 66.5% and banks loans from 31.0% to 67.4%. On the other hand, the percentage of public and private bonds in the GNP increased only from 2% to 4.5%, and the market value of listed stocks outstanding as a percentage of the GNP increased from 8.3% to 15.2%. Since bonds and equity cost business less than loans, more financial deepening in the area of bonds issuance and development of the capital market are called for. A development of bond markets which facilitate active bond transactions is a precondition of active bond issuance. To allow bonds to be traded by the existing bills companies would be one of the quickest ways to develop the bond market.

2. Intensify the Money Market

An official money market was established in 1976 to pave the way for more flexible interest rate movements and to channel financial savings from the unorganized private money market to businesses. Money market instruments consist of commercial paper, bankers' acceptances, negotiable certificates of deposit and treasury bills. Interest rates in the money market are not subject to ceiling regulation. Over the one-and-a-half-year period from the end of 1981 to May 1982, the ratio of the value of money market instruments outstanding to total banking loans increased from 8.6% to 15.6%. Bankers' acceptances had the fastest growth, increasing 5.4 fold; CDs came next with a 2.4-fold growth, and commercial paper increased 40%. Compared with the growth of bank loans, which increased 20%, money market instruments grew very rapidly except for treasury bills, which decreased 25%. Since interest rates on money market instruments are allowed to fluctuate, the relative expansion of the money market paved the way for interest liberalization. Many improvements are still conceivable in the money market, however, in terms of both quantity of transactions and management techniques.

3. Interest Liberalization

According to the present banking law, the maximum rates for different kinds of deposits are prescribed by the Central Bank of China. The spread of interest rates on different kinds of loans are proposed by the Bankers' Association and submitted to the Central Bank of China for confirmation and enforcement. Also, minimum loan rates must exceed the maximum deposit rates.

In order to move toward interest liberalization under these regulations, the Central Bank of China promulgated the "Essentials of Interest Rate Adjustment" in November 1979. In this Essentials a bigger range of difference between maximum and minimum interest rates is permitted and free interest rates on CDs are allowed. However, due to the fact that the Regulations for Interest Rate Management do not allow maximum deposit rates to exceed minimum loan rates, and since demand for money through the banking system was very strong, the allowance of a wider gap between maximum and minimum loan rates caused banks to raise most of their actual loan rates close to the ceiling. As a result the range was reduced gradually to prevent banks from earning too much excess profit.

One of the key obstacles to interest rate liberalization lies in the present regulation stipulating that maximum deposit rates shall not exceed minimum loan rates. This regulation eliminates the possibility of approving a wider range of loan rates and deposit rates by the Central Bank of China. In order to allow interest liberalization, therefore, an amendment of the regulation is necessary. On the other hand, however, interest liberalization does not aim at perfection. For example, in the United States, Regulation Q is to be phased out by 1986 and the first step was supposed to have been taken in December 1981; however, action was delayed to March 1982. Even then, no action was taken. Although innovations in U.S. financial markets through creation of interest-carrying transaction balances and large amounts of MMF and MMC made the interest rates move toward liberalization, they also created new and difficult financial problems. For interest liberalization, a careful plan with a concrete timetable is thus called for.

4. Modernization of the Banking System

The banking system provides external help to other sectors, particularly manufacturing. The role of the banking system changes in response to the environment. As the economy becomes more industry-oriented in the 1980s, the upgrading of banking operations will be necessary. From the point of view of banking operations, there is an urgent need for computerization, mechanization, and management improvement. Form the point of view of banking services rendered to businesses, repayment of loans in installments has become a particularly important factor in improvement, because banks had few operations of that kind. Without bank reform in the area of installments, the development of the machinery industry will be very limited.

Loans extended for housing construction should be studied and intensified. Most housing construction in the 1980s will likely be on a large scale. Bank loan operations should be designed to support a modernized housing construction and sales system. From the point of view of the services that banks extend to consumers, new financial services should be provided to meet consumers' new needs. For example, credit cards, installment payment of loans for purchases of durable consumption goods, etc. should be intensified as the level of society advances in the 1980s. Lagging financial development in these areas would give rise to illegal services from the unorganized money market. Thus, in order to meet the new requirements of the advanced society, new financial commodities should be provided at the proper time.

5. Foreign Exchange

The foreign exchange system was converted from a fixed system into a floating system in February 1979. Since then, the value of the New Taiwan dollar has fluctuated. The fluctuation has been very mild; during the period from February 1979 to June 1982, the New Taiwan dollar depreciated about 10%. The economic indicators did not reveal any obvious depreciation signals, for both current accounts and the basic balance were in surplus continuously over the six-year period of 1976—81. The real effective exchange rates have been less than 100 (with 1980 as the base year) for all the six-year period, indicating that in terms of the weighted foreign exchange rate, with the relative price change (domestic prices against foreign prices) taken into account, the value of the New Taiwan dollar has been favorable for foreign trade during 1976–81.

In the coming years, the important goals in the foreign sector are continuous export expansion and net inflow of foreign capital. For continuous export expansion, the value of the New Taiwan dollar should be protected from over-valuation. The best way for this is through import liberalization. For, otherwise, export expansion together with a net inflow of foreign capital will force the value of the New Taiwan dollar to appreciate, which in turn will not be good for export expansion. Here again we see the importance of import liberalization.

V. Manpower

A shortage of unskilled labor has been experienced in recent years, due largely to the fact that structural change in industry lagged behind structural change in the labor supply. Due to government emphasis on higher education over the last three decades, the labor structure advanced quickly and will continue to advance in the 1980s. Over the 1968–89 period, for example, the proportion of the total work force with a less than junior high school education will decline from 86% to 66%; over the same period, the proportion having received senior high school and vocational school education will rise from 10% to 22%, and the proportion with advanced education (college or above) will increase from 4% to 12%. To continuously maintain full employment and at the same time fully utilize manpower in production, the demand for manpower must adjust itself to these changes in manpower structure and supply. That is, through the upgrading of production and the expansion of technology-intensive and higher value-added industries, there will be a greater demand for labor of higher quality to meet the needs of the upgraded labor structure. Looked at from another angle, an improvement in the caliber of labor can lay the basis for a further upgrading of the nation's industry and facilitate efforts to increase the value-added proportion of total output, thus helping to maintain long-term economic growth.

However, in order for senior high school and vocational school graduates to play an optimum role in industrial production, numerous improvements and shifts in emphasis must be made in vocational education and training, in terms of both quality and quantity.

VI. Technology

The rate of technical progress measures the speed of increase in output that is caused not by an increase in inputs but by an advancement in the efficiency of production. Technical progress contributed greatly to the growth of the Taiwan economy, accounting for about 50% of the growth of all sectors in the 1950s. A slowdown in technical progress started in the 1960s, however, and took a change for the worse in the 1970s. In order to provide for a more effective utilization of resources, the following are the major directions needed for the advancement of technology:

(1) Entrepreneurs should recognize the importance of upgrading management through the increased use of experts; that is, they must understand that family operations are not efficient. Material management and labor management become much more important in the management of heavy industry.

(2) Encouraging R & D through proper public policies is considered highly fruitful, for the social return exceeds the private return. Tax exemptions on the R & D expenditures of businesses, and direct government subsidies to some particular businesses, are also beneficial to society. For this reason, the expansion of the government spending on R & D is recommended.

As for the allocation of R & D funds, scaling down the proportion of basic research and scaling up the proportion of experimentation and development are considered highly beneficial. For there is now convincing evidence that the typical process of technical change is not one of dramatic breakthroughs but of a host of improvements in existing products, processes and techniques that are implemented by engineers, production supervisors and designers without any direct contribution from scientific research. A big proportion of government grants and loans should be given to private businesses. Research carried out with public funds should be oriented towards commercial objectives, and support at the development stage should be given to those activities that will generate external benefits for a number of users.

(3) The importance of improving vocational education cannot be over-emphasized. Vocational schools, both public and private, should be better equipped. Also their coordination with industries should be actively planned and implemented.

(4) Efficiency should be increased through the encouragement of automation and standarization. Automation should be emphasized not only for physical production, but also for management. In order to accelerate office automation through the use of computers, Chinese language inputs into computer software should be standardized. In addition, standardization of products is important for improving efficiency.

(5) Amendments of laws and regulations are urgently needed at this stage; for changes in some laws and regulations have been unable to match the speed of industrialization, and thus hinder production and commerce. It is necessary to review the relevant laws and regulations with a view to transforming government intervention into assistance for development.

(6) Quality control should be advanced through all practical means. The subcontracting of Japanese parts and garment production would help raise the level of quality control through a process of learning by doing.

(7) Much attention should be given to royalties and patents, and product piracy must be heavily punished. Continuation of the present situation would damage the incentive to innovate.

(8) Acceleration of depreciation should be allowed in order to encourage replacement of machinery and equipment.

The government and the people of the Republic of China have overcome many difficulties in the past three decades to achieve their present success.   If quick responses to new problems and prompt adjustments to new circumstances are made in the challenging 1980s, they will continue to have a prosperous economy and bright future.

Appendix I
A Review of Unemployment Rates

Various sources of employment data seem to indicate that in the 1950s Taiwan had large scale unemployment; the rate of unemployment declined during the mid 1960s; and by 1971 the economy had reached full employment. However the available employment data series differ in definition, sampling size and methods of compilation, which makes them diverge from one another. In order to grasp the general idea of the level of and changes in the rates of unemployment in Taiwan, a review of the unemployment rates based on all sources available is presented in this appendix.

1. Existing Unemployment Data

The existing unemployment data can be classified into two categories in terms of time, i.e., continuous and fragmentary.

The two kinds of continuous employment data are Household Registration Statistics and the Labor Force Survey. The household registration statistics have been published annually with the unemployment figures available since 1954. The labor force survey has been reported quarterly since October, 1963.

The two kinds of fragmentary employment data are Population Censuses and an Unemployment Survey. Before 1976 three population censuses were carried out, in 1956, 1966 and 1970. One unemployment survey was conducted, in 1953. The unemployment data based on these four sources will be reviewed respectively through the identification of their definition and the cross checking of their reliability.   Data are adjusted when necessary.

(1) Household Registration Statistics

The household registration statistics, being a by-product of the civil registration system, have the quality of economically active population data which is inferior to that of demographic data. Unemployment figures in these statistics have been available since 1954; however, the figures before 1967 are considered inappropriate.   The reason is that for the period 1954—60, both the unemployed and jobless persons without the desire to work were all classified as "jobless". As a result, these data show an inflated amount of unemployment based on a faulty definition. From 1961 to 1966, unemployment was distinguished from the category "jobless", but the rates of unemployment derived from this source were as low as 0.2% to 0.3%; these figures are inconsistent with the 1966 Census data.   The statistics have been improved since 1967 and now provide rather reasonable figures.

Thus, the household registration statistics provide reasonable unemployment figures only for the period 1967—73 (Table AI.1); however, for the whole period 1964—73, figures are shown in Table AI.5for reference.

(2) Labor Force Survey

The labor force survey was initiated by the Taiwan Provincial Labor Force Survey & Research Institute in October 1963.   Since then, it has been conducted quarterly without interruption in January, April, July and October every year.   The collection of unemployment data has been stipulated as one of the major purposes of conducting this survey.   Not only are the breakdowns detailed enough for various analyses, but the concepts and sample design adopted by the institute are also quite close to those used by advanced countries.   The lower age limit for unemployment was 12 in 1963, and it has been raised from 12 to 15 since 1968.

According to the definition adopted by the Taiwan Provincial Labor Force Survey and Research Institute, unemployed persons fit into these basic categories: (a) without a job, (b) available for work and (c) looking for work.   It seems that these criteria are more meaningful for developed

Table AI.1   Unemployment Data Based on Household Registration

Year	Unemployment	
	No. of Persons (Persons)	Unemployment Rate (%)
1967	250,069	5.71
1968	206,649	4.55
1969	202,045	3.93
1970	216,153	4.10
1971	189,232	3.36
1972	165,874	2.77
1973	176,212	2.81

Source: Ministry of Interior, *The Statistical Report of Household Registration for Taiwan-Fukien Area,* various years.
Note: The unemployed were counted as persons aged 12 and over before 1968. Since then, the lower age limit has been raised from 12 to 15.

countries than for developing countries. In development countries, an effective labor market mechanism has not yet been established, and the employment relations are in the main set up through the instrumentality of friends and relatives. In rural areas, the unemployed usually do not know whom to contact about, nor where to find, jobs.   Hence, use of this definition tends to underestimate the level of unemployment. If the activity of job hunting is not taken as a necessary   condition, and the unemployed are considered to be those who are jobless but have the ability and willingness to work, the results are more likely to reflect the facts.   In this aspect, the Institute has classified one group as "willing to work but not job hunting" under the potential labor force category in its quarterly report. The status of this group shows not too much difference from that of unemployment derived from the usual definition, except that it includes those people who are not actively looking for jobs. This will be called "unemployment in broad terms," and is calculated as shown in the second part in Table AI.2.

(3) Population Census

Three population censuses were conducted prior to 1976: in 1956,

1966 and 1970. The census of 1970 was conducted in response to the UN's call for a world-wide unification of the census year based on a 5% sample census of population. The unemployment data obtained from these censuses are presented in Table AI.3.

(4) Unemployment Survey

The Unemployment Survey was conducted by the Taiwan Provincial Department of Social Affairs in September, 1953. The characteristics of unemployment covered in this survey included sex, age, educational attainment, causes of unemployment and occupation of last job. However, the unemployed included only those who had lost their jobs and were jobless and available for work in the age group of 18 to 60, without counting first-job seekers or those persons below 18 and above 60. Therefore, this survey of unemployment covered only part of the unemployed, and gave a total unemployment figure as low as 39,099 persons; the unemployment rate based on these figures was only 1.37%.

2.   Overall View of Unemployment in Taiwan

The foregoing statements can be summarized as follows:

(1) The quality of unemployment data seems inadequate before the Labor Force Survey data became available beginning in 1963. Estimates derived from census and household registration data tend to overestimate the level of unemployment.

(2) Generally, the definition of unemployment adopted by the Labor Force Survey and Research Institute follows the concept used by advanced countries. However, the socio-economic background and stage of development of the advanced countries differ from those of the developing ones. This leads to underestimation of the level of unemployment. In order to reflect the present situation, necessary adjustments have to be made.

(3) Before 1962, there was little unemployment information other than that obtained from the 1953 Unemployment Survey and the 1956 Census. The 1953 Unemployment Survey covered only part of the unemployed. It excluded first-job seekers and those who had lost their jobs at the age 61 years and over, or below the age of 17. In order to be definitionally appropriate and comparable to other years, some necessary esti-

Table AI.2   Unemployment Data Based on Labor Force Survey

Year	Total Unemployment with Activity of Seeking Jobs		Total Unemployment Including Persons Intending to Work but Not Seeking Jobs (i.e., in Broad Terms)	
	No. of Persons	Unemployment Rate	No. of Persons	Unemployment Rate
1963	198,000	5.25	–	–
1964	166,000	4.34	250,000	6.40
1965	128,000	3.34	203,000	5.20
1966	120,000	3.12	161,000	4.15
1967	95,000	2.31	140,000	3.36
1968	74,000	1.72	120,000	2.76
1969	84,000	1.86	157,000	3.42
1970	79,000	1.70	142,000	3.01
1971	80,000	1.66	147,000	3.01
1972	75,000	1.49	141,000	2.77
1973	68,000	1.26	122,000	2.24
1974	85,000	1.53	150,000	2.66
1975	136,000	2.40	214,000	3.73
1976	85,000	1.48	153,000	2.63

Source: Taiwan Provincial Labor Force Survey & Research Institute, *Quarterly Report on the Labor Force Survey in Taiwan, Republic of China,* various years.
Note: 1963 data refer to October figures.

mates have to be made based on these incomplete data. With the adjusted data of the 1953 Unemployment Survey, 1956 Census and adjusted Labor Force Survey, unemployment figures for 1954–55 and 1957–63 are interpolated in Table AI.4. The denominators needed for calculation of unemployment rates for the period of 1953–63, when the Labor Force Survey had not yet been established, are estimated in Appendix II.

Unemployment rates, some of which are adjusted or estimated, are presented in Fig. 4.1.

These rates give a general idea about the level of and changes in the rates of unemployment during the period of 1953 through 1980. The unemployment rate was high before 1965. It dropped rapidly from 1965

Table AI.3   Unemployment Data Based on Population Census

Year	Age	Total Unemployment	
		No. of Persons	Unemployment Rate
1956	12 and over	293,070	9.84
	15 and over	175,844	6.34
1966	12 and over	434,294	9.45
	15 and over	261,203	6.14
1970	15 and over	232,151	4.57

Source:
   1956: Office of Population Census, Taiwan Provincial Government, *The 1956 Census Report of Population, Republic of China.*
   1966: Office of Population Census, Taiwan Provincial Government, *The 1966 Census Report of Population & Housing, Taiwan-Fukien Area, Republic of China.*
   1970: Census Office of the Executive Yuan, *The 1970 Sample Census of Population and Housing, Taiwan-Fukien Area, Republic of China, General Report.*

to 1968. By 1971 the unemployment rate had reached 3.36% according to the household registration statistics, and 3.01% according to the labor force survey in broad terms. Thus, if 3% is viewed as a criterion of full employment, it can be said that by approximately 1971, the Taiwan economy had successfully reached the full employment level after a period of extensive labor absorption.

Table AI.4   Unemployment Rate

Year	No. of Unemployed (per 1,000 persons)	Unemploy- ment Rate (%)	Year	No. of Unemployed (per 1,000 persons)	Unemploy- ment Rate (%)
1953	194	6.29	1967	140	3.36
1954	188	6.02	1968	120	2.76
1955	182	5.79	1969	157	3.42
1956	176	5.63	1970	142	3.01
1957	185	5.73	1971	147	3.01
1958	194	5.88	1972	141	2.77
1959	204	5.99	1973	122	2.24
1960	213	6.12	1974	150	2.66
1961	222	6.21	1975	214	3.73
1962	231	6.32	1976	153	2.63
1963	241	6.38	1977	138	2.27
1964	250	6.40	1978	173	2.69
1965	203	5.20	1979	145	2.21
1966	161	4.15	1980	137	2.05

Source:
   1953: Adjusted as in Note 1, based on Department of Social Affairs, Taiwan
   Provincial Government, *1953 Unemployment Survey.*
   1954–1955: Estimates.
   1956: Office of Population Census, Taiwan Provincial Government, *The 1956
   Census Report of Population, Republic of China.*
   1957–1963: Estimates
   1964–1980: Directorate-General of Budget, Accounting and Statistics, Executive
   Yuan, *Yearbook of Labor Statistics, Republic of China, 1981.*
Notes:
   1. The 1953 unemployment figure is adjusted as follows:
      a. Unemployed persons aged 18 to 60 in the 1953 Unemployment Survey
         were estimated at 39,099, and it is assumed that the proportions of first-
         job seekers and the unemployed who had lost their jobs at ages in the 16 to
         60 range were the same as those in the 1956 Census period.
      b. Numbers of the unemployed with work experience in the age bracket of
         18-60 were 35,441, and those aged 15 and over in 1956 Census Report
         totaled 37,574. Therefore, the total unemployed persons 15 years old and
         over can be calculated proportionally as 41,452 persons in 1953.
$$39,099 \times \frac{37,574}{35,441} = 41,452$$
      c. In the 1956 Census Report, the total unemployed aged 15 and over were
         175,844. It is assumed that the ratio of the unemployed with work ex-
         perience to the total unemployed in 1953 was identical with that in 1956,
         so that the total unemployed in 1953 can be calculated as follow:
$$41,452 \times \frac{175,844}{37,574} = 193,993$$
   2. The unemployed figures from 1964 to 1980 are derived from LFS, which
      includes persons intending to work but not seeking job opportunities.

Table AI.5   Household Registration Statistics
(at End of Year)

(person)

Year	Total Population	Employed Population	Unemployed Population	Others	Housekeeping	Student
1946	6,090,860	2,325,768		1,587,200		
1947	6,497,734	2,481,465		1,760,590		
1948	6,807,601	2,614,475		1,847,751		
1949	7,396,931	2,828,149		2,070,395		
1950	7,554,399	2,848,849		2,118,324		
1951	7,869,247	2,880,623		1,885,138		351,735
1952	8,128,374	2,936,097		1,932,825		388,208
1953	8,438,016	2,953,838		2,005,737		462,469
1954	8,749,151	2,999,617	407,925		1,657,733	507,137
1955	9,077,643	3,025,849	415,569		1,719,109	567,021
1956	9,390,381	3,015,182	438,474		1,772,061	624,595
1957	9,690,250	3,109,885	445,598		1,842,168	555,749
1958	10,039,435	3,177,677	448,388		1,934,093	542,310
1959	10,431,341	3,272,384	463,936		1,984,834	598,545
1960	10,792,202	3,343,711	494,349		2,039,005	652,155
1961	11,149,139	3,428,525	6,775	505,323	2,098,498	736,025
1962	11,511,728	3,503,623	7,580	569,535	2,156,347	798,281
1963	11,883,523	3,616,023	8,205	613,183	2,217,393	898,388
1964	12,256,682	3,710,555	10,333	669,617	2,289,019	983,607
1965	12,628,348	3,755,289	8,431	726,926	2,320,739	1,179,773
1966	12,992,763	3,870,442	11,724	774,267	2,393,134	1,271,923
1967	13,296,571	4,129,953	250,069	402,102	2,169,963	589,599
1968	13,650,370	4,336,613	206,649	395,107	2,256,206	661,608
1969	14,334,862	4,942,072	202,045	366,732	2,262,060	755,752
1970	14,675,964	5,053,095	216,153	384,121	2,340,035	861,421
1971	14,994,823	5,440,274	189,232	392,211	2,247,185	920,739
1972	15,289,048	5,811,700	165,874	378,147	2,156,283	980,349
1973	15,564,830	6,090,596	176,212	383,139	2,162,753	982,931

Source:
    1946–1966: Bureau of Accounting & Statistics, Taiwan Provincial Government,
        Statistical Abstract of Taiwan Province, Republic of China (Oct.
        1971).
    1967–1973: Same as Table AI.1.
Note: Others include jobless, old or sick, institutionalized.

Population Aged 15 & under (1966 and before, Aged 12 & under)
2,177,892
2,255,679
2,345,375
2,498,387
2,587,226
2,751,751
2,871,244
3,015,972
3,176,739
3,350,095
3,540,069
3,736,850
3,936,967
4,111,642
4,262,982
4,373,993
4,476,362
4,530,331
4,593,551
4,637,190
4,671,273
5,754,885
5,794,187
5,806,201
5,821,139
5,805,182
5,796,695
5,769,199

Appendix II
A Review and Recompilation of Employment

The review and recompilation of employment here are aimed at consistency of definition and adjustments for over-estimation and under-estimation.

The original employment data are available from two sources. The Household Registration gives employment data for the total economy and for sub-industries for the period 1952–66; but the employed in this source refer to those aged 12 and over, and occupations are classified under the old definitions. The Labor Force Survey provides employment data only from 1964; but it includes those aged 15 and over, and is based on the new classification of occupations.

Aiming at consistency of definition and at the adjustment of abused definitions, the data are estimated and/or adjusted for the period 1952–66. The procedure of estimation is as follows:

(1) New and old classifications of occupations are compared.

(2) The data based on the old classification are reclassified into the new classification.

(3) The primary, secondary, and tertiary industries are identified, based on the new classification.

(4) In order to have a consistent series of employment data for ages 15 and over, it is necessary to link the two sources of employment, i.e., the Labor Force Survey which starts in 1964 with employment for ages 15 and over, and the Household Registration which runs from 1952 to 1966 with employment for ages 12 and over.

For three years, 1964, 1965 and 1966, employment data are available

339

from both sources. Thus, for these three years, the ratios of employment aged 15 and over to employment aged 12 and over are calculated and the average ratio is obtained as 0.9778. Utilizing this ratio, the employment in the Household Registration is adjusted to employment for ages 15 and over for the years 1952–63 (see column (4) of Table AII.2).

(5) Due to the characteristic of registration its mechanism, the Household Registration has an obvious over-estimation of primary-industry employment and under-estimation of secondary-industry employment. The distribution of employment among industries is more reliable in the Labor Force Survey; however, the Labor Force Survey provides this distribution data only from 1966 (although it provides total employment of the economy from 1964). The only comparable year, 1966, shows that the percentage of primary-industry employment to total employment was 43.4% according to the Labor Force Survey, while it was 50.3% according to the Household Registration; the percentage of secondary-industry employment to total employment was 23.4% according to the Labor Force Survey, while it was 12.3% according to the Household Registration. Thus, when we put the two sources of employment figures together, we find an obvious discontinuity of percentage distribution in 1966 (see Table AII.3).

In order to adjust the primary-industry employment of the Household Registration downward, the difference between the two sources in 1966 for this item (53.0% − 43.4%) is deducted from the Household Registration for the period 1952–65. In order to adjust the secondary-industry employment of the Household Registration upward, the difference between the two sources in 1966 for this item (23.4% − 12.3%) is added to the Household Registration for the period 1952–1965. The tertiary-industry figure is obtained as a residual.

(6) With total employment for ages 15 and over (Table AII.2) and the ratio of employment for each industry to total employment (Table AII.4), the number of employed aged 15 and over for each industry is obtained in Table AII.5.

Table AII.1   A Comparison of the New and Old Classifications
              of Occupations

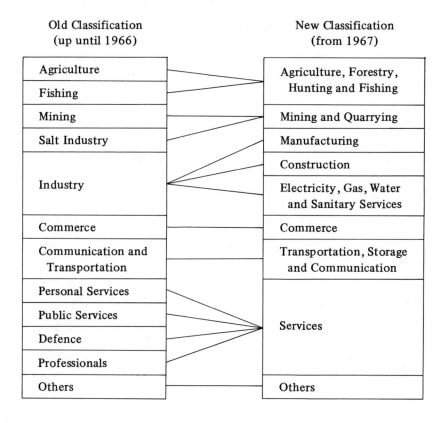

Old Classification   New Classification
(up until 1966)   (from 1967)

Table AII.2   Employment of the Whole Economy

(1,000 persons)

Year	Labor Force Survey Data (15 and more then 15 years old, mid-year figure)	Household Registration Data (12 and more than 12 years old, end-of-year figure)		Total Laborers (15 and more then 15 years old)
	(1)	(2)	(3)=(1)/(2)	(4) = (2)×0.9778
1952		2,936		2,871
1953		2,954		2,888
1954		3,000		2,933
1955		3,026		2,959
1956		3,015		2,948
1957		3,110		3,041
1958		3,178		3,107
1959		3,272		3,199
1960		3,344		3,270
1961		3,429		3,353
1962		3,504		3,426
1963		3,617		3,537
1964	3,658	3,710	0.9860	3,658
1965	3,701	3,755	0.9856	3,701
1966	3,722	3,870	0.9618	3,722
1967	4,022			4,022
1968	4,225			4,225
1969	4,433			4,433
1970	4,576			4,576
1971	4,738			4,738
1972	4,948			4,948
1973	5,327			5,327
1974	5,486			5,486
1975	5,521			5,521
1976	5,663			5,663
Average			0.9778	

Source:
1. 1964–1976: Taiwan Provincial Labor Force Survey & Research Institute, *Quarterly Report on the Labor Force Survey in Taiwan, Republic of China*, Vol. 55 (April 1977) p. 39.
2. 1952–1963: column (2) is original Household Registration data; column (4) is the adjusted data.

Table AII.3   Distribution of Employment by Industry Origin
(Unadjusted Data)

(%)

Mid-year	Primary Industry		Secondary Industry	
	Labor Force Survey Data	Household Registration Data	Labor Force Survey Data	Household Registration Data
1952		61.0		9.3
1953		61.3		9.2
1954		60.4		9.6
1955		59.9		9.8
1956		59.9		9.9
1957		58.2		10.4
1958		57.1		10.9
1959		56.6		11.1
1960		56.1		11.3
1961		55.8		11.3
1962		55.3		11.5
1963		54.5		11.7
1964		54.2		11.8
1965		53.7		12.0
1966	43.4	53.0	23.4	12.3
1967	42.8		25.2	
1968	39.7		24.9	
1969	38.9		26.5	
1970	36.7		28.3	
1971	35.1		30.3	
1972	33.0		32.1	
1973	30.5		34.0	
1974	30.9		34.5	
1975	29.9		35.5	
1976	29.1		36.4	

Source: Labor Force Survey Data: Taiwan Provincial Labor Force Survey & Research Institute, *Quarterly Report on the Labor Force Survey in Taiwan, Republic of China,* Vol, 55, (April, 1977) p. 49.
Household Registration Data: Economic Planning Council, Executive Yuan,
Taiwan Statistical Data Book, (1977) p. 8.

Table AII.4   Distribution of Employment by Industry Origin
(Adjusted for 1952—1965)

(%)

Mid-year	Primary Industry	Secondary Industry	Tertiary Industry
1952	51.4	20.4	28.2
1953	51.7	20.3	28.0
1954	50.8	20.7	28.5
1955	50.3	20.9	28.8
1956	50.3	21.0	28.7
1957	48.6	21.5	29.9
1958	47.5	22.0	30.5
1959	47.0	22.2	30.8
1960	46.5	22.4	31.1
1961	46.2	22.4	31.4
1962	45.7	22.6	31.7
1963	44.9	22.8	32.3
1964	44.6	22.9	32.5
1965	44.1	23.1	32.8
1966	43.4	23.4	33.2
1967	42.8	25.2	32.0
1968	39.7	24.9	35.4
1969	38.9	26.5	34.6
1970	36.7	28.3	35.0
1971	35.1	30.3	34.6
1972	33.0	32.1	34.9
1973	30.5	34.0	35.5
1974	30.9	34.5	34.6
1975	29.9	35.5	34.6
1976	29.1	36.4	34.5

Source: 1966—1976: Taiwan Provincial Labor Force Survey & Research Institute,
Quarterly Report on the Labor Force Survey in Taiwan, Republic of China,
Vol. 55, (April 1977) p. 49.
1952—1965: Adjusted Data.

Table AII.5   Employment by Industry Origin
(Adjusted for 1952—1965)

(1,000 persons)

Mid-year	Primary Industry	Secondary Industry	Tertiary Industry
1952	1,476	586	809
1953	1,493	586	809
1954	1,490	607	836
1955	1,488	619	852
1956	1,483	619	846
1957	1,478	654	909
1958	1,476	683	948
1959	1,504	710	985
1960	1,521	732	1,017
1961	1,549	751	1,053
1962	1,566	774	1,086
1963	1,588	806	1,143
1964	1,631	838	1,189
1965	1,632	855	1,214
1966	1,617	870	1,235
1967	1,723	1,013	1,286
1968	1,676	1,051	1,498
1969	1,726	1,172	1,535
1970	1,681	1,295	1,600
1971	1,665	1,435	1,638
1972	1,632	1,590	1,726
1973	1,624	1,810	1,893
1974	1,697	1,891	1,898
1975	1,652	1,961	1,908
1976	1,649	2,063	1,951

Source: Same as Table AII.4.

Appendix III
Decomposition of Sources of Demand

Using the same notations as in the text (on pages 144-145), we explain the supply-demand balance equation of the input-output system as:

(1) $X = A^d X + A^m X + C + B + E - M^w - M^f$

$$\text{(where } A^m X = M^w)$$

Thus, in domestic terms

(2) $X = A^d X + \hat{U}_c C + \hat{U}_b B + E$

i.e.,

$$
\begin{bmatrix} X_1 \\ X_2 \\ \cdot \\ \cdot \\ \cdot \\ X_n \end{bmatrix}
=
\begin{bmatrix} a^d_{11} & a^d_{12} & \cdots & a^d_{1n} \\ a^d_{21} & a^d_{22} & & a^d_{2n} \\ \cdot & & & \cdot \\ \cdot & & & \cdot \\ \cdot & & & \cdot \\ a^d_{n1} & a^d_{n2} & \cdots & a^d_{nn} \end{bmatrix}
\begin{bmatrix} X_1 \\ X_2 \\ \cdot \\ \cdot \\ \cdot \\ X_n \end{bmatrix}
+
\begin{bmatrix} U_{1c} & 0 & \cdots & 0 \\ 0 & U_{2c} & & 0 \\ \cdot & & & \cdot \\ \cdot & & & \cdot \\ 0 & 0 & \cdots & U_{nc} \end{bmatrix}
\begin{bmatrix} C_1 \\ C_2 \\ \cdot \\ \cdot \\ \cdot \\ C_n \end{bmatrix}
$$

$$
+
\begin{bmatrix} U_{1b} & 0 & \cdots & 0 \\ 0 & U_{2b} & & 0 \\ \cdot & & & \cdot \\ \cdot & & & \cdot \\ 0 & 0 & \cdots & U_{nb} \end{bmatrix}
\begin{bmatrix} b_1 \\ b_2 \\ \cdot \\ \cdot \\ b_n \end{bmatrix}
+
\begin{bmatrix} e_1 \\ e_2 \\ \cdot \\ \cdot \\ e_n \end{bmatrix}
$$

Solving (2) for X, we have

(3) $X = (1 - A^d)^{-1} (\hat{U}_c C + \hat{U}_b B + E)$

i.e.,

$X = R^d (\hat{U}_c C + \hat{U}_b B + E)$

Based on this basic equation, the increment of each sector over the two periods, ΔX, can be calculated as follows.

(4) $\Delta X = X_2 - X_1$

$= R_2^d (\hat{U}_c^2 C_2 + \hat{U}_b^2 B_2 + E_2)$

$- R_1^d (\hat{U}_c^1 C_1 + \hat{U}_b^1 B_1 + E_1)$

$= R_2^d [(\hat{U}_c^2 C_2 - \hat{U}_c^2 C_1) + (\hat{U}_b^2 B_2 - \hat{U}_b^2 B_1) + (E_2 - E_1)]$

$+ R_2^d (\hat{U}_c^2 C_1 + \hat{U}_b^2 B_1 + E_1)$

$- R_1^d (\hat{U}_c^1 C_1 + \hat{U}_b^1 B_1 + E_1)$

$= R_2^d (\hat{U}_c^2 \Delta C + U_b^2 \Delta B + \Delta E)$

$+ R_2^d [(\hat{U}_c^2 C_1 - \hat{U}_c^1 C_1) + (\hat{U}_b^2 B_1 - \hat{U}_b^1 B_1)]$

$+ R_2^d (\hat{U}_c^1 C_1 + \hat{U}_b^1 B_1 + E_1)$

$- R_1^d (\hat{U}_c^1 C_1 + \hat{U}_b^1 B_1 + E_1)$

$= R_2^d (\hat{U}_c^2 \Delta C + \hat{U}_b^2 \Delta B + \Delta E)$

$+ R_2^d (\Delta \hat{U}_c C_1 + \Delta \hat{U}_b B_1)$

$+ (R_2^d - R_1^d)(\hat{U}_c^1 C_1 + \hat{U}_b^1 B_1 + E_1)$

But

$$(R_2^d - R_1^d) (\hat{U}_c^1 C_1 + \hat{U}_b^1 B_1 + E_1)$$

$$= R_2^d (I - A_1^d) (I - A_1^d)^{-1} (\hat{U}_c^1 C_1 + \hat{U}_b^1 B_1 + E_1)$$

$$- (I - A_2^d)^{-1} (I - A_2^d) R_1^d (\hat{U}_c^1 C_1 + \hat{U}_b^1 B_1 + E_1)$$

$$= R_2^d (I - A_1^d) R_1^d (\hat{U}_c^1 C_1 + \hat{U}_b^1 B_1 + E_1)$$

$$- R_2^d (I - A_2^d) R_1^d (\hat{U}_c^1 C_1 + \hat{U}_b^1 B_1 + E_1)$$

$$= R_2^d (I - A_1^d) X_1 - R_2^d (I - A_2^d) X_1$$

$$= R_2^d (A_2^d - A_1^d) X_1$$

Thus

$$(5) \quad \Delta X = R_2^d (\hat{U}_c^2 \Delta C + \hat{U}_b^2 \Delta B + \Delta E)$$

$$+ R_2^d (\Delta \hat{U}_c C_1 + \Delta \hat{U}_b B_1) + R_2^d (A_2^d - A_1^d) X_1$$

Further, the term $(A_2^d - A_1^d)$ can be written as

$$(6) \quad A_2^d - A_1^d = (A_2 - A_1) - (A_2^m - A_1^m)$$

The first term on the right-hand side of (6) is the change in the input matrix that is caused by a change in production technology. The second term contains the change due to both technology change and import substitution. For example, the import of iron ore for the production of one unit of steel, a_{ij}^m , would be decreased if production efficiency increased and/or domestic production could be further substituted. In order to separate these two effects contained in $A_2^m - A_1^m$, we will construct an import matrix $\tilde{A}_2^m$, which can express how much import would have been needed in period 2 if there were neither technology change nor import substitution. A typical element in $\tilde{A}_2^m$ can be shown as

$$\tilde{a}_{ij2}^m = a_{ij2}^m \times \frac{a_{ij1}}{a_{ij2}}$$

where it indicates that actually a_{ij2}^{m} is imported, but if there is no technology change nor import substitution, then $\tilde{a}_{ij2}^{m}$ should be imported.

Let us rewrite $(A_2^m - A_1^m)$ as

(7) $A_2^m - A_1^m = (A_2^m - \tilde{A}_2^m) + (\tilde{A}_2^m - A_1^m)$

The elements of the first term on the right-hand side can be written as

(8) $a_{ij2}^{m} - a_{ij2}^{m} \dfrac{a_{ij1}}{a_{ij2}} = \dfrac{a_{ij2}^{m}}{a_{ij2}} (a_{ij2} - a_{ij1})$

Thus, we can write

(9) $A_2^m - \tilde{A}_2^m = [m_{ij}^2 \cdot \Delta a_{ij}]_{(n \times n)}$ where $m_{ij}^2 = \dfrac{a_{ij2}^{m}}{a_{ij2}}$

This is the change in the input coefficient (change in production technology) multiplied by import ratio of period 2. Hence, the term $(A_2^m - \tilde{A}_2^m)$ measures the extent to which imports would have increased due to the change in technology if the import ratio for intermediate goods had been fixed.

In turn, the elements of $(\tilde{A}_2^m - A_1^m)$ can be written as

(10) $a_{ij2}^{m} \dfrac{a_{ij1}}{a_{ij2}} - a_{ij1}^{m} = \left(\dfrac{a_{ij2}^{m}}{a_{ij2}} - \dfrac{a_{ij1}^{m}}{a_{ij1}} \right) a_{ij1}$

Thus, we can write

(11) $\tilde{A}_2^m - A_1^m = [\Delta m_{ij} \cdot a_{ij1}]_{(n \times n)}$

This is the change in the import ratio multiplied by the input coefficient in period 1. Hence, the term $(\tilde{A}_2^m - A_1^m)$ measures how much additional imports would have been needed if technology had not changed.

Accordingly, the negative of $(\tilde{A}_2^m - A_1^m)$ measures the output increment from domestic production for import substitution.

Incorporating (7) through (11) into (6), we have:

$$\therefore \qquad A_2^d - A_1^d = (A_2 - A_1) - (A_2^m - A_1^m)$$

$$= \Delta A - [(A_2^m - \tilde{A}_2^m) + (\tilde{A}_2^m - A_1^m)]$$

$$\therefore (12) \ (A_2^d - A_1^d) X_1$$

$$= \left\{ -(\tilde{A}_2^m - A_1^m) + [\Delta A - (A_2^m - \tilde{A}_2^m)] \right\} X_1$$

$$= \qquad IS_w \qquad + \qquad TC$$

In Equation (12), the two terms on the right-hand side explain the change in domestic production due to import substitution of intermediate goods at fixed technology (IS_w), and due to technology change at a fixed import ratio of intermediate goods (TC), respectively.

Assuming $X_j = 1,000$, a simple numerical example may be used for clarification. Let us assume that in order to produce 1,000 units of commodity j, the following units of input i are needed, respectively, for the two periods:

$$a_{ij1}^d \times 1,000 = 10, \quad a_{ij1}^m \times 1,000 = 110, \quad a_{ij1} \times 1,000 = 120$$

$$a_{ij2}^d \times 1,000 = 20, \quad a_{ij1}^m \times 1,000 = 40, \quad a_{ij2} \times 1,000 = 60$$

Then, $\quad \tilde{a}_{ij2}^m = a_{ij2}^m \dfrac{a_{ij1}}{a_{ij2}} = 40 \times \dfrac{120}{60} = 80$

This means if technology did not change and there were no import substitution, the import of i for intermediate use should have been 80 units. According to (12),

$$IS_w \text{ for } i = -(\tilde{a}_{ij2}^m - a_{ij1}^m)$$

$$= -(80 - 110) = 30$$

$$\text{TC} \quad \text{for } i = [\Delta a_{ij} - (a^{m}_{ij2} - \tilde{a}^{m}_{ij2})]$$

$$= [(60 - 120) - (40 - 80)] = -20$$

Thus, IS_w and TC together explain the expansion in output, which is $a^{d}_{ij2} - a^{d}_{ij1} = 10$. In other words, 10 units of output expansion of commodity i is partly due to import substitution with fixed technology (+30 units) and partly due to technology change (technology improvement in this case) with a fixed import ratio (−20 units).

Also, since $m_{ij} = a^{m}_{ij} / a_{ij}$, m_{ij} can be written as $m_{ij} = 1 - U_{ijw}$, where U_{ijw} is the ratio of the supply of intermediate goods i that is produced domestically. Therefore, $\Delta m_{ij} = \Delta (1 - U_{ijw}) = -\Delta U_{ijw}$. Thus, the terms in Equation (12) can also be written as:

$$(A^{m}_{2} - \tilde{A}^{m}_{2}) = [m^{2}_{ij} \, \Delta a_{ij}] = [(1 - U^{2}_{ijw}) \Delta a_{ij}]_{(nxn)},$$

$$[\Delta A - (A^{m}_{2} - \tilde{A}^{m}_{2})] = [U^{2}_{ijw} \, \Delta a_{ij}],$$

and $\quad (\tilde{A}^{m}_{2} - A^{m}_{1}) = [\Delta m_{ij} \, a_{ij1}] = [-\Delta U_{ijw} \cdot a_{ij1}]$

Incorporating those into Equation (5), we can write ΔX as:

$$(13) \quad \Delta X = R^{d}_{2} (\hat{U}^{2}_{c} \Delta C + \hat{U}^{2}_{b} \Delta B + \Delta E)$$

$$+ R^{d}_{2} \left\{ \Delta \hat{U}_{c} C_{1} + \Delta \hat{U}_{b} B_{1} + [\Delta U_{ijw} \, a_{ij1}] X_{1} \right\}$$

$$+ R^{d}_{2} [U^{2}_{ijw} \, \Delta a_{ij}] X_{1}$$

This is the equation of the Laspeyres version, which appeared as Equation (4) in the text (page 147).

The other version, the Passche version of the decomposition equation can be shown as the following:

$$\Delta X = X_2 - X_1$$

$$= R_2^d (\hat{U}_c^2 C_2 + \hat{U}_b^2 B_2 + E_2) - R_1^d (\hat{U}_c^1 C_1 + \hat{U}_b^1 B_1 + E_1)$$

$$= R_2^d (\hat{U}_c^2 C_2 + \hat{U}_b^2 B_2 + E_2) - R_1^d (\hat{U}_c^2 C_2 + \hat{U}_b^2 B_2 + E_2)$$

$$+ R_1^d \ [(\hat{U}_c^2 C_2 - \hat{U}_c^1 C_1) + (\hat{U}_b^2 B_2 - \hat{U}_b^1 B_1) + (E_2 - E_1)]$$

$$= (R_2^d - R_1^d)(\hat{U}_c^2 C_2 + \hat{U}_b^2 B_2 + E_2)$$

$$+ R_1^d \left\{ [(\hat{U}_c^2 C_2 - \hat{U}_c^1 C_2) + \hat{U}_c^1 \Delta C] \right.$$

$$\left. + [(\hat{U}_b^2 B_2 - \hat{U}_b^1 B_2) + \hat{U}_b^1 \Delta B] + \Delta E \right\}$$

$$= (R_2^d - R_1^d)(\hat{U}_c^2 C_2 + \hat{U}_b^2 B_2 + E_2)$$

$$+ R_1^d (\hat{U}_c^1 \Delta C + \hat{U}_b^1 \Delta B + \Delta E)$$

$$+ R_1^d (\Delta \hat{U}_c C_2 + \Delta \hat{U}_b B_2)$$

But $(R_2^d - R_1^d)(\hat{U}_c^2 C_2 + \hat{U}_b^2 B_2 + E_2)$

$$= (I - A_1^d)^{-1}(I - A_1^d) R_2^d (\hat{U}_c^2 C_2 + \hat{U}_b^2 B_2 + E_2)$$

$$- R_1^d (I - A_2^d)(I - A_2^d)^{-1}(\hat{U}_c^2 C_2 + \hat{U}_b^2 B_2 + E_2)$$

$$= R_1^d (I - A_1^d) R_2^d (\hat{U}_c^2 C_2 + \hat{U}_b^2 B_2 + E_2)$$

$$- R_1^d (I - A_2^d) R_2^d (\hat{U}_c^2 C_2 + \hat{U}_b^2 B_2 + E_2)$$

$$= R_1^d [(I - A_1^d) - (I - A_2^d)] X_2$$

$$= R_1^d (A_2^d - A_1^d) X_2$$

$\therefore$ (14) $\Delta X = R_1^d (\hat{U}_c^1 \Delta C + \hat{U}_b^1 \Delta B + \Delta E)$

$+ R_1^d (\Delta \hat{U}_c C_2 + \Delta \hat{U}_b B_2)$

$- R_1^d (\tilde{\tilde{A}}_2^m - A_1^m) X_2$

$+ R_1^d [\Delta A - (A_2^m - \tilde{\tilde{A}}_2^m)] X_2$

$$\left[\begin{array}{l} \text{But a typical element of } \tilde{\tilde{A}}_{ij1}^m, \ \tilde{\tilde{a}}_{ij1}^m \text{ is defined} \\[2mm] \text{as } \ \tilde{\tilde{a}}_{ij1}^m = a_{ij1}^m \times \dfrac{a_{ij2}}{a_{ij1}} \end{array} \right]$$

Also $\Delta X = R_1^d (\hat{U}_c^1 \Delta C + \hat{U}_b^1 \Delta B + \Delta E)$

$+ R_1^d \left\{ \Delta \hat{U}_c C_2 + \Delta \hat{U}_b B_2 \right.$

$+ [\Delta U_{ijw} a_{ij2}] X_2 \left. \right\}$

$+ R_1^d [U_{ijw}^1 \Delta a_{ij}] X_2$

Thus, we obtain Equation (4)' in the text (page 147).

Appendix IV
Input-Output Sector Classifications

Reclassified 58 Sectors

1. Paddy Rice
2. Sugarcane
3. Other Common Crops
4. Livestock
5. Forestry
6. Fisheries
7. Coal & Products (excluding Gas)
8. Metallic Minerals
9. Crude Petroleum & Natural Gas
10. Salt
11. Non-Metallic Minerals
12. Rice
13. Sugar
14. Canned Foods
15. Tobacco & Alcoholic Beverages
16. Monosodium Glutamate
17. Wheat Flour
18. Edible Vegetable Oil & By-products
19. Non-Alcoholic Beverages
20. Misc. Food Products
21. Artificial Fibres
22. Artificial Fabrics
23. Cotton Fabrics
24. Woolen & Worsted Fabrics
25. Misc. Fabrics & Apparel, Accessories
26. Lumber
27. Plywood
28. Products of Wood, Bamboo & Rattan
29. Pulp, Paper & Paper Products, Printing, Publishing & Bookbinding
30. Leather & Products
31. Rubber & Products
32. Chemical Fertilizer
33. Medicines
34. Plastics & Products
35. Petroleum Products
36. Industrial Chemicals
37. Misc. Chemical Manufactures
38. Cement & Cement Products
39. Glass, Misc. Non-Metallic Mineral Products
40. Steel & Iron
41. Steel & Iron Products
42. Aluminum & Aluminum Products
43. Misc. Metals & Products
44. Machinery
45. Household Electrical Appliances
46. Communication Equipment
47. Other Electrical Apparatus & Equipment
48. Transportation Equipment
49. Misc. Manufactures
50. Construction
51. Electricity
52. Gas
53. City Water
54. Transportation and Warehousing
55. Communications
56. Wholesale and Retail Trade
57. Misc. Services
58. Undistributed

Index